The Politics of Official Apologies

Intense interest in past injustice lies at the center of contemporary world politics. Most scholarly and public attention has focused on truth commissions, trials, lustration, and other related decisions, following political transitions. This book examines the political uses of official apologies in Australia, Canada, New Zealand, and the United States. It explores why minority groups demand such apologies and why governments do or do not offer them. Melissa Nobles argues that apologies can help to alter the terms and meanings of national membership. Minority groups demand apologies in order to focus attention on historical injustices, the rectification of which, they argue, should guide changes in present-day government policies. Similarly, state actors support apologies for ideological and moral reasons, driven by their support of group rights, responsiveness to group demands, and belief that acknowledgment is due. Apologies, as employed by political actors, play an important, if underappreciated, role in bringing certain views about history and moral obligation to bear in public life.

Melissa Nobles is an associate professor of political science at the Massachusetts Institute of Technology. Professor Nobles' teaching and research interests are in the comparative study of racial and ethnic politics and issues of retrospective justice. She is the author of *Shades of Citizenship: Race and the Census in Modern Politics* (2000), which received the 2001 Outstanding Book Award from the National Conference of Black Political Scientists, as well as honorable mention of the Ralph Bunche Book Award from the American Political Science Association. Nobles has been a Fellow at Boston University's Institute on Race and Social Division (2000–1) and Harvard University's Radcliffe Center for Advanced Study (2003–4).

The Politics of Official Apologies

MELISSA NOBLES

Massachusetts Institute of Technology

CAMBRIDGE
UNIVERSITY PRESS

CAMBRIDGE UNIVERSITY PRESS
Cambridge, New York, Melbourne, Madrid, Cape Town, Singapore, São Paulo, Delhi

Cambridge University Press
32 Avenue of the Americas, New York, NY 10013-2473, USA

www.cambridge.org
Information on this title: www.cambridge.org/9780521872317

First published 2008

Printed in the United States of America

A catalog record for this publication is available from the British Library.

Library of Congress Cataloging in Publication Data
Nobles, Melissa.
The Politics of official apologies / Melissa Nobles.
p. cm.
Includes bibliographical references and index.
ISBN 978-0-521-87231-7 (hardback) – ISBN 978-0-521-69385-1 (pbk.)
1. Civil rights – North America – History. 2. Civil rights – Australia – History.
3. Civil rights – New Zealand – History. 4. Reconciliation – Political aspects – North
America. 5. Reconciliation – Political aspects – Australia. 6. Reconciliation –
Political aspects – New Zealand. 7. Apologizing. I. Title.
JC599.N66N63 2008
323.1–dc22   2007023442

ISBN 978-0-521-87231-7 hardback
ISBN 978-0-521-69385-1 paperback

For Fritz

Contents

Preface and Acknowledgments

The Turkish government's insistence on denying the Armenian geno-cide – specifically article 301 of Turkey's penal code, which authorities have used to interpret discussion of the genocide as an insult to "Turk-ishness" – has garnered a great deal of attention here in the United States and in Europe. The press, lawmakers, and political pundits present such Turkish insistence as excessive, an assault on free speech and creative thought, and, most seriously, an assault on truth itself. Indeed, in October 2006, the French Assembly passed a law that makes denial of the genocide a crime, presumably to counteract and highlight the wrong of Turkish historical and moral denial. (The law must still be approved by the French Senate and president.) The press writes sym-pathetically of Armenians' desire to have their stories told and history known.

If these collective reactions are to be believed, it is as if Turkey's behavior is somehow incomprehensible to Europeans and Americans. But continuing debates in France about the Algerian War, for example, or the deafening silence about the experiences of Native Americans tell another story. Of course, most countries' behaviors are far closer to Turkey's than they or we would care to admit. Governments and citizenries have many reasons to ignore or deny historical injustices, and they have long done so, in perhaps more subtle but no less effective ways than Turkey has. Like many aggrieved groups, Armenians have long asked for acknowledgment and even apology. Their demands are often met with mixed reactions. Why would an apology be desired or regarded as necessary?

My desire to better understand and explain official apologies motivates this book. Skepticism about apologies is well understood. After all, apologies serve as indicators of moral codes, illuminating what is considered "right" and "wrong" in social behavior and interactions. Coming from politicians, is this basic quality of apologies not violated from the start? What could an apology mean or accomplish? Yet, on the other hand, skepticism about apology is also puzzling. We recognize the importance of apologies in our personal lives and interactions. We value acknowledgment of wrongdoing and expressions of remorse. As importantly, we make judgments about the worth of apologies, usually on a case-by-case basis. Sometimes, we judge an apology to be sincere, warranted, and helpful in resolving disagreement. In other instances, we judge an apology less than satisfactory, exacerbating a disagreement rather than helping to resolve it. There are, of course, important differences distinguishing apologies between individuals from those made by governments to a segment of their citizenry or to other governments. But all apologies share basic characteristics: They require judgments and reflection, both ideational and moral, on what the apologies are being asked for and on what the expected consequences of the apologies are. What purposes are they going to advance?

In this book, I argue that apologies are desired, offered, and given in order to change the terms and meanings of membership in a political community. Membership in democratic polities provides citizens with the basic political language of rights, obligations, and responsibilities. They have certain expectations about the proper relationships between government and citizenry, and citizens press their claims accordingly. Group claims toward governments may also be rooted in grievances, not just expectations. These two sources of claims are here related: Grievances are connected to violated expectations of just treatment and respect, if not full inclusion. Yet grievances may be addressed without an apology as such. They may well simmer and even fuel group demands, but this does not mean that groups will ask for an apology. Instead, groups may demand simply that governments attend to their concerns without mention of apology. Governments may pass laws and implement policies but never apologize. What is it, then, that makes apologies desirable? Apologies, I argue, help to bring history into the conversation, providing justification for political and policy changes and reforms. Central to the addressing of contemporary grievances is the focus on the historical injustices that created the grievances. Apologies focus on a neglected past and demand that moral reflection be bought to bear and that some attempt at remedy be undertaken.

But, if I am right in my intuitions, then the question still remains, why would governments apologize? I argue that certain political elites may also judge the current situation in need of reform. Furthermore, for ideological reasons, they are supportive of minority group rights and are responsive to group demands and claims. These elites also express a certain guilt and sense of responsibility for righting wrongs. Sometimes, these political elites will themselves initiate offers of apology, although as often they apologize when pressured. On the other hand, political elites will not apologize when they do not agree with minority group demands, do not favor group rights, and do not think that the past provides a way forward. But whether political elites support or oppose apologies, political ideology and moral reflection drive their interpretations of history and its political and moral obligations. Neither money nor electoral prospects are as influential as is often speculated, precisely because lawmakers hold the most powerful cards. They may pay nothing, if they choose, and they often choose this course of action. Also, and relatedly, indigenous issues are of little electoral salience, especially in national elections. In short, my theoretical proposition makes the perhaps obvious claim that big ideas and moral judgments matter in political life. I should state, finally, that I am careful not to overstate what apologies do or can do. They do not by themselves effect direct changes in political, economic, and social arrangements. Rather, they provide justifications for reforms today that are grounded in acknowledgment of historical injustices. As important as I think that ideas and specifically apologies are, my theoretical claims and their anticipated outcomes are intentionally modest. Apologies, as employed by political actors, play an important if underappreciated part in bringing certain views about history and moral obligation to bear in public life.

The beginnings of this book came with the frontpage headlines of a 1998 *New York Times* article reporting that the Canadian government had apologized to its indigenous citizens for historical mistreatment and decades of abuse at residential schools. At the time, I was admittedly suspicious of the Canadian government's motivations and skeptical of the apology's likely outcomes. But at the same time, I was pleasantly surprised because I was well aware of the evident discomfort in public, and much scholarly, discussion about U.S. slavery, Jim Crow racial segregation, and the widespread silence about the dispossession and treatment of Native Americans. I thought then, as I think now, that whatever else the apologies managed to accomplish, a discussion about those events would not and could not be a bad thing. This is not to suggest that I thought the histories produced would be any less contentious; however, an effort at inclusion and the courage to address deeply troublesome but fundamental facts about national histories seemed to be an undeniably positive development.

This project has benefited from the assistance of many people. I began initial fieldwork in August 1999, when I traveled to Australia. There, Dr. Jan "Jindy" Pettman, then director of the Centre for Women's Studies at the Australian National University in Canberra, generously provided me a desk, computer, and access to the university's resources. Jan also introduced me to one of the centre's graduate students, Tikka Wilson, who was enormously generous with her time and knowledge. She assisted me by making valuable introductions and contributed to my understanding of Australia, as one copatriot to another. (Tikka, an American, now calls Australia her home.) She had been involved in Link-Up, a New South Wales community organization of Aboriginal Australians dedicated to reuniting persons separated from their families, communities, and culture by the state policy of child removal. Tikka kindly introduced me to members of that organization, thus enriching my research. In 2000, I traveled to Ottawa and Vancouver, Canada. In Vancouver, I met with professors David Elkins, Arthur Ray, and Paul Tennant, all of the University of British Columbia, who all gave generously of their time and expertise.

This book has also benefited from my participation in various fora where I have presented my work in various stages of development. Of these many gatherings, participation in the following have been especially influential in shaping my thinking and sharpening my ideas: In May 2001, I presented my first ideas at the Massachusetts Institute of Technology's (MIT) MacArthur Transnational Security Seminar. In February 2002, I participated in an interdisciplinary conference, "Apologies: Mourning the Past and Ameliorating the Present," organized by Elazar Barkan of the Claremont Graduate University. The conference, dedicated specifically to apologies, proved especially useful in highlighting to all what political science is best able to explain:

the political motivations and likely outcomes of apologies. In March 2005, I presented certain of my ideas at an interdisciplinary conference at Brown University, "Historical Injustices: Restitution and Reconciliation in International Perspective," where I learned and received helpful feedback from British and Australian scholars. Finally, although I had not yet embarked on this particular project, I knew that I was interested in issues of retrospective justice. During the 1998–9 academic year, I was fortunate to participate in a yearlong seminar series, "Retrospective Justice," organized by Professor Jon Elster of Columbia University. There I was first introduced, through papers and stimulating discussion, to especially useful ways of coherently thinking about and studying an increasingly important topic.

I am grateful for the valuable financial support, time, and, most important, intellectual engagement provided by my appointments in 2000–2001 as a Fellow at Boston University's now defunct Institute on Racial and Social Division, led by Professor Glenn Loury, and in 2003–2004 at Harvard University's Radcliffe Institute for Advanced Study, led by Professor Drew Gilpin Faust. Finally, I extend my appreciation to Josh Cohen for useful discussion about and comments on earlier chapter drafts, and to two anonymous readers for their careful and constructive reviews.

Toward a Membership Theory of Apologies

Governments are not in the habit of apologizing for their own injustices, let alone those perpetrated by former governments in distant and not-so-distant pasts. Yet they sometimes do, most often in response to the demands of organized citizen groups or former adversaries, but not always. In widely known instances, former belligerents have apologized for crimes committed during World War II. Similarly, in democratizing nations, former perpetrators of state crimes have apologized for their past actions. For both, the desired outcomes are clear, if not always achieved. Former belligerents may apologize, thereby easing relations between the two, as in the case of France and Germany. In contrast, Japan's repeated failures to apologize unambiguously for its war crimes have made reconciliation with neighboring countries difficult. For new democracies, proponents assert that apologies will advance societal reconciliation and strengthen democratic consolidation.

But neither the latest wave of democratization nor World War II crimes account for all present-day apologies or demands for them. Groups have demanded and governments have offered apologies for historical injustices. Australian Aboriginal peoples have urged Prime Minister John Howard to apologize for the state policy, begun in the early twentieth century, of removing "half-caste" Aboriginal children from their parents' care, usually forcibly. Aboriginal Canadians and New Zealand Maori continue to press for greater political and economic autonomy, after receiving official apologies from the Canadian government and the British Crown, respectively. African Americans call for apology and reparations for two hundred years of slavery. Existing scholarship on World War II war crimes and democratization says little about these cases, if mostly because they fall outside of its established topical parameters.

In the cases of indigenous peoples and African Americans, the motivations for either asking for or offering an apology and the desired outcomes are less clear.[1] The passage of time makes the rectification of most claimed injustices difficult, if not impossible. Without the possibility of direct remedy, might an apology be regarded as empty rhetorical gesture, without much impact? Moreover, in established democracies such as Australia, Canada, New Zealand, and the United States, neither the survival nor the consolidation of a new democratic regime is at stake. Indeed, in these democracies, grievances may be addressed through several channels, without an apology, thus raising the question of why and how "apology politics" emerge at all. What do such politics accomplish?

I argue that in Australia, Canada, New Zealand, and the United States, organized groups and state actors demand and provide apologies in order to help change the terms and meanings of national membership. The power of apologies, and what distinguishes them from other types of symbolic gestures, such as monuments and pronouncements, is that they not only publicly ratify certain reinterpretations of history, but they also morally judge, assign responsibility, and introduce expectations about what acknowledgment of that history requires. Thus, although apologies focus our attention on the past, they also have implications for the future. This is not surprising. In everyday life and politics, we routinely use the past to inform our judgments and justify our decisions about present and future conduct. We reevaluate our past, in light of new information or simply for new reasons, and come up with revised understandings that guide our actions as we move forward.

---

[1] Although there is legal and political disagreement over what constitutes "indigeneity" and who may claim such an identity, "indigenous" denotes "originating or occurring naturally, native," in reference to people and products. In our cases, indigenous connotes first occupation of a given territory prior to European settlement. Hodgson (2002: 1037–49).

Yet, because our views of the past change and are governed, in part, by our evaluations of present and future needs, apologies for that past are bound to be contentious. With official apologies, political elites, groups, intellectuals, and the public at large disagree about historical facts, about how they should be interpreted, and about what bearing such facts should have on present-day and future policy making. There is disagreement also over whether the moral culpability that an apology implies is warranted. One might expect state officials and aggrieved groups to be willing to endure such contention because of the anticipated benefits – electoral or monetary – of receiving or offering an apology (or not). Yet, as we shall see, these motivations are weak in practice and are largely overridden by ideological commitments and moral concerns. All parties recognize the symbolic power of apology, which they treat not as a form of political evasion, "cheap talk," or mere means to an end, but as a political act, with intrinsic significance. Apologies help to shape politics, by publicly acknowledging injustice and by registering support of certain views of national membership and history while displacing others.

This book proposes a membership theory of official apologies, which explains apologies by focusing on their ideological and moral stakes and not only on anticipated material gains or losses. Political actors provide and seek apologies to register their ideological support of minority group claims and to advance the political, economic, and social objectives that flow from group demands. Apologies are the likely outcomes when political elites and aggrieved groups favor them, but of the two, political elite support is absolutely essential to obtaining an apology. Apologies, in turn, are most effective indirectly and diffusely, strengthening historical justifications for present-day recognition and government support of indigenous claims and contributing to greater public acceptance of, if not deep agreement with, indigenous demands.

My explanation focuses on government apologies, which are part of a larger universe of apologies. Although I do not analyze these other apologies, it is important to locate within this larger set those cases that are the focus of this book (those of indigenous peoples in Australia, Canada, New Zealand, and the United States, and of African Americans) in order to specify further their frequency and characteristics.

A Sorry World

Journalists have taken notice of the swell of apologies, asking in often skeptical tones, "Who's sorry now?"[2] Their observations about the increase of apologies are borne out by existing data, even if their skepticism is not. Public apologies and gestures of regret became more frequent over the second half of the twentieth century and continue to be offered in the early years of the twenty-first. Heads of state, governments, religious institutions, individuals, and nongovernmental organizations have offered them (see Appendix A). Drawing from the few studies and compilations of apologies, I divide them into six separate categories organized according to who offers the apology: (1) heads of state and government officials; (2) governments; (3) religious institutions; (4) organized groups or individual citizens; (5) nongovernmental organizations and institutions; and (6) private institutions.[3] My compilation is undoubtedly incomplete, relying as it does on public English-language sources (newspaper and magazine articles, books, and Internet searches). These shortcomings notwithstanding, it does provide a fairly full view of apologies in the twentieth and twenty-first centuries.

Of the seventy-two apologies I list, over half of them (thirty-nine) have been offered by heads of state. Moreover, nearly half (nineteen) of their apologies are related to World War II, thus explaining their appearance in the postwar period. Most (thirteen) of these World War II apologies were offered in the 1990s, in conjunction with fifty-year commemorations of the war. Religious institutions, and principally the Catholic Church, have offered a significant number of apologies covering a range of issues. Two apologies refer to the Catholic Church's silence and inaction toward the slaughter of European Jews during World War II.

As important, although I do not discuss them, are the large – indeed incalculable – number of apologies neither asked for nor given and refusals to apologize. The former group might well include, for

---

[2] For example, O'Connor (2004: L-01); Fallow (2005: 3).

[3] My categories are similar to those used in Cunningham (1999). By far the most useful chronological compilation is provided in an unpublished paper written by Graham G. Dodds for the Penn National Commission on Society, Culture, and Community. See Dodds (1999). This paper was later published, without the chronological list of political apologies, in an edited book; see Mitchell (1998: 46–7); Brooks (1999); Barkan (2000); Dodds (2003).

example, an apology from the Dominican Republic for the week-long massacre in October 1937 of approximately eight thousand Haitians by the Rafael Trujillo government. Under pressure from the United States and Haiti, Trujillo agreed in December 1937 to arbitration and an international commission to investigate the massacre. However, before the investigation began, Trujillo offered to pay $750,000 to the Haitian government to end the matter immediately. In the end, Trujillo paid only a fraction of the promised amount and offered no apology. As Eric Roorda writes, "One element missing from Trujillo's effort to repair the damage of the Haitian massacre was any expression of remorse."[4] The Haitian government, for its part, accepted the money, along with a personal payment to the president, and did not demand an apology.

Among the refusals to apologize, perhaps the most notorious is the Turkish government's refusal to apologize for the Armenian genocide of 1915. Armenians have long demanded that Turkey acknowledge the massacre as genocide and apologize for it. Turkey claims that there was no genocide, that the numbers dead are wildly exaggerated, and that the Armenians rose up against the Ottoman Empire and fought with the Russian army.[5] This refusal to acknowledge, let alone apologize, persists, even with Turkey's entry into the European Union partly hanging in the balance and in the wake of historical reexaminations undertaken by a small, and growing, number of Turkish historians.[6]

In this book, I focus on the apologies offered by and requested of governments, as opposed to heads of state. This distinction is an important one that requires explanation. Apologies by heads of state are verbal utterances made by an executive and, in a few cases, a government official. These utterances bear official weight, of course, by virtue of the speaker's prominence and position. But they do not carry the weight of government apologies, which are (or so far have been) the results of deliberative processes and have frequently been accompanied by monetary compensation. There are exceptions, however. The establishment of a national center of medical bioethics at Tuskegee University, for example, followed President Bill Clinton's 1997 apology to the eight survivors of the Tuskegee syphilis study.

[4] Roorda (1998: 142).
[5] Smith (1992).
[6] See, for example, Kolbert (2006: 120–4).

In keeping with this distinction between heads of state and governments, all but two of the government apologies have been directed toward domestic populations, whereas the majority of apologies offered by heads of state have concerned international matters.[7] Moreover, certain of the head-of-state apologies possess an unexpected quality not present in government apologies. A leader may or may not have consulted with advisors and other politicians before offering it. For example, during his 1970 visit to the site of Poland's Warsaw ghetto, West German Chancellor Willy Brandt fell to his knees, expressing German guilt, sorrow, and responsibility for the Holocaust. In contrast, government apologies most often have been highly scripted affairs, the products of consultations and official government bodies.

Governments have apologized or have been forced or asked to apologize for historical and catastrophic wrongs – wrongs committed during World War II, at the end of colonial rule, or over the course of national founding and settlement. Of the eight that I count in the twentieth and twenty-first centuries, three resulted from actions committed during World War II: Germany's apology and payments (now totaling an estimated 100 billion DM) to Israel, to surviving Jews for the Holocaust, and to other victims[8]; the United States' apology and payments of $20,000 to surviving Japanese Americans for their internment; and Canada's apology and payments of CAN$21,000 to surviving Japanese Canadians for their internment.[9] There was one for the decisions undertaken by a former European colonizer. In February 2002, the Belgian government apologized for its role in the 1961 assassination of Patrice Lumumba, the first prime minister of Congo, Belgium's former colony.[10] The Belgian government also "announced the creation of a $3.5 million fund in Lumumba's name to promote democracy in Congo . . . "[11] The remaining four apologies have been for national founding and historical treatment of indigenous populations

---

[7] The two exceptions are the German government's apology to Jews who survived the Holocaust and to the state of Israel, and the Belgian government's apology to the Congolese for Belgium's role in the assassination of Patrice Lumumba.

[8] The figure of 100 billion DM is based on German government estimates up to the year 2000. It includes all reparations claims to all those persecuted by the Nazis, including non-Jews. Pross (1998: 170–3).

[9] Hatamiya (1993); Torpey (2006: ch. 3).

[10] Agence France-Presse (2002).

[11] Idem (2002).

TABLE 1.1. *Origins and Outcomes of Demands for Apology*

I. Apology asked for and given	II. Apology given but not asked for
Aboriginal Australians from state governments, police forces, and churches for government policy of child removal	Queen Elizabeth/ New Zealand government to Maori groups for land confiscation
Indigenous Canadians from Canadian government for federal policies and for the residential school system	U.S. Bureau of Indian Affairs (BIA) to American Indians for BIA federal policies
U.S. congressional resolution to Native Hawaiians for 1893 overthrow of the Hawaiian Kingdom	
III. Apology asked for but not given	**IV. Apology neither asked for nor given**
Aboriginal Australians from the Australian federal government for government policy of child removal	Latin American states and their indigenous and black populations for dispossession and slavery
Rep. Tony Hall (D-OH) and some African American leaders for American slavery	

in Australia, Canada, New Zealand, and the United States.[12] In addition, in 2000 the U.S. Bureau of Indian Affairs apologized for its treatment of American Indians, and in 2005 the U.S. Senate apologized for its historical failure to pass antilynching laws. Finally, there is a pending congressional apology resolution to Native Americans, and there has been widespread discussion about and demands for an apology and reparations to African Americans for slavery and Jim Crow segregation.

We now have a sense of the wider set of public apologies and the comparatively smaller set of government apologies, and of where the Australian, Canadian, New Zealand, and U.S. apologies and nonapologies that I will examine fit within both. They are few in number, but most often broader in scope, addressing national founding, settlement, and historical mistreatment. Yet these cases themselves have separate origins and outcomes, based on the instigator(s) of the apology and on the resultant action. Table 1.1 identifies these origins and outcomes

[12] The U.S. case refers to the 1993 Joint Congressional Resolution to the people of Hawaii.

in four cells: cell I, "Apology asked for and given"; cell II, "Apology given but not asked for"; cell III, "Apology asked for but not given"; and cell IV, "Apology neither asked for nor given."

Cell I lists apologies that were both asked for and given. In Australia, a government commission recommended apologies to Aboriginal peoples. In 1993, the governing Labor Party's attorney-general, Michael Lavarch, established a national inquiry and authorized the Human Rights and Equal Opportunity Commission (HREOC) to investigate the state policy (in effect from 1910 to 1970) of removing "half-caste" Aboriginal children from their parents' care. The HREOC's resultant report, *Bringing Them Home*, offered fifty-four recommendations, of which one called for apologies and acknowledgment from the Commonwealth and state parliaments and their police forces and from churches. In Canada, indigenous groups have long demanded an apology for their treatment by the Canadian government. Although Canada's 1996 Royal Commission on Aboriginal Peoples (RCAP) did not explicitly recommend an apology, the tone of its recommendations strongly suggested that governmental contrition, publicly displayed, was due. RCAP also recommended that CAN$38 billion be allocated to Aboriginal affairs, including Aboriginal self-governance and economic development, over a twenty-year period. The Canadian government included a formal apology in its 1998 policy response to RCAP, along with a CAN$350 million "healing fund" to assist victims of sexual and physical abuse in the residential school system and CAN$250 million to put toward Aboriginal economic development and self-governance initiatives. In 1993, the U.S. Congress passed a resolution apologizing for the U.S. government's role in the Hawaiian kingdom's overthrow, on its one-hundredth anniversary. Pressure from the Hawaii sovereignty movement and Hawaii's federal senators were largely responsible for that resolution.

Cell II lists apologies given but not directly requested. In 1995 and 1998, the British Crown (in the person of Queen Elizabeth) and the New Zealand government issued formal apologies to the Waikato-Tainui people for land confiscation and to the Ngai Tahu for breaches of the Treaty of Waitangi, respectively. The 1995 apology accompanied a NZ$170 million land settlement agreement with the Waikato-Tainui, and the 1998 apology to the Ngai Tahu came with a NZ$170 million payment plus an additional NZ$2.5 million to resolve thirty small private claims. Neither group had explicitly requested the apologies, although both groups welcomed them. Similarly, in 2000, Kevin Gover, then assistant secretary of the U.S. Bureau of Indian Affairs (BIA), offered a formal apology on behalf of the BIA for its historical treatment of Native Americans, although such an apology had not been demanded. Neither the Congress nor the president publicly endorsed Gover's apology. They did not oppose it, either.[13]

Cell III lists cases where apologies were demanded, but not given. As mentioned, the Australian *Bringing Them Home* report recommended apologies from each of the state parliaments and their police forces, the Commonwealth Parliament, and churches. Of these, all except Prime Minister Howard issued an apology, who has steadfastly refused to do so. Former Representative Tony Hall (D-OH) twice proposed, in 1997 and 2000, a House concurrent resolution that apologized for slavery; on neither occasion did the resolution make it out of the House Committee on the Judiciary. Representative Hall explained publicly that he was guided largely by moral concerns.

The cases listed in cells I through III share four characteristics:

- All of the countries involved are former British colonies and all are democracies, with historically open channels of participation for the propertied, for men, and eventually for women and racial or ethnic minorities.
- All of the groups involved are small, even tiny, minorities. According to the most recent census data, indigenous people constitute 1.5 percent of the total U.S. population, 2.5 percent of Australia's, and 4.4 percent of Canada's. New Zealand's Maori are 14 percent and African Americans are 12 percent.
- In all of the cases, there were sharp views of the purportedly insurmountable cultural and racial differences between the majority and minority group(s). And in all, complex administrative and legal apparatuses were created to manage these differences.
- In all but one case (Australia), the central governments entered into treaties with indigenous group(s) and during certain historical periods allowed for separate, albeit severely constrained, indigenous self-governance.

---

[13] Tsosie (2006: 191).

These similar historical experiences are especially amenable to structured comparison, as the historical trajectory of government–indigenous interactions has followed quite a similar course, occurring in five stages over time, from independence to mutual relations, dependency, marginality, and political resurgence.[14] With these commonalities, that apologies have been offered or demanded in certain of our cases but not in others requires analysis and explanation.

Cell IV refers to circumstances where apologies were neither asked for nor received. Of course, any number of peoples in different countries could fit within this cell. However, I include the cases of Latin America's indigenous groups and black Latin Americans because their historical experiences in New World settler societies are most comparable. Yet even with analogous historical experiences of dispossession, slavery, and contemporaneous disadvantage, demands for apologies do not seem forthcoming. Similarly, state officials have indicated neither an intention nor a desire to apologize for historical injustices, while apologizing in at least one case for crimes committed during twentieth-century military rule.[15] What might these null cases, when compared with the others, tell us about the likely conditions that lead to apologies?

The cases that fall into cell IV share four circumstances:

- There were extended periods of undemocratic rule in twentieth-century Latin America and previously during the colonial period.
- There is the view, no longer dominant but still widely held, of Latin America comprising culturally and racially homogeneous populations. According to Latin American intellectual and political elites, extensive "racial mixture" has resulted in the formation of new national races (Brazilian, Cuban, Mexican, and others). Accompanying these ideas were concrete state policies to "reconstitute Indians as national peasants" within corporatist political arrangements that provided Indians access to economic resources (such as land and agricultural subsidies) in an illusory exchange for their self-identifications as Indians.[16] Latin American states sought also

---

[14] Nichols (1998: xiv).

[15] For example, the former Chilean president Patricio Aylwin publicly presented that country's Truth Commission's key findings. In his televised presentation, President Aylwin called for a "societal apology." Teitel (2000: 84).

[16] Yashar (1999: 61, 81).

to "whiten" their policies through immigration policies targeted to Southern Europeans and social mores that maintained a flexible skin-color hierarchy. It is important to note that it has been noticeably easier for indigenous movements to discredit cultural homogeneity and reclaim cultural distinctiveness than it has been for black movements to create and sustain a distinct black racial identity.[17]

- In spite of the image of homogeneous and assimilated populations, indigenous groups constitute substantial pluralities in some countries, the inherent problems of classification and enumeration notwithstanding. Although indigenous peoples make up approximately 10 percent of the region's population, they constitute 60 to 70 percent of Bolivia's population, 45 to 60 percent of Guatemala's, and 38 to 40 percent of Peru's, for example.[18] Less is known about the size of Latin America's black population precisely because of the meanings of and values attached to "black," "brown," and "white." Nonetheless, Brazil's nonwhite population is approximately 49 percent. Most other Latin American countries do not yet include a "race" question in their national censuses, despite domestic and international pressures to do so.[19]

- Spanish and Portuguese colonial administrations rarely entered into treaties with indigenous peoples.[20] During the colonial period, the Crown's efforts were focused on three main objectives: maintaining and fortifying the Crown's authority, ensuring Indian labor, and protecting Indians from excessive exploitation by settlers. The devised solution was "juridical separation of the rights and obligations" of each: Spaniards were subjects of the Crown and Indians were wards.[21] Within this legal regime, the Crown recognized Indian communal landholdings, but it did not recognize indigenous sovereignty – thus the absence of treaties.[22] The encomienda system was designed principally to guarantee Indian labor, and not to

---

[17] Hooker (2005).
[18] Yashar (2005: 19).
[19] Nobles (2005).
[20] In 1641 the Spanish Crown signed the Treaty of Quillin with the Mapuche Nation of today's Argentina and Chile. The treaty demarcated the boundaries of the Mapuche Nation. With the break from Spanish rule by the newly formed states of Argentina and Chile, the new states repealed the treaty and initiated efforts to overtake Mapuche territory.
[21] Williamson (1992: 110); Cook and Lindau (2000: 11).
[22] Ibid.

advance land alienation, as such. (Under the feudal-like encomienda system, settlers mostly coerced Indians into working for them in exchange for care, wages, and Christian instruction.) With independence, indigenous land possession worsened dramatically as the separate legal system – which had, paradoxically, provided some protection for Indian landholdings – was abolished and replaced by liberal legal reforms requiring conversion of communal land ownership to individual.[23] Such land reforms led to steep declines in Indian landholding, as Latin American Creole landowners bought or otherwise obtained these properties. By the end of the nineteenth century, many Indians were reduced to landless laborers and forced to migrate to cities or to seek work on large rural estates or other extractive enterprises. Moreover, slavery in Latin America, although comparable to American slavery in its brutality, also allowed for a sizable class of persons known as "free people of color," whose free status made a strict correspondence between skin color and slave status impossible.

Latin America's experiences highlight the significance of legal, institutional, ideational, and political histories and demographic factors. As importantly, they point to the necessity of motivation, political strategy, and opportunity in accounting for demands or offers of apology. For most of the twentieth century, indigenous and black mobilization in Latin America was largely ineffective and episodic, in significant measure because neither ethnic nor racial identity was an effective basis for mobilization. This lack of mobilization resulted, in turn, from three of the aforementioned factors: undemocratic rule, dominant ideologies of "mestizaje" and "whitening," and corporatist policies that promoted local autonomy based on collective identities as peasants first and as Indians second. Recent democratization and state encroachment on local Indian autonomy has helped to make Indian and black identities politically salient. Like indigenous peoples in Australia, Canada, New Zealand, and the United States, Indians in Latin America desire both equal rights and rights to self-governance. Black Latin Americans, like black Americans, demand greater political power, economic parity, and regard.

---

[23] Williamson (1992: 245–7).

Although indigenous groups constitute large pluralities, if not majorities, in several countries, such as Ecuador and Bolivia, they also constitute small minorities (less than 3 percent) in other countries, such as Columbia and Venezuela. However, in each of these four countries, indigenous parties have won legislative and gubernatorial seats.[24] More important, then, than demographic size for understanding the direction and success of indigenous political mobilization is the openness of Latin American political institutions and electoral systems.[25] Scholars have provided distinct and largely complementary explanations for indigenous mobilization, focusing on neoliberal economic adjustment policies that threatened indigenous autonomy and livelihoods, constitutional reforms that promised long-sought rights and protections, and a more accessible party system.[26]

Indigenous groups have not demanded that political elites establish a commission or any other investigative body to reexamine past state policies and elites have expressed neither a desire nor intention to do so. Instead, indigenous groups have mobilized to gain political power, creating ethnic political parties and becoming active players in shaping national political institutions and public policies. This is not to suggest that history or past injustices are absent from political rhetoric. To the contrary, as Donna Lee Van Cott observes, indigenous groups often frame "their alternative political projects by invoking the historical roots of the modern state in a history of conquest, violence, and domination."[27] Nonetheless, at the moment, the overriding political issue for the entire citizenry is democratic governance itself. It remains to be seen whether apology politics will someday emerge in response to the terms of citizenship being decided upon today.[28]

The Determinants of Apologies

In important ways, democratizing states (after war and/or regime change) and long-established democracies face the same basic issues, albeit at different times: Dealing with past injustices is an ongoing

---

[24] Cott (2005: 2).
[25] Ibid.
[26] Cott (2000); Cott (2005); Yashar (2005).
[27] Cott (2000: 18).
[28] Yashar (2005).

process, not a one-shot deal. In newly democratizing states, the incoming leadership must decide how to address the political abuses of outgoing regimes. First they must decide whether to do anything at all, and if so, what and for how long. The same is true in long-established democracies. Yet in older democracies, these decisions are in need of more explanation precisely because the claimed injustices, many dating back to national beginnings, are seemingly too deeply and complexly implicated in founding and settlement to be effectively remedied by actions taken today.

Despite differences, both the old and the new share this fundamental similarity: There are injustices that are seen to require attention and action, even if they cannot be fully remedied. Indeed, although Jon Elster finds that the desire for retribution diminishes the longer the period between the injustice and the political transition and the longer the period between the injustice and trials, he also finds that "counteracting mechanisms may keep memory and resentment alive for a century or more."[29] In this book's cases, chief mechanisms that keep memories alive are past state policies and individual and group perceptions of their ongoing deleterious effects. This all underscores the point that an explanation of apologies in long-established democracies requires analytics similar to those employed in the study of transitional justice: identification of the independent variables and causal mechanisms that lead to demands or offers of apologies.[30]

Actors

There are three principal groups of actors: mobilized minority groups, state officials, and public intellectuals, principally historians. The first set of actors is mobilized minority groups. In Australia, Canada, New Zealand, and the United States, groups' historical treatment as "Aborigines," "Indians," and "blacks," separate and apart from other citizens, has done as much as, if not more than, shared cultures to enforce group identity and to obscure important cultural and experiential differences within the group. This sharp differentiation between minority and majority group members on the one hand, and

---

[29] Elster (2004: 77).
[30] My identification of the determinants is adapted from Elster's discussion of the framework of transitional justice and independent variables in Elster (2004, ch. 4).

the imposed homogenization of the minority group itself on the other, characterizes numerous state policies in the four countries.

At the same time, somewhat incongruously, states implemented assimilation and "antimiscegenation" policies affecting Aboriginal and black people. As scholars have documented, these policies were driven, in significant measure, by economic imperatives. State policies sought either to assimilate Aboriginal peoples or physically eliminate them, thereby facilitating alienation from their lands.[31] In contrast, antimiscegenation policies affecting African Americans and other "nonwhites" helped to isolate and secure a subordinate workforce.[32]

Assimilation and antimiscegenation policies were also driven by ideological imperatives, based in racial ideas. For example, Australian advocates of Aboriginal assimilation over time expressed different and, at times, conflicting views about Aboriginal racial origins and their suitability for and hence prospects in "White Australia." On one side, Australian scientists concluded that Aboriginal people, especially "full-bloods," were doomed for extinction.[33] However, others thought that European and Aboriginal peoples shared a common ancestry, however remote, which meant that extinction was not inevitable and that assimilation was a possible, if onerous and prolonged, undertaking. The idea of "blood kinship," Russell McGregor observes, was useful in arguing for Aboriginal inclusion in the body politic.[34] This was especially true for purported "half-castes." However, in regard to African Americans, American race scientists deemed "racial mixture" undesirable, as it resulted in white racial contamination.

Finally, differences in political standing between indigenous peoples and African Americans distinguish their experiences, historically and presently, and bear directly on their political objectives. Indigenous peoples were prior inhabitants of the land, and their political relationship with European settlers was determined largely through treaties and/or warfare. American federal authorities, for example,

---

[31] Cornell (1988: 40–5).

[32] Wolfe (2001).

[33] Australian scientists were not alone in their views about Aboriginal extinction. As Patrick Brantlinger analyzes, from the late eighteenth century to the twentieth century, European and American beliefs and theories about extinction explained and justified the decimation of indigenous populations. Brantlinger (2003).

[34] McGregor (1996: 14).

treated Native Americans as "aliens," in keeping with the view that tribes constituted separate nations.[35] Native Americans were presumed to be members of tribes that "were sovereign enough to give protection to and demand allegiance from their members."[36] Citizen status for individual Native Americans was gained through tribal treaties and congressional acts – that is, positive government action – and not an individual's decision to leave ("expatriate") from his or her tribe.[37] The 1924 General Citizenship Act finally declared Native Americans to be American citizens while still allowing for tribal membership.[38] In sum, the loss of land and accompanying political subjugation did not necessarily mean the extinction of Aboriginal rights or native land title. Indeed, much of the legal and political contention today in all four countries centers on determining the content and scope of Aboriginal rights, native title, and self-government.

In contrast, the political status of African Americans was determined first by slavery and then by a racial caste system. Enslaved persons were thought of and treated as property, not as citizens, thereby evading the prevailing legal assumption that American citizenship was acquired through birthright. As James Kettner explains, "as long as slaves could be viewed in some sense as property, judges could avoid fitting them into established categories of membership or non-membership."[39] In the case of Native Americans, such avoidance also was not necessary, since, as earlier discussed, the quasisovereign status of Native American tribes made their members "aliens" and overrode issues of American citizenship through birthright. Such was not the case with free African Americans, whose citizenship should have been unassailable, given they that were either born in free states or of free parents or had been manumitted, and were not slaves or Native Americans.

Yet, their citizenship was assailable precisely because recognition of it "raised complex questions about manumission that could easily challenge the idea that black slaves were property."[40] Recognition

---

[35] Kettner (1978: 296).
[36] Ibid.
[37] Ibid. (297).
[38] Wilkins (2002: 55).
[39] Kettner (1978: 301).
[40] Ibid. (310).

also required that whites include African Americans in the political community, extending to them the full rights and privileges of citizenship. The Civil War amendments, specifically the thirteenth – which abolished slavery and involuntary servitude – and the fourteenth – which affirmed both national and birthright citizenship while also guaranteeing enjoyment of the basic rights of life, liberty, and property and equal protection of the law – seemingly settled the basic principles of American citizenship. As is well known, de jure racial segregation in the southern American states and de facto segregation throughout the rest of the country vitiated, to varying degrees, these constitutional rights and privileges until the mid-1960s.

The second set of actors is state officials: elected politicians, government officials, and political appointees. In several of our cases, either a government official or a legislature enabled an official commission and charged that these bodies investigate a given issue. With their completed reports, these bodies advised the legislature and/or executive of their findings and recommendations, which often include apology. Members of these commissions have included government agency heads, judges, elected politicians, minority group leaders, and scholars. For example, Canada's Royal Commission of Aboriginal Peoples, cochaired by the former national chief of the Assembly of First Nations and a former judge of the Quebec Appeals Court, included former heads of Aboriginal organizations, an attorney and professor, a professor and former provincial deputy minister, a former Canadian Supreme Court justice, and a former premier of Saskatchewan.

The third set of actors is intellectuals, principally historians, who have emerged as important players because their scholarship contributes both to the public record and influences public opinion, to varying degrees. Their participation extends far beyond serving on the aforementioned official commissions. They are also outspoken actors in public debates about national histories, offering not only the "historical facts," but also inescapably their interpretations of said facts. Historical scholarship has often corresponded with, or is at least perceived as corresponding with, a political viewpoint, which has led in turn to charges of bias and partisanship. Australia's "history wars" are but the latest examples. Here, historians have provided, both intentionally and unintentionally, understandings of Australian history that support the views of the two main competing political parties, the currently ruling

Liberal Party and opposition Labor Party.[41] For the Liberal Party, Australian history is basically good, full of achievements and reflective of cultural values that should be a source of pride for Australians. For the Labor Party, Australian history is good, but still needs to fulfill its profoundly egalitarian promise of fraternity ("mate-ship"), especially toward Aboriginal peoples. Furthermore, recent interpretations of Australian history that emphasize Aboriginal dispossession not only seemingly challenge the moral authority of the state, but also support the 1992 pivotal High Court *Mabo v. Queensland* decision affirming native title.[42]

Motivations

Elster identifies three interrelated motivations that are nearly universal in transitional justice: reason, emotion, and interest.[43] These three motivations are certainly at work in each of our cases, with reason and emotion being the more powerful and determinative. In general, indigenous groups are opposed to formal equality because it establishes symmetrical terms of citizenship, where indigenous peoples are treated the same as and assumed to have the same political allegiances as everyone else. But, of course, their claims to sovereignty and unjust dispossession distinguish them from every other group of citizens. The currently prevailing view of a "differentiated citizenship," aptly captured in the Canadian term "citizens plus" reflects attempts to maintain Canadian unity while still recognizing historical circumstance. As Alain Cairns explains, in devising this term for the government's 1965 Hawthorn Report, the term "plus" "referred to ongoing entitlements, some of which flowed from existing treaties, while others were to be worked out in the political processes of the future, which would identify the Indian peoples as deserving possessors of an additional category of rights based on historical priority."[44] Yet, for some indigenous activists, a "citizens plus" status is not enough. The ultimate goal is the establishment of "nation-to-nation" arrangements. On this view,

---

[41] Bonnell and Crotty (2004).

[42] As Stuart Macintyre and Anna Clark note, the justices based their decision "on the 'full facts' of Aboriginal dispossession; among the sources they used was the research of the historian Henry Reynolds." Macintyre and Clark (2003: 126).

[43] Elster (2004: 82).

[44] Cairns (2000: 12).

indigenous peoples seek to advance an agenda leading to political, economic, and social arrangements that approximate their former independence. Because indigenous groups view themselves as "nations," with a political existence that predates that of the settler states, the apologies they seek are analogous to those sought between states.

Their desire for change is rooted in a deep sense of grievance of having been subjugated and disregarded. Attending to their grievances, as they see it, requires both apology and concrete political and economic alterations. Their larger political strategy is, in some respects, backward looking, although the ultimate desired goal is to reshape their political future. Apologies, then, are logical, although not inevitable, outgrowths of this larger strategy. For African Americans, the circumstances are different, and the demands for apology and reparations are rooted less in dissatisfaction with the goals of formal equality than with their nonachievement and limits. African Americans are still not treated like everyone else, usually in negative ways. Demands for an apology and reparations might be viewed as reactions not only to the failures of formal equality (such as those of civil rights laws), but also to the inability of circumscribed race-conscious policies to remedy persistent and deeply rooted inequities.[45]

State actors are similarly driven by ideological and moral concerns. They are dissatisfied with the current state of affairs and desire to alter policies toward Aboriginal peoples. The decision to offer (or decline to offer) an apology can suggest a marked change in government policy. Political ideology points the direction of such change. In general, liberal parties, in keeping with their view of the sanctity of individual rights and the virtues of limited government, have advocated for undifferentiated citizenship and against group rights for indigenous peoples.[46] For example, in 1969 Prime Minister Pierre Trudeau's government issued a now infamous White Paper that advocated repealing Canada's Indian Act (and thus ending Indian legal status), terminating federal obligations, and dismantling the Department of Indian Affairs.[47] Trudeau's government officially withdrew the paper in 1971,

---

[45] Forum (2000); Ghannam (2000); Robinson (2000).
[46] Christian and Campbell (1990); Bennett (1999: 57–75).
[47] The White Paper was formally titled "The Statement of the Government of Canada on Indian Policy."

in the face of indigenous resistance. Today, Australian Prime Minister Howard ignores calls for a treaty and recognition of Aboriginal group rights. He refuses to apologize largely because an apology would signal agreement with Aboriginal demands. In contrast, labor parties, in keeping with their commitments to collectivism and social equality, have been more supportive of group claims. In Australia, for example, Labor Party governments since the early 1970s have advocated Aboriginal "self-determination," secured the passage of antiracial discrimination legislation, and significantly increased federal spending.

It is important to note, however, that for much of the twentieth century, political parties in Australia, Canada, New Zealand, and the United States paid little attention to indigenous issues. A study of Canadian political party platforms from 1867 to 1960, for example, found only "one innocuous reference to Aboriginal peoples in 1887," followed seventy-one years later, in 1958, by a "Liberal Party endorsement of 'voluntary integration of the Canadian Indians into our national life as full citizens.'"[48] Similarly, political scientist Scott Bennett describes early efforts (from 1900 to the 1960s) by Aboriginal peoples to garner support from mainstream Australian political parties (that is, both the Labor and Liberal parties) as "futile," because none except the Communist Party showed "great sympathy for Aboriginal claims."[49] These examples are not to suggest that political parties were unaware of Aboriginal issues, but rather that a near consensus on government policy existed, rendering partisan divisions inconsequential, and that such issues were of marginal electoral importance. Bennett describes approaches to Australian Aboriginal policy for much of the twentieth century as bipartisan because all major parties supported specific policies of "assimilation" and general goals of Aboriginal "betterment." Describing legislation regarding Native Americans as "minor," because it affects a tiny and politically weak segment of the population and because lawmakers have largely treated it as such, Charles C. Turner finds that up to the mid-twentieth century, federal American Indian legislation was characterized by a "lukewarm bipartisanship," which has since been replaced by an observable partisanship.[50] The point is, then,

[48] Cairns (2000: 20).
[49] Bennett (1999: 58).
[50] Turner (2005: 1–17).

that when political parties have differed in their approaches to indigenous policies, these differences have been largely along ideological and partisan lines.

For certain state actors, an apology is the morally correct action in light of the historical record. Australia's former Labor Prime Minister Paul Keating once remarked, "I'm more convinced than ever that we've got to make peace with the Aborigines to get the place right."[51] By "make peace," he did not mean stop war or curb violence; rather, he meant that it was time to reach a just and fair arrangement. Likewise, former Representative Tony Hall (D-OH), in arguing for a congressional resolution for slavery, claimed that while an apology is "not easy," it is "the right thing to do."[52]

These moral judgments are often rooted in feelings of guilt. Recent research postulates that "collective guilt" is a powerful motivator for apologies and other efforts of rectification. Drawing from social identity theories in social psychology, researchers have found that when persons identify with a group, and accept that their group is responsible for harmful actions against another group, they feel guilty, even if they themselves are not personally responsible.[53] This group-based guilt, research shows, is a powerful predictor of support for apology.[54] Representative Hall's proposed slavery resolution broadly conforms to the theory's postulates. He attempted to evoke collective guilt in order to get the Congress to act, admonishing fellow members to accept what Congress as an institution had historically done while recognizing that they were not personally responsible: "No member of Congress today voted on measures to perpetrate slavery. But the Congress as an institution bears responsibility." He also reminded them that acceptance of the good also requires acceptance of the bad. In keeping with social identification theory, individuals, not surprisingly, are much more likely to "bask in the glory" of group membership than recognize group transgressions.[55]

In the end, efforts to evoke collective guilt do not automatically result in apologies, for at least two reasons: First, a prerequisite for

[51] Markus (1994: 221).
[52] U.S. House of Representatives (1997: H3890).
[53] Branscombe and Dooseje (2004: 3).
[54] McGarty et al. (2005).
[55] Ibid. (4).

feeling guilty is the perception of being responsible for said injustices; second, pride and honor seem also to override feelings of guilt. For example, Prime Minister Howard has justified his decision not to apologize by both rejecting the premise of responsibility ("Australians of this generation should not be required to accept the guilt and blame for the past actions and policies over which they had no control"[56]) and by expressing pride in Australian history (the negative portrayal of Australian history "...deliberately neglects the overall story of great Australian achievement..."[57]). Research on the attitudes of ordinary Australians confirms that individuals who did not believe that their group was responsible for Aboriginal disadvantage neither felt guilty nor were supportive of apology.[58]

Resources and Constraints

Whatever their motivations, the ability of actors to act on them can be both enabled and constrained by the political contexts in which they operate. Democratic institutions best enable, imperfectly and incompletely, the expression and pursuit of preferences. In this book's cases, historical treaties as well as other legal, political, and administrative arrangements are political resources for minority groups, although they might not readily appear as such. These treaties and arrangements anchor minority claims in institutional processes and not mere complaint. They also provide the language and implements needed for effective mobilization by highlighting the relevance of historical claims of injustice to contemporary politics. Indigenous groups refer to broken treaties and to designated bureaucratic policies, constitutional protections, and laws. In calls for apology and reparations, African American advocates refer to slavery, Jim Crow segregation, and violence, and to General William Sherman's "40 acres and a mule."[59]

---

[56] Behrendt (2003: 3).

[57] Howard (1997).

[58] McGarty et al. (2005).

[59] On January 16, 1865, Sherman declared the Georgia Sea Islands and a strip of South Carolina rice country as rice settlements. Each family of freed slaves was to be given 40 acres and a mule. President Andrew Jackson nullified the Field Order and ordered that the Freedman's Bureau return the land to pardoned Confederate landowners. In 1867, Republican representative Thaddeus Stevens proposed a slave-reparations bill that did not pass.

Groups also use international law as a resource; examples include the United Nation's *International Covenant on Civil and Political Rights* (1976) and the United Nation's *Draft Declaration on the Rights of Indigenous Peoples* (1994). The calls for self-determination and autonomy are supported explicitly by the UN's International Covenant on Civil and Political Rights, adopted by the UN General Assembly in 1966 and entered into force in 1976.[60] Aboriginal activist Mick Dodson justifies the desired domestic political status of Australia's Aboriginal peoples in terms of human rights as follows:

As the First Peoples of this land we are unique with distinct communal values. We are different, but this difference does not preclude a dichotomous approach to the enjoyment of human rights, both individual and collective. It should be understood that our rights are different from but equal to the rights of non-indigenous people.[61]

Moreover, the commission that produced the official report (*Bringing Them Home*) on Australia's policy of forced child removal policies was itself a direct result of international law. The Human Rights and Equal Opportunity Commission is empowered to handle complaints, review legislation, and conduct research, all in light of the Racial Discrimination Act of 1975 and other laws. The 1975 act was Australia's legislative response to the International Convention on the Elimination of All Forms of Racial Discrimination, to which Australia became a signatory in 1966 and which it ratified in September 1975.[62]

Obvious political constraints for minority groups derive from both the absolute and relative paucity of resources (political and economic) in relation to state authorities and the groups' small demographic size. Their minority status often requires that they seek out allies and build coalitions with majority groups. Indigenous leaders and African Americans use rhetorical strategies to move minority concerns from the periphery to the center, suggesting, for example, that the majority's welfare in some way depends on the minority's welfare. For vulnerable and disadvantaged groups, moral appeals are often central to political argument and action. As Native American scholar and activist Vine Deloria observes, "The Aboriginal peoples can only argue the morality

---

[60] Pritchard (1998: 184).
[61] Dodson (1999: 45).
[62] Chesterman and Galligan (1997: 196).

of their case. Overwhelmed by the European peoples, they cannot look forward to the day when they regain control of their lands."[63] But at the same time, group members also express skepticism about the ultimate worth of moral appeals because although they may be essential, they are infrequently followed by action. This paradox is revealed in Hoopa leader Lyle Marshall's reactions to the 2000 Bureau of Indian Affairs' apology: "Until the government and Congress are bound to action, no apology will be sufficient. Indian survival depends on the American conscience."[64]

State officials, being the far more powerful actors, can do as much or as little as they choose. However, even with this vast power differential, constraints influence their decision to apologize (or not). These constraints are political, electoral, legal, and affective. The political constraint is largely of their making. As mentioned, in most of our cases, the executive and/or legislature created the very commissions that recommended an apology. Here, the executive and legislature must decide whether to abide by the commission's recommendations. Australia's Prime Minister Howard chose mostly to disregard them, and Canada's Jean Chrétien opted to abide by them, albeit in modified form.

Attention to public opinion in general and elections in particular can potentially affect the decision to apologize. Will elected politicians be rewarded, punished, or left unaffected by their decision to endorse (or not endorse) an apology? The apologies appear not to have been of electoral significance, except, to a small degree, in Australia and the United States. In Australia, the opposition Labor Party made the ruling Liberal Party's refusal to apologize a central issue in the 2001 federal elections. Prime Minister Howard was reelected to a third term in October 2001 and to a historic fourth term in October 2004. Yet his 2001 victory cannot be seen unambiguously as public support for his refusal to apologize, in part because Australians were themselves divided on the issue. A 1999 poll sponsored by the Council of Aboriginal Reconciliation reported that 57 percent opposed an apology and 40 percent supported it.[65] Rather, his tough stance on immigration in light of the September 11 terrorist attacks in the United States overwhelmed all

---

[63] Quoted in Manuel and Poslums (1974: xi).
[64] Tsosie (2006: 186).
[65] Newspoll, Saulwick & Muller and MacKay (2000: 33–52).

other issues, including economic and social welfare policies along with Aboriginal policy and apology.[66] Prior to September 11, apology had been an issue of some electoral salience. In 2004, Republican members of the U.S. Congress sponsored an apology resolution to Native Americans because, according to press reports, they hoped to garner votes in tight congressional races in the 2004 election, where Native American votes were crucial.[67] Although Native American voter participation increased in key states, they tended to vote Democratic and to base their decisions on local issues.[68] By contrast, Canadian public opinion polls conducted one month before the government issued its 1998 apology showed that 75 percent of Canadians supported the government making an apology to all Aboriginal peoples. The apology was itself not an issue by the time of the 2003 federal elections.

The legal constraint has been raised by state officials concerned with introducing legal liability through apology. The threat of such liability has been more feared than real, however, precisely because lawmakers can invoke sovereign immunity. In 2000, for example, the presiding judge of one of the first test cases of Australia's child-removal policy (*Cubillo v. Commonwealth*) commented on the legality of a formal federal apology, although the issue had not been raised in the case.[69] Judge Maurice O'Loughlin observed that such an apology would be covered by absolute parliamentary privilege.[70] The proposed U.S. congressional apology to Native Americans expressly immunizes the federal government from making claims.

Finally, as earlier mentioned, state actors who judge that neither they as individuals nor their fellow citizens were responsible for said injustices do not feel guilty and therefore do not favor apology. Feelings of "nonresponsibility" are powerful constraints against state support for apologies. Feelings of national pride, derived from certain interpretations of national history, also play a role.

---

[66] Hugo (2002).
[67] Editorial (2004).
[68] Lehman and Macy (2004).
[69] In the *Cubillo v. Commonwealth* case, Lorna Cubillo and Peter Gunner sued the Commonwealth government for having been removed from their mothers' care and placed in detention homes, run by two religious organizations. "They claimed damages for loss of cultural and other aspects of Aboriginal life and loss of rights..." Clarke (2001: 228).
[70] Senate Legal and Constitutional References Committee (2000: 113–14).

Organizational and Institutional Mechanisms

Demands for or offers of official apologies do not just happen. Rather, they are mediated through organizational and institutional mechanisms. The two critical and related mechanisms are pressure and the power and authority of a deliberative institutional body. Groups pressure and persuade, by means of lobbying, networking, and/or protesting. They do not necessarily lobby directly or only for an apology, but rather for attention to be paid to a specific issue or range of issues. In Australia, for instance, several years before the apology issue emerged, government officials, child welfare advocates, and Aboriginal organizations began to call for a national investigation into the state's child removal policy. Similarly, Canada's seemingly ongoing constitutional crisis and an armed standoff between the Mohawk nation and state and federal officials over land prompted Prime Minister Brian Mulroney to establish RCAP.

The other means is institutional, where an official (either elected or appointed) uses the authority of his or her office to propose an apology or where a special body is created to investigate a given issue and to provide recommendations, one of which may be an apology. These two mechanisms are related because outside pressure usually, but not always, precipitates an official taking a stand or a commission being established. Similarly, once a lawmaker proposes or a legislative body recommends an apology, groups apply more pressure so that lawmakers' efforts are supported or the commission's recommendations are followed. Thousands of non-Aboriginal Australians, for example, initiated grass-roots efforts to encourage Prime Minister Howard to apologize and themselves signed "sorry books." When the Canadian government was slow in formally responding to the RCAP report, Aboriginal organizations conducted public demonstrations.[71]

The Stakes of Apologies

Identifying the factors and mechanisms that lead to an apology (or not) does not provide all of the information required to construct a complete theory of apologies. Required also is a fuller discussion of apologies

---

[71] Hurley and Wherrett (2000a).

themselves and of the judgments that political actors make about both their propriety and efficacy. In the first instance, current debates among liberal theorists regarding indigenous claims usefully lay out the ideas that animate competing views about apologies' suitability.[72] As earlier discussed, indigenous claims include demands for the return and control of traditional lands, meaningful self-government, and respect for and preservation of cultures. It may not be immediately clear what, if anything, an apology has to do with these claims. The connection between claims and apology is made when thinking about how history should be taken into account in response to indigenous demands.

On the view of proponents of formal equality, apology would not seem a pressing concern, since the proper way of addressing indigenous claims is to extend formal equality – that is, that all of the rights and protections afforded to other citizens also be extended to indigenous citizens. On this view, the past has no bearing on their status as citizens, because they are to be treated as individuals, not as group members. Their claims to prior land ownership and political autonomy, which are based on group membership, are tangential to what contemporary political life and justice requires. Thus, if the past has no bearing on their present status, it follows logically, although not inevitably, that an apology has no place, especially if that apology – in acknowledging group identity, land loss, and political and cultural autonomy – implies that such lands and autonomy should be somehow restored. In principle, an apology need not be automatically ruled out if one is a proponent of formal equality. One can recognize group identity and past injustices without either endorsing group rights or group-based remedies. But, in the real world, the two appear to be diametrically opposed, with politicians and other advocates of formal equality usually objecting to apology.

For supporters of indigenous claims, there is a logical connection between such claims and apology. Indigenous demands for land return, self-government, and cultural preservation rest on historical experiences of dispossession and political and social subordination. Contemporaneous indigenous disadvantage, they argue, is linked directly to these past experiences. An apology, then, supports indigenous claims by identifying the past as a major, if not only, source of harm and by

[72] Ivison et al. (2000); Ivison (2002: ch. 5).

implying that the remedy of current disadvantage requires a more just distribution of resources, with an eye toward meaningfully restoring what was lost. Just as formal equality need not stand in opposition to apology, an apology need not automatically follow from support of indigenous group rights, although the two are quite compatible. Yet, the case can be made to separate the two. Jeremy Waldron argues that historic injustices have been "superseded" by present-day realities.[73] According to Waldron, there is no straight line from evidence of historical injustice to restitution for said injustices, because over time material and social circumstances have changed radically. The "supersession argument" posits that

> ... in certain sequences of circumstances, dispossession may not continue to count as an injustice even though the events that led to it were undoubtedly an injustice. And if the dispossession does not continue to count as an injustice, then reversion cannot be conceived as an appropriate remedy.[74]

Instead, Waldron argues that attention to injustice today and in the future, which would necessarily include attending to indigenous disadvantage, should guide our thinking. Present-day exigencies require that we distribute "the resources of the world in a way that is fair to all of its existing inhabitants."[75] Apologies, accompanied by some sort of symbolic reparations, are especially desirable because "the payments give an earnest of good faith and sincerity to acknowledgement."[76] Here, one can support an apology, precisely because it acknowledges historical injustice, and still oppose indigenous demands for full restitution of land, reparations, and self-governance.

At bottom, an apology is an acknowledgment and moral evaluation of wrongdoing.[77] It can stand alone, disconnected from a position on indigenous claims. However, more often than not, an apology is so attached precisely because historical injustices are at the heart of

---

[73] Waldron (1992): idem (2002).

[74] Idem (2004: 245). For an argument challenging the supersession thesis, see Patton (2005).

[75] Waldron (1992: 26).

[76] Ibid. (4–7).

[77] Sociologist Nicholas Tavuchis defines apology as "an acknowledgement and painful embracement of our deeds, coupled with a declaration of regret." Tavuchis (1991: 19).

indigenous claims. It is not a big leap from acknowledgment and moral evaluation of historical injustices to an expectation that some attempt at repair be initiated. Making that leap is what proponents of indigenous claims and apologies advocate. It is also the leap that opponents of indigenous claims resist.

Resistance to this connection takes three main discursive forms. Most often, actors first register their opposition by calling historical reinterpretation into question. Apologies, after all, ratify certain reinterpretations of history. National histories are reexamined; justifications are looked at anew; aspects of history that were ignored draw focus; and actions that were denied are acknowledged. The objective is to cast doubt on both the "small facts" and the "big picture" in ways that undermine the rationale for giving an apology.

The linkages connecting apology to indigenous claims begin with the acknowledgment of past wrongdoing and lead to the attribution of contemporary minority disadvantage to past state actions. Dependency, extreme poverty, and marginalization today are perceived as best explained by earlier state policies, and not by purported cultural deficiencies and racial inferiority. For apology opponents, it does not follow that all, or even most, of indigenous or minority disadvantage today is rooted in past mistreatment. Finally, the linkages between apology and indigenous claims end with a critical reappraisal of the fundamental boundaries and obligations of national community. Indigenous peoples were often treated as "wards" of the state, judged incapable of self-direction, unsuited for white civilization, and unqualified for citizenship. State officials and citizens assumed a paternalistic and racist sense of obligation, not one of mutual regard or respect. Disavowal of past practices, as signified through an apology, strengthens demands and proposals for new political arrangements, since the old way of doing things usually meant disregarding indigenous ideas and preferences. Opponents of apologies do not think that past bad practices, if we today judge them as such, obligate states to agree now with indigenous demands.

Apologies, then, are admissions of past injustices that can be, in turn, pressed into service, providing justifications for changes in the content and direction of state policies. It is these central features of acknowledgment and judgment that make apologies attractive to some and objectionable to others. Moreover, as distinctive as apologies are, certain of their tasks are also carried out by other processes. For example, legal trials during periods of political transitions call attention to and sanction new historical interpretations and make moral judgments, just as apologies do. As Ruti Teitel writes, "Through investigatory and condemnatory processes, the law exposes and delegitimates the value system associated with past rule."[78] However, official apologies differ from trials and other legal measures in three important respects. The first, and most obvious, is that apologies are not legally binding. There is no legal sanction for not apologizing, and there are no legal consequences for reneging on the implied agreement of apology, namely that certain acts will not be committed again. Second, although often publicized, trials and judicial decisions are not open to public participation in the ways that official commissions and public debates about apologies and history are. Third, the law and a given legal case establish individual guilt or innocence, whereas official apologies assign (or urge acceptance of) collective guilt.

Proponents also think that apologies can effectively achieve desired ends, namely, reconciliation. Although reconciliation is best understood in its specific context, at minimum it refers to positive changes in emotional dispositions. These dispositions can lessen the animus between individuals, groups, or countries. Evidence partially supports these expectations for individuals. For example, recent research on legal dispute resolution has found that apologies that are perceived as genuine can "reduce the risk of litigation and help to resolve legal disputes once they arise."[79] However, research also shows partial apologies can actually aggravate matters when evidence clearly points to liability on the apologizer's part. Here, a partial apology is viewed as an attempt to evade full responsibility, not accept it. Similarly, scholars of international relations expect that apologies will ease interstate relations by lessening threat perceptions. However, as with disputes between individuals, perception of the apology's quality matters. Aggressive nationalist or nonrepentant views, shared by certain segments of the citizenry and political elite, can undermine how an apology is delivered and hence perceived. The need to preserve national

---

[78] Teitel (1997: 2078).
[79] Matthews (2005: 5).

"honor and face" overrides the desire to apologize sincerely and fully.[80] For example, the well-documented divisions within Japanese political leadership between "hard-line" nationalists, who minimize or glorify Japan's past aggression, and "soft-line" nationalists, who express regrets about that past, partly explain the ambiguity of Japanese apologies.[81]

In democratizing countries, apologies are presumed to ease political transition and help in strengthening democracy. This idea received its strongest endorsement in South Africa's Truth and Reconciliation Commission (TRC). Apology became a key component of the TRC's amnesty policy and procedures. The policy granted amnesty to anyone who had engaged in gross human rights violations if they testified before the TRC. Frequently, these testimonies resulted in apologies. Research shows that these apologies, when perceived as sincere, mattered to victims and their families and helped to generate "popular acceptance of amnesty."[82] In most other transitional experiences, the consequences for apologizing are neither as directly beneficial to the alleged perpetrators nor as demanding of the apology's recipients. After all, receiving amnesty for self-incriminating testimony is a powerful incentive to participate. For victims or their families, satisfaction with perpetrator testimony in lieu of criminal punishment requires a great deal of generosity. In sum, when reconciliation is discussed in affective terms, it refers to the strengthening of a sense of sharing, regard, and having "come to terms," in some emotional way, with the past. Apologies are presumed to contribute to reconciliation; the ways by which they do so are usually not well specified, other than through education (that is, citizens learn about harms through the public debates about apology) and increased and more "honest" interactions between individuals and groups, in both structured settings (such as the TRC) and unstructured ones. Generally, it is not asserted that apologies alone will lead to affective reconciliation, but rather that they are sometimes important contributors.

However, detractors point out that apologies can lead to resistance and backlash. The invocation of guilt required to receive an apology

---

[80] O'Neill (1999: 177).
[81] Yoshibumi (1999).
[82] Gibson (2004: 285).

may have undesired effects, because few want to feel guilty or want to be made to feel guilty. For example, just the mention of an apology and reparations for American slavery produces very strong opposition from white Americans, as registered in public opinion polls.[83] In a more neutral way, apologies may foster indifference or disinterest, which is also a less desirable result. For example, Leslie Hatamiya found that most senators and representatives, in voting for apology and reparations for Japanese Americans, faced neither a "noticeable Japanese (or Asian American) community nor a vocal and organized opposition."[84] Thus, although the apology was successfully achieved, it was not accompanied by nor did it generate widespread public debate about or interest in societal reconciliation.

As importantly, for our purposes, reconciliation has other meanings beyond affect and extending to law and politics. Generally, reconciliation is tied to desired political arrangements. In Australia, competing political views of reconciliation are most sharp, where reconciliation, on one side, means supporting Aboriginal rights, and, on the other, it means support of Prime Minister Howard's "practical reconciliation" and formal equality. Similarly, in South Africa, reconciliation has taken on several meanings. James Gibson argues that it has included at least four concepts, of which two pertain to acceptance of the legitimacy of South African laws and political institutions.[85] The point here, then, is that reconciliation may be understood to include not just better, more harmonious relations among citizens, but also greater confidence in political institutions as well as concrete alterations in laws and political arrangements governing national membership.

A Membership Theory of Apologies

We are now at the point where I can outline my membership theory of apologies. Political actors offer and/or demand apologies in the service of minority group claims. Apologies are most achievable when both political elites and aggrieved groups desire them, but the sanction of the political elite is absolutely essential to their obtainment. Political elites

---

[83] Dawson and Popoff (2004).
[84] Hatamiya (1993: 75).
[85] Gibson (2004: 4).

who favor minority rights and are responsive to minority pressure support apology. The elites' backing of indigenous claims is based in their views of citizenship and related views of national history and its moral obligations. Regret and guilt about past injustices often accompany this elite support. Similarly, indigenous groups have long demanded autonomy while also fighting for the end of discriminatory treatment. Over the course of the twentieth century, indigenous mobilization has contributed to the end of formal exclusion, and has also made possible the pursuit of strategies aimed at retrieving lost land as well as political, cultural, and economic autonomy. Apologies put historical loss and restoration at the center of indigenous argument, which accounts for their appeal.

The objectives that apologies advance are multiple, and are often referred to simply as "reconciliation," which is itself broadly defined. Reconciliation is here understood to mean not only more harmonious societal relations, but also alterations in political, economic, and, possibly, legal arrangements. State actors may use apologies to change or fortify the content and direction of public policies in order to support and further indigenous autonomy.

Conversely, political elites do not offer apologies when they neither support nor seek to advance indigenous or minority group claims. They do not recognize group rights, nor do they believe that the facts of historical injustice require them to do so. Nor do they define reconciliation in expansive ways, choosing instead to view reconciliation narrowly and in largely affective ways, without referring to fundamental political, legal, or economic alterations.

In deciding whether to apologize, political actors are guided most significantly by their ideological positions on group claims and their related understandings of national history and its moral burdens. The prospect of electoral gains, the desire to avert reparations and other material compensation, and international norms and influence each fail to explain apologies' emergence or the stakes attached to them. The "winners" in apology politics are those domestic actors whose views about national membership and national history prevail.

Narrow electoral considerations do not typically explain the decision to apologize (or not) because political elites recognize that the direct electoral effects of apologies are likely to be negligible. Public support for or opposition to apologies is tied to partisan positions on larger indigenous issues, which are, in turn, usually of low electoral salience at the national level. There are exceptions, however, to this general observation of low electoral salience. For example, political scientists Scott Bennett and James Jupp suggest that backlash against the Australian Labor Party's support of Aboriginal issues among its own supporters contributed to its 1996 loss to the Liberal Party.[86] In the wake of this defeat, however, the Labor Party has remained attentive to and supportive of Aboriginal concerns. (Apology did not become a national issue until 1997, with the release of the *Bringing Them Home* report.) The proposed 2004 U.S. congressional apology to Native Americans is an instance where narrow electoral concerns seem to explain best elite motivations, at least according to press reports. Republican legislators hoped that a Republican-initiated apology would redound to the party in several tight congressional races where Native American votes were anticipated to make the difference. In the end, Native Americans voted in large numbers for the Democratic Party, conforming to an observed partisanship since the 1970s, with the proposed apology having no effect.[87] Since the 2004 election, Senate subcommittee hearings on the apology continue, suggesting that motivations beyond electoral gain are also at play.

Neither do desires to avert or to acquire material gains best explain the giving or demands for apology nor the refusals to give one. First, lawmakers can and do invoke the principle of sovereign immunity, parliamentary privilege, or some other disclaimer to disallow upfront reparations or restitution payments. Reparations are offered only when they are the intent of lawmakers. The Canadian government's apology, for example, was accompanied by a $350 million "healing fund" for Aboriginal victims of residential school abuse. Moreover, indigenous groups have pursued native title and treaty claims largely independently of demands or requests for apologies. These claims predate

---

[86] Citing an article from an Australian newspaper, Scott Bennett writes: "Ironically, however, research conducted after the 1996 election debacle suggested that Labor's support for Aboriginal people was an important factor in turning away many long-term Labor voters." Bennett (1999: 62). James Jupp writes simply, "The ministers most closely identified with Labor's Aboriginal policy, Michael Lavarch and Robert Tickner, both lost their seats." Bean et al. (1997: 81).

[87] Wilkins (2002: 194).

demands for apologies and continue in the courts, legislatures, and federal bureaucracies long after an apology is given or not.

More broadly, however, apologies do effect material claims insofar as political elites use them discursively to support changes in federal policy favoring indigenous political autonomy and economic self-sufficiency. For example, if the recommendations of Canada's RCAP and subsequent executive policy statements are followed through in any meaningful, if incomplete, way, they would result in substantial material gains for many indigenous peoples. In the end, the ability of apologies to influence or alter policy is tied to an overall determination of elites to change policy. The point here is that apologies do not themselves lead to an opening of the public till, nor are they solely or primarily desired in order to do so. Rather, they provide justification for why such payment is warranted, and they often accompany decisions to reformulate federal policies and/or actually to dispense funds and redistribute lands and resources.

Finally, scholars have stressed the role of international actors and norms in accounting for the emergence of demands and/or offers of domestic apologies. It is true that international law and norms buttress domestic indigenous mobilization. Groups have used them to support their demands both for indigenous rights and entitlements and for the cessation of racial discrimination. The government commissions that recommended apologies judged said injustices as violations both of national principles and of international human rights laws and norms. It is also likely that proponents of apologies looked abroad for positive examples. This is certainly true in the Australian case, where in the wake of Prime Minister Howard's "Motion of Reconciliation," which many judged insufficient, legislators identified Canada as an example of a proper and successful apology.[88]

Nonetheless, it seems an overstatement to suggest that international law and norms or even demonstration effects lead directly to the apologies offered. For example, in offering the U.S. Bureau of Indian Affairs 2000 apology, Assistant Secretary Kevin Gover explained that his own moral sensibilities and those of his staff guided him.[89] The Canadian

---

[88] Senate Legal and Constitutional References Committee (2000: ch. 4).
[89] Author's telephone interview with Kevin Gover, December 6, 2000.

government's apology was a direct, if belated, response to the RCAP report. The Australian National Parliament in 1998 commissioned a background paper that compared Australian indigenous and non-indigenous relations with those of several countries, including Canada, New Zealand, Norway, Sweden, and the United States. One point of comparison was whether apologies had been offered or not. Through this study, Australian lawmakers learned that Canada, New Zealand, Norway, and the United States had apologized to indigenous populations and Sweden had not.[90] The Australian National Parliament, as we know, did not formally apologize. If international norms had any effect, in this case it would be negative, fortifying a government's decision to buck international trends and to demonstrate national independence. In sum, the impact of international factors varies, according to their instrumental utility to political actors. The overriding determinants are the desires and intentions of political elites to apologize, which are driven by ideology and the seeming imperatives of moral reflection.

Apologies and National Membership

The theoretical claim is that political actors use official apologies in ongoing efforts to reshape the meanings and terms of national membership. Membership in a political community exists along three dimensions: legal, political, and affective. The three are inextricably linked. The legal status of one's membership as a citizen (whether one is or is not a citizen) profoundly affects one's feeling of belonging, the political rights one may exercise, and one's perception and treatment by others. Conversely, feelings of detachment or satisfaction with membership may lead to lesser or greater civic participation, which may lead to the further loss or enhancement of political rights. All three, then, are bound together, and along all three dimensions indigenous people and African Americans were excluded or severely constrained in ways that made meaningful participation extremely difficult, when not impossible. As earlier discussed, the successful fulfillment of these three dimensions contributes to a broader conceptualization of reconciliation.

The acknowledgment of historic injustices, which an apology announces, is directly tied to altering membership. As Duncan Ivison

[90] Dow and Gardiner-Garden (1998).

writes, "The injustice of expropriation of Aboriginal lands, for example, is not only about the dispossession of property, or the violation of negative rights of non-interference, but a violation of just terms of association," between indigenous peoples and the state.[91] If such injustices are recognized, then, rectification of some sort is required, so the argument goes, and such rectification can mean policy support of indigenous claims and self-determination, however defined.

There is the obvious fact, however, that the enormity and complexity of the attendant issues dwarf whatever expected effects apologies would or could have. The evidence from our cases, as we shall see, confirm that intuition insofar as the effects of apologies are largely indirect, reinforcing, and diffuse. But it also remains true that the denial, nonacknowledgment, and minimizing of historical injustices have long neutralized the potency of indigenous claims and undercut government efforts at remedy precisely because the wrongs themselves have gone unacknowledged. The relationship between the state and indigenous groups has been and continues to be an interconnected but profoundly unequal one, with each successive generation negotiating terms of association on an uneven and seemingly overdetermined political field. Apologies, in their own specific ways, can help to reorient that field, as political actors recognize.

Successful apologies can affect national membership, in ways consistent with indigenous demands. Predictably, in none of the cases analyzed in this book has an apology affected the legal status of group members as citizens. However, political actors have used apologies to shape political arrangements in nearly all of our cases, to greater and lesser degrees. The influence of apology is most evident in Canada, where the then-governing Liberal Party used it to justify the further strengthening of institutions of Aboriginal self-governance, in keeping with the general direction of federal Aboriginal policy making since the 1970s. Government officials identified dealing with the past, both learning from and apologizing for it, as a means to renew and fortify Aboriginal policy. However, concrete changes in policy have been far more limited, according to Canada's Assembly of First Nations, with the government assisting a small number of bands in their transition to self-government and funding a number of economic development

---

[91] Ivison (2000: 362).

programs, but with little to no progress on the major policy changes recommended by RCAP.[92]

By contrast, outcomes are more complex in Australia, as there are competing views about both the propriety of apology and the proper direction of Aboriginal policy making. Prime Minister Howard has long held that his understanding of reconciliation, known as "practical reconciliation," does not require an apology, because, he argues, a more robust commitment to formal equality, and not to Aboriginal rights, is required. Aboriginal leaders, along with opposition party leaders, criticize practical reconciliation both on its own terms and on their understanding of reconciliation. They link their advocacy for an apology directly to their view of reconciliation, which they have taken to mean a formal treaty and/or eventual political autonomy and economic self-sufficiency. In less forceful and evident ways, apology has supported and advanced current state policies of self-determination in the United States and New Zealand, respectively. Discussion about an apology for slavery has not been linked in any way to issues of African American political representation (such as minority–majority districting) or voting rights.

Finally, in nearly all of the cases, the apologies have involved the affective sides of membership – that is, feelings of belonging and mutual obligation – although not in the ways usually predicted. As with political arrangements, apologies' effects on collective sentiments vary. Perhaps not surprisingly, public opinion polls taken before and after the Canadian government's 1998 "Statement of Reconciliation" show that the Canadian public widely supported the apology itself and the direction of government Aboriginal policies. By contrast, in Australia, polls and surveys show that the majority of white Australians, including Prime Minister Howard, also decouple apology from reconciliation:

---

[92] Ten years after the report's release, the Assembly of First Nations produced a study of the government's adherence to the RCAP's recommendations. The Assembly gives the Canadian government an overall grade of "F," but gives individual grades for particular initiatives. It gives the government a "C" on the establishment of the Aboriginal government transition centre, a "C" on cojurisdiction and comanagement of land and resource initiatives, and a "C–" in the financing of Aboriginal economic and business development, through the funding of Aboriginal capital corporations. Assembly of First Nations (2006).

They support reconciliation, but oppose an apology, suggesting that an apology is not necessary for certain understandings of reconciliation. I have not found any polls of New Zealanders' views on the Queen's 1996 and 1998 apologies.

In the United States, we have a nonapology in the matter of slavery, and an apology for Native Americans, with opposite effects. Just the mere mention of an apology for slavery has raised far more attention, public discussion, and ire than either the actual Bureau of Indian Affair's apology or the proposed congressional resolution. As Christopher Buck observes, the BIA apology has "suffered a death by silence."[93] Societal reconciliation presumes and requires broad awareness and acceptance. By contrast, public opinion research on apologies and reparations reveal these two issues to be extremely polarizing, thus making "racial reconciliation" a highly unlikely result. In a 2000 survey of white and black Americans, political scientists Michael Dawson and Rovana Popoff found that 79 percent of African Americans favored a government apology for slavery, while 21 percent did not. At the other pole, 70 percent of whites were against a government apology and 30 percent favored it.[94]

Plan of the Book

Chapter 2 provides an abbreviated and analytical history of government indigenous policies in Australia, Canada, New Zealand, and the United States. Such history is indispensable to understanding the subsequent actions and demands of state and group actors. Although the U.S. Senate apology and public debates about apology and reparations for slavery are discussed in later chapters, the history of slavery and racial segregation are not included in this chapter, for two reasons. First, the broad contours of this history are better known (especially among American readers), and second, African American–related apologies (and nonapologies) are not among the book's main cases.

Using government documents, newspaper articles, and scholarly literatures, Chapter 3 closely analyzes the instances of the apologies

---

[93] Buck (2006: 97).
[94] Dawson and Popoff (2004: 61).

themselves, identifying the relevant actors, their motivations and actions, and the course of events leading to offers or lack of offers of apologies. It finds that successful apologies are the result of the support of the political elite and organized pressures or only of the political elite. These elites ideologically endorse indigenous claims, are responsive to appeals, and seek to advance group demands. They are also guided by guilt and their views about history's moral obligations. The chapter also examines how political actors, recognizing the qualities of apologies, use them either to ratify or reject reinterpretations of national histories in order to advance preferred political aims and to displace others.

Chapter 4 considers the outcomes of the apologies. It assesses the effects of apologies on the three dimensions of national membership, drawing on public opinion surveys, government reports, policy analyses, and scholarly works. How do apologies affect one's legal status as citizen? Are claims to self-governance affected by apologies, and if so, how? In which ways, if any, is societal reconciliation advanced by apologies? The chapter shows that apologies have no effect on the legal status of citizens, but that the effects on political arrangements are indirect and uneven in force. Apology has been at its most influential in underscoring a government's stated commitment to self-governance, as in Canada, and at its least influential, when it is largely disconnected from policy making, as in New Zealand or the United States. The chapter finds also that in nearly all of the cases, apologies have generated public debate about national histories and meaning of reconciliation. Whether and how apologies have furthered the affective dimensions of reconciliation varies across the cases, with the apology having some positive effects in Canada (as inferred from public opinion polls) and either no effect or potentially negative effects in the United States, for example.

Finally, Chapter 5 examines apologies through another lens, comparing them with reparations. Apologies are often judged as useless when compared with reparations as remedy, but they may be more valued if understood on their own terms – that is, as forward-looking tactics in the service of membership claims. Moreover, there are ways in which the work of reparations and apologies converge and are mutually reinforcing in that they both rely on and often lead to critical reexaminations of history. Yet, how these new histories are interpreted and their significance for present and future policy making is another matter. This chapter maintains that prior ideas about the legitimacy of group claims and citizenship provide the scale by which political actors weigh the historical facts and assess attendant moral obligations. The chapter concludes by arguing for the positive value of symbolic acts, such as apologies, to minority group politics.

2

History of National Memberships in Australia, Canada, New Zealand, and the United States

This chapter analyzes the national histories of Australia, Canada, New Zealand, and the United States in light of their policies affecting the national membership of indigenous peoples. Although national histories are sometimes vigorously disputed, as we shall see, there is ample agreement about the thrust of government policies affecting indigenous peoples and the motivations and ideas that supported those policies. These histories are essential to my argument in two ways. First, governments have apologized for (or have been asked to apologize for) specific acts and for the larger policies of which these acts were a part. Second, the past terms of national membership have, to a great degree, shaped both the ways in which indigenous groups have mobilized and the claims they have made. The discussion that follows is organized according to the three dimensions of national membership – legal, political, and affective – and analyzes the actions of state actors who have and continue to decide, although not without resistance from or sometime in consultation with indigenous peoples, the extent and meaning of indigenous membership. Apologies politics should be understood as part of this ongoing dynamic of negotiation, where state officials and indigenous groups have each sought to structure and restructure the terms of membership, usually in diametrically opposed ways. State officials built nation-states, at the expense of substantial indigenous political, economic, and social autonomy. Indigenous peoples, in turn, have fought to preserve and regain some measure of autonomy to shape their collective futures.

The Legal Dimension of Membership: Wards, Not Citizens

In all four countries, the British Crown overruled indigenous peoples' claims to sovereignty and effectively diminished indigenous understandings of landownership. The Royal Proclamation of 1763, issued after the French and Indian War, incorporated lands acquired from France upon its defeat and established British political authority over British North America. It declared that "all lands that had not been ceded to or purchased by Britain" were to be considered "reserved lands" for indigenous peoples.[1] The proclamation, while recognizing indigenous title to those lands not ceded by duly constituted indigenous leadership, claimed ultimate British sovereignty over all of the land and extended Crown protection to indigenous inhabitants. The proclamation's conciliatory tone was intended to appease indigenous authorities, who were both deeply dissatisfied by increasing settler encroachment on their lands and resistant to claims of British political authority.[2] The proclamation's "provision for sale of Indian lands to the Crown formed the basis for the land surrender treaties in Canada."[3] With confederation in 1867, all plenary power was invested in the Constitution, which did not recognize indigenous rights, and governance was divided between federal and provincial governments, with no recognition of indigenous governance structures.[4] Instead, colonial and then Canadian legislation created the conditions of Indian "wardship" and spelled out the requirements for becoming Canadian. (All Canadians were classified as British subjects until passage of the Canadian Citizenship Act of 1947.)

Similar assumptions about sovereignty guided British policy in the American colonies prior to the Revolution. The British Crown declared itself to be the ultimate sovereign, although Native Americans were sovereign over the lands they possessed. Diplomacy, treaties, and warmaking, all in the service of land acquisition, characterized the American colonial experience and extended well into the early decades of the republic. The founders inscribed their view of Native American nations as nations in the treaty clause of the American Constitution,

---

[1] Dickason (1997: 161).
[2] Tobias (1983: 40); Armitage (1995: 73).
[3] McNeil (2001: 59).
[4] Schouls (2003: 41).

recognizing Native American tribes as similar, if not equivalent, to foreign powers, and vesting the federal government with the sole power to make treaties with these nations. Article 1, section 8, clause 3 gave to Congress the power "to regulate Commerce with foreign Nations, and among the several States, and with Indian Tribes." Although Native American sovereignty was strongly implied in Article 1, its meanings soon required greater political and constitutional attention. By the 1830s, both Supreme Court decisions and settler encroachment resulting in substantial land losses gave "autonomy" and "sovereignty" different and diminished meanings.[5] Independent nations were reduced to, in the Supreme Court's words, "domestic dependent nations," and their members were rendered noncitizens, and sometimes subjects of the American government.

In contrast, the British Crown declared Australia to be *terra nullius*, an empty land, and thus did not recognize Aboriginal sovereignty or native title. State governments, for their part, did not alter the legal status of Aboriginal peoples who were viewed and treated as noncitizens during the colonial period.[6] To be sure, the absence of treaty making in Australia has been highly consequential for Aboriginal land and self-government claims in the twentieth and twenty-first centuries. However, legally, the idea of *terra nullius* accompanied ward status for Aborigines, similar to that status for indigenous peoples in Canada and to a lesser extent in the United States.

In all four countries, lawmakers spelled out in national and subnational legislation the parameters of wardship status – its entitlements and restrictions – with varying detail and consistency. With confederation in 1867, Canada established, through Section 91 (24) of its Constitution Act, federal jurisdiction over "Indians and lands reserved for Indians."[7] Enabled by this legislation, the Canadian Parliament passed the Indian Act of 1876. This Act excluded all persons designated

---

[5] Wallace (1999); Wilkins (2002: ch. 4).
[6] Using colonial Victoria as an example, Chesterman and Galligan point out that "aboriginal natives" were excluded from citizenship, but provided assistance from the Victoria Board for the Protection of Aborigines. "Preversely," they note, "half-castes were forcibly removed from stations and denied supporting benefits in the name of making them 'free and equal citizens', a status denied to 'aboriginal natives'." Chesterman and Galligan (1997: 12).
[7] Russell and Jones (1997).

as Indians from full inclusion or exercise of political rights and privileges.[8] Although lawmakers amended the Act nine times between 1914
and 1930 and substantially revised it in 1951 and 1985, it has been and
continues to be the anchor of Canadian Aboriginal policy: "'Indian'
refers to a person who, pursuant to the Indian Act, is registered as an
Indian or is entitled to be registered as an Indian," and is thus a person of "federal concern."[9] Being designated a "status" or "registered"
Indian has both given Canadian Aboriginals access to certain federal
programs and benefits and subjected them to a host of exclusions and
limitations.

For most of the Act's history, to be defined as Indian meant that
one was formally excluded from Canadian political membership
and the rights and privileges accorded its non-Indian members. It
was impossible to be Indian and Canadian at the same time. To
become a member of the Canadian community, or enfranchised, one
had to demonstrate competent English language skills and exhibit
"good" moral character. Individual, not communal, ownership of
land was also a requirement for enfranchisement. Thus the Indian
Act stipulated that reserve lands be divided into individual lots. Once
an Indian had demonstrated the requisite "civilizational" skills, he
was placed on probation for three years, during which time he had to
demonstrate that he would use the land as a white Canadian would.
Upon successful completion of the three-year probationary period,
"he was enfranchised and given title to the land."[10] Because the Indian
Act conferred Indian status through male lineage, an Indian woman
lost her Indian status if she married a non-Indian. Any Indian who
was enfranchised lost his or her legal Indian status and reserve land,
but was then given entrance into the Canadian political community,
including the right to vote. The 1951 amendment extended provincial
laws over Indian affairs and removed the Act's most paternalistic
features, such as the prohibition of specific cultural activities.[11]

In the late 1960s, the government first introduced, in its two-volume
Hawthorn Report (1966–7), the idea of "citizens plus," by which it

---

[8] The Indian Act itself drew largely on the Gradual Civilization of the Indian Tribes of
Canada Act passed in 1857, ten years prior to confederation. Dickason (1997: 225).
[9] Frideres (1998: 25).
[10] Tobias (1983: 44).
[11] Bartlett (1988: 7).

was meant that Indian status should be combined with common Canadian citizenship. The report endorsed an "asymmetrical" notion of citizenship for Aboriginal peoples, aptly captured by the term "citizens plus."[12] Yet just two years later, in 1969, the Pierre Trudeau government issued a White Paper that completely rejected the Hawthorn Report by calling for the elimination of the Indian Act altogether. Its elimination would have terminated both separate Indian status and federal obligation. It also would have undermined Aboriginal self-government, as will be discussed later in this chapter. The government withdrew the White Paper, largely in response to indigenous objections. Having survived the 1969 White Paper, the Indian Act was amended by Parliament again in 1985. The 1985 amendment (Bill C-31) not only expunged several discriminatory provisions, including most notably the enfranchisement provision, but also "increased band control over membership and other aspects of community life."[13] Indeed, with the 1985 amendment, the Indian Act remains a fundamental, if embattled, component of Aboriginal policy, precisely because it codifies Indian status.

Unlike in Canada, Australian lawmakers decided that the legal status of Aboriginal peoples should rest in state rather than national legislation. Although the Constitution offers a general framework of governance, it provides neither positive rights of citizenship nor a national definition of citizenship, as, for example, the American Constitution has since ratification of the Fourteenth Amendment in 1868.[14] Instead, the Australian Constitution has provided only a guarantee of subjecthood to the queen, the rights of citizenship being conferred through state-level laws and bureaucratic procedures. The Constitution's use of the term "Subject of the Queen" rather than "citizen" enabled Australian lawmakers to ensure that the former colonies, now states, could retain their authority over the citizenship rights of certain categories

---

[12] Cairns (2000: 52).

[13] Furi and Wherrett (2003: 1).

[14] The Constitutional Commission of 1988 recommended a number of changes to the Australian Constitution, including a bill of rights and a formal statement of citizen status, but a referendum on the issue was "defeated disastrously." Davidson (1997: 133). Moreover, "the Commission cautiously refused any enlargement of the notion of citizenship and refused to consider the introduction here of the notion that 'once a citizen, always a citizen' (the rule of Article 1 of the Fourteenth Amendment of the United States Constitution)." Ibid. (251).

of persons at the state level. Predictably, state laws denied Aboriginal residents the basic rights of citizenship conferred to white Australians through these very same state laws. In effect, lawmakers rendered Australian Aborigines aliens on their own soil. Although they were technically British subjects (as were immigrants from other parts of the British Empire), Aborigines were always excluded by state laws that differentially distributed rights and benefits to immigrants according to racial/ethnic categories.[15]

The Australian Constitution itself referred to Aboriginal people twice in its 128 sections – both in exclusionary terms. Section 51 and clause 26 declared, "The Parliament shall, subject to this Constitution, have power to make laws for the peace, order, and good government of the Commonwealth with respect to . . . [t]he people of any race, other than the Aboriginal race in any State, for whom it is deemed necessary to make special laws."[16] The census clause prohibited Aboriginal population data from being used in the apportionment of parliamentary seats and the allocation of public funds. The "special laws" clause disallowed the Commonwealth from making "special laws" in the states, when deemed necessary, for Aboriginals. In other words, the Commonwealth's "special laws" powers were restricted only in regard to the Aboriginal population. Thus Aboriginal people had no Commonwealth protection from state laws, whereas, in the words of the Constitution, "The people of any race, other than the Aboriginal race in any State," did.[17] Indeed, although the Northern Territory came under the legislative control of the Commonwealth in 1911, its Aboriginal policies differed little from those of the other states, thus underscoring the absence of federal protection or provision of rights for Aboriginal people. Australian legislators, at both the Commonwealth and state levels, passed laws that excluded Aboriginals from the range of federal and state government benefits and rights extended to Australian citizens, "natural-born" or "naturalized."[18] Instead, legislators and policy makers devised laws and policies suitable for people they perceived and treated as noncitizens or aliens. Aboriginal peoples were trapped

---

[15] Chesterman and Galligan (1997: ch. 4).
[16] Ibid. (58).
[17] Ibid. (58).
[18] Ibid. (82–3, 120)

within the regulatory web of state protection boards and reserves that controlled virtually all aspects of their existence.

As a result of the 1948 Nationality and Citizenship Act, Aboriginal people, along with other Australians, became Australian citizens. Yet the Act "actually changed very little by way of actual citizenship rights," owing to "the distinct separation between the acquisition of Australian 'nationality,' now termed citizenship, and the restrictions on individual rights at the Commonwealth and State levels."[19] Of even greater consequence, then, for Aboriginal peoples was the undoing of exclusionary and restrictive laws at the state level, where citizenship traditionally resided and from which they had been excluded. This dismantling occurred gradually over the following decades.[20] In 1967, Australians approved in a national referendum – known famously as the 1967 Referendum – reforms of the two federal constitutional clauses that referred to Aboriginal people: Aboriginal Australians would thereafter be included in the national census, and the federal government would thereafter be "authorized to enter the jurisdiction of states to make laws relating to the Aboriginal population."[21]

In the United States, it was not until the Citizenship Act of 1924, which extended U.S. citizenship to all Native Americans born in the country, that Native Americans became American citizens by birthright. (U.S. citizenship does not extinguish tribal membership, which itself can be federally or tribally recognized or denied.) Prior to the Act, Native Americans acquired citizenship through treaties, statutes, receipt of land allotments, marriage, or military service.[22] Similar to provisions of the Canadian Indian Act, the Dawes Act of 1887 stipulated that every Native American who accepted an individual plot of land would automatically "become a citizen of the United States and of the state or territory in which he or she resided, subject to its criminal and civil laws."[23]

In New Zealand, the Maori were given, in principle, the legal status of citizens on par with white New Zealanders. According to English interpretations of the 1840 Treaty of Waitangi, New Zealand's foundational document, the Maori were recognized as British subjects,

---

[19] Ibid. (119).
[20] Ibid. (ch. 6).
[21] Fletcher (1997: 409).
[22] Cohen (1988: 153).
[23] Cornell (1988: 59)

like New Zealand's other inhabitants, in exchange for surrendering sovereignty.[24] (Maori groups did not interpret the treaty to mean that they surrendered sovereignty.) Although the Maori were assigned the same legal status as white colonists, their experience of citizenship was quite dissimilar. As with Canadian and American Indians and Australian Aborigines, they were subject to a host of policies designed to force their assimilation and to undercut their autonomous political power, cultural traditions, and economy.

The Political Dimensions of Membership: Self-Governance under Constraints

In all four countries, legal status and political rights are inextricably linked. The denial of legal citizenship was nearly always accompanied by the denial of the franchise. In Canada, only enfranchised Indians were allowed to vote. The government finally extended the federal franchise to all Indians in 1967, without their having to relinquish their status as Indians. According to the Australian Constitution, the right to vote in both federal and state elections was determined at the state level. However, there were no uniform franchise laws among the states, and the state of South Australia allowed Aboriginal men and women to vote, whereas the states of Queensland and Western Australia explicitly denied them.[25] There was no consistent protection of federal franchise rights until 1949, when the Commonwealth government guaranteed Aboriginal people who had been enfranchised under state law the Commonwealth franchise. (However, indigenous Australians in Queensland and Western Australia still could not vote in federal elections because these states denied them the state vote. Queensland would hold out until 1965, making it the last state to grant this right.) Also in 1949, indigenous Australians who had served in the military during World War II were guaranteed the Commonwealth franchise. Finally, in 1962 the Commonwealth granted all indigenous Australians the right to vote in Commonwealth elections, independently of state voting restrictions, although enrollment was not compulsory until 1983.[26] Although the

[24] Sorrenson (1993: 32).
[25] Summers (2000–1: 7).
[26] Norberry (2001–2: 3).

Fifteenth Amendment of the U.S. Constitution prohibited the denial of the vote on the basis of color or race, several states denied Native American citizens the franchise on questionable constitutional, legal, and cultural grounds.[27] New Zealand's 1853 electoral franchise was open to Maori men who met the individual property ownership requirement, although few did because Maori land was communally owned.

Governments justified this exclusion from national political participation, in part, on the argument that indigenous peoples constituted sovereign nations that should be allowed to conduct their own political affairs, albeit under increasingly unfavorable and constrained conditions. (Australia is here the exception.) Indeed, treaty making had reflected this "sovereign" to "sovereign" relationship. Self-government was somehow to be maintained and respected, even as the Canadian and American governments in particular worked, for most of the nations' histories, to undermine such governance and to force the full assimilation or marginalization of indigenous peoples. For example, Canada's Indian Act, its amendments, and other federal and provincial legislation effectively made politically autonomous lives for indigenous bands and individuals nearly impossible. Although the Indian Act allowed for self-government, the ultimate goal of official indigenous policy was enfranchisement and assimilation.

Indigenous bands resisted the government's enfranchisement efforts, thus leading to more, not fewer, measures by the Canadian government to impose on and restrict indigenous political life. The Indian Act set out an electoral system for the election of leaders to band councils. With an amendment to the act in 1884 (known as the Indian Advancement Act), for example, the Canadian superintendent general or his agent "was empowered to call for band elections, supervise them, call band meetings, preside over them, record them, advise the band council, and participate in the meetings in every manner except to vote and adjourn the meetings."[28] In short, the Act greatly extended the Canadian government's reach into the internal workings of band governance. Nonenfranchisement meant that Indians remained members of their own bands, living on band reserves, and self-governing within the Indian Act's severe constraints.[29] Yet even with the government's ever-tighter

[27] Wilkins (2002: 193); McCool, Olson, and Robinson (2007).
[28] Ibid. (46).
[29] Armitage (1995: 192).

grip on band governance, voluntary enfranchisement remained abysmally low: "Between 1847 and 1940, fewer than 500 men had chosen to enfranchise."[30] Aborigines preferred self-governance, however constrained, to enfranchisement.

The Revised Indian Act of 1951 significantly increased the political power of indigenous bands by allowing them, for example, to manage "surrendered and reserve lands, band funds, and the administration of by-laws."[31] Perhaps most consequential for eventual Aboriginal mobilization, the act finally made it possible for bands to use their monies to fund lawsuits.[32] The Act also significantly weakened the minister's control over indigenous affairs. Yet even with this devolution and redistribution of power, official policy remained fully committed to assimilation and the ultimate termination of separate Aboriginal governance, as revealed by the aforementioned 1969 White Paper of the Trudeau government.

With the government's withdrawal of its White Paper in 1971, the Indian Act lives on. It remains a fundamental, if embattled, component in the strengthening of indigenous self-governance insofar as the Act now authorizes indigenous bands to determine band membership.[33] Equally important to Aboriginal self-governance as the Act's survival were Canada's constitutional debates beginning in the early 1970s, which led eventually to the constitutional recognition of Aboriginal rights in 1982.

Emergent Quebec nationalism in the 1960s raised to a new level ongoing wrangling over Canada's constitutional arrangements, especially the amending formulas. In the late 1970s, successive rounds of constitutional talks began to address a range of fundamental issues, including "patriation of the Constitution, a Charter of Rights and Freedoms, and the division of powers" between the central and provincial governments. At the beginning, in 1978, numerous constitutional conferences were held and "a Continuing Committee of Ministers was established to co-ordinate efforts for constitutional change" in response to the government's earlier proposed constitutional amendment, allowing the federal government "to unilaterally

---

[30] Dickason (1997: 225).
[31] Ibid. (305).
[32] Ibid. (305).
[33] Furi and Wherrett (2003: 1).

change the structure of central government" without consultation from
the provinces. Government officials did not include Aboriginal groups
in any of these discussions.[34]

Just as the White Paper triggered a reaction from Aboriginal groups,
so too did the constitutional talks. This time, Aboriginal groups, principally the National Indian Brotherhood, demanded both that constitutional reforms include the "entrenchment of Aboriginal and treaty
rights," and that Aboriginal peoples be included in the deliberations
as equal partners. The government responded by assigning Aboriginal groups status as observers. But that status did not satisfy Aboriginal demands, and the Aboriginal leadership took their demands
to England in 1979, where they received substantial support. Finally,
in 1981, the federal government and all provinces, except Quebec,
reached an accord that "included patriation, a domestic amending for-
mula, a Charter of Rights and Freedoms, linguistic rights, and the
strengthening of provincial control over natural resources."[35]

Since Quebec had elected not to enter into the accord, that province's
representatives claimed in the courts that the accord was invalid and
required its government's consent. In the end, the Quebec Appeals
Court ruled that Quebec did not have veto power. The Supreme Court
of Canada subsequently affirmed this decision. Consequently, Canada's
written constitution recognized Aboriginal and treaty rights for the first
time in the country's history. Specifically, section 35 of the Constitution
Act of 1982 read as follows:

1. The existing aboriginal and treaty rights of the Aboriginal peoples of Canada
are hereby recognized and affirmed. 2. In this Act, "aboriginal peoples of
Canada" includes the Indian, Inuit and Metis peoples of Canada.

Also, section 25 of the Canadian Charter of Rights and Freedoms,
which is Part I of the Constitution Act of 1982, included provisions to
"protect the special rights of Aboriginal peoples." Although the Constitution Act was widely viewed as contributing crucially to the advancement of Aboriginal self-government, its passage did not settle that issue.
Rather, first ministers' subsequently met with Aboriginal groups to clar-
ify further the Constitution Act's terms. For example, in March 1983,

---

[34] Russell and Jones (1997: 12–14).
[35] Ibid. (13–14).

sections 25 and 35 clarified "future land claims agreements." However, enduring contention between Aboriginal leaders and government officials turned on the meaning of self-government itself and the Constitution's role in recognizing it. Aboriginal leaders argued that as the right to self-government was inherent and had not been extinguished by conquest and settlement, it was not necessary for the Constitution to create that right.[36] Government took the opposite view, with both Prime Minister Trudeau and his successor, Mulroney, "adopting a 'contingent right approach' that required the content of self-government to be defined by agreement among federal and provincial government prior to any entrenchment in the Constitution."[37] In concrete terms, Aboriginal leaders demanded recognition of Aboriginal governments as "'the third order of government,' equal in jurisdiction to the other two levels of government."[38] The two sides did not reach an agreement and ended their talks.

At the same time that the Canadian government was negotiating with Aboriginal groups, it was also quietly negotiating with Quebec province over its constitutional demands. Quebec presented five demands that had to be met if Quebec were to accept the 1982 Constitutional Act. (Recall that Quebec had not signed the accord.) These demands were designed to protect Quebec's autonomy and strengthen its power within central decision making. The compromise devised by the first ministers was "to 'provincialize' Quebec's demands, by extending them to all of the provinces."[39] That 1987 compromise, known as the Meech Lake Accord, required ratification by all of the provincial legislatures to guarantee passage. In the end, two provinces, Manitoba and Newfoundland, did not ratify the accord. In the case of Manitoba, Elijah Harper, the only Aboriginal member of that province's legislature, cast the lone "no" vote. Not surprisingly, Aboriginal leaders strongly opposed "both the content and the process of the Meech Lake Accord."[40] Their demands, like those of Quebec, were based on recognition of their distinctness (Quebec had demanded to be recognized

---

[36] Morse (1999: 19–20).

[37] Ibid. (20); Russell and Jones (1997).

[38] Ibid. (17).

[39] "The only section that could not be provincialized was the distinct society clause for Quebec." Ibid.

[40] Ibid.

as a "distinct society"). The Canadian government seemed unable or unprepared to perceive the distinctness of Aboriginal peoples, although it could do so for Quebec.

The Canadian government then went back to the drawing board. In addition to establishing the Royal Commission on Aboriginal Peoples (RCAP) in August 1991, the government (federal and special parliamentary committees) began in September 1991 to develop "a more comprehensive set of constitutional proposals" and engaged in another round of negotiations in March 1992. This time, the negotiations included "national Aboriginal leaders, ministers or first ministers from all provinces and territories except Quebec, and the Right Honourable Minister Joe Clark as convenor and federal representative." The Charlottetown Accord was the final result of this effort. It "offered more compromise and more promise for all. It contained most of the Meech Lake package for Quebec, a triple-E Senate for the West, further transfer of federal powers to the provinces, and a comprehensive package for Aboriginal peoples, including the elusive inherent right and a treaty-renewal process."[41] However, the Canadian public defeated the accord in a national referendum.

With the Charlottetown Accord's defeat, Aboriginal groups and the Canadian government have looked to avenues besides the Constitution to advance Aboriginal self-governance. In that regard, RCAP has provided direction. Its report, *Partners in Confederation: Aboriginal Peoples, Self-Government, and the Constitution*, "concluded that as a matter of law and as a matter of proper public policy the inherent right of self-government already exists within section 35 of the Constitution, and that negotiations should be commenced immediately to implement that right."[42] In what appears to be an end run around Charlottetown's defeat, RCAP suggests that a constitutional amendment may not be necessary "to accommodate the inherent Aboriginal right of self-government."[43] Nevertheless, the issue remains far from settled, at least as far as the Canadian Constitution is concerned.[44] Yet

---

[41] Morse (1999: 22–4).
[42] Ibid. (25).
[43] Royal Commission on Aboriginal Peoples (1993: 1).
[44] "Significant doubt remains as to whether or not Canadian law, as it stands, acknowledges the inherent right of Aboriginal peoples to determine their own futures and govern their own affairs." Morse (1999: 41).

in another way, the issue is being settled on the ground, as Aboriginal bands enter into agreements with both provincial governments and the federal government, which set out Aboriginal jurisdiction.

Australia's policy of assimilation was similar to that of Canada, although it differed significantly in its deliberate and permanent disenfranchisement of Aboriginal peoples and absence of recognition of preexisting forms of Aboriginal governance. For the first half of the twentieth century, the policies of the Australian states were overwhelmingly "protectionist," allowing for virtually no self-government among those Aboriginal persons who were under state governments' control.[45] Instead, states passed legislation that delegated considerable administrative and regulatory power to Aboriginal protection boards. These boards, known as the Board for the Protection of Aborigines in Victoria, the Aborigines Welfare Board in New South Wales, and the Aborigines Protection Board in South Australia, controlled virtually all aspects of Aboriginal lives, including the choice of marriage partners, employer, and movement (travel from remote reserves to towns was severely restricted). Queensland's Native Affairs Department even possessed the power of taxation and compulsion, taxing Aboriginal persons not living on reserves a small percentage of their wage (5 percent) and forcing their Aboriginal charges to save a certain amount. The department funneled the monies collected from nonreserve Aborigines into an Aboriginal Provident Fund, which was in turn open to other Aboriginal inhabitants.[46] In general, separation, regulation, and assimilation were the hallmarks of official Australian policy, with no legislative provisions for Aboriginal self-governance.

The Australian government's conception of Aboriginal self-government did not appear until the last decade of the twentieth century. Described by one scholar as the "boldest and most controversial reform" of policy toward Aboriginal peoples, the Robert Hawke government in 1990 established the Aboriginal and Torres Strait Islander Commission (ATSIC), which permitted Aboriginal participation in policy making and administration.[47] ATSIC and its less powerful predecessors (that is, the National Aboriginal Consultative Committee [NACC]

---

[45] Chesterman and Galligan (1997: ch. 5).
[46] Ibid. (126).
[47] Pratt (2003: 1).

and the National Aboriginal Conference [NAC]) were all broadly committed to Aboriginal self-representation and participation in policy formulation. Yet the nature and extent of Aboriginal participation has always been complicated and worked at cross-purposes. ATSIC possessed both advocacy and delivery functions. Its representatives, elected to serve on regional councils, were expected to represent and advocate for their respective Aboriginal communities. At the same time, ATSIC also administered government programs. The tension between the two roles of advocate for Aboriginal communities within the government and administrator of government programs, compounded by ongoing public charges of ineffectiveness, incompetence, and insufficient accountability, led to ATSIC's demise in 2003. In April 2004, Prime Minister Howard announced that ATSIC would be formally and permanently abolished and that all of ATSIC's programs would be mainstreamed.

From its inception and throughout its existence, government officials and segments of the public closely scrutinized ATSIC, owing largely to its expressed commitment to Aboriginal leadership and participation (ATSIC's enabling legislation was at the time of its passage the "second-most amended piece of legislation since Federation" in 1901[48]). The Howard government has vowed to take Aboriginal involvement seriously and to improve services by way of an Aboriginal advisory council and a still-evolving system of "Australian Government Indigenous Coordination Centres." But Howard made it quite clear that he would not replace ATSIC, judging "the experiment in separate representation, elected representation for indigenous people," to have been "a failure."[49] If this view prevails, Aboriginal people in Australia will not have separate institutions (as they do in the United States and Canada), but will be expected to take part in national and state-level governance, both as the electors and the elected. At this writing in 2007, there have been only two Aboriginal members of the Commonwealth Parliament: Senator Neville Bonner (Liberal Party, Queensland) served from 1971 to 1983, and Senator Aden Ridgeway (Democrats Party, New South Wales) was elected to a six-year term in July 1999. Since 1974, approximately fourteen Aboriginal persons have served in the state parliaments

[48] Ibid.
[49] Howard (2004).

of the Northern Territory, Queensland, Western Australia, and New South Wales.[50]

New Zealand's Treaty of Waitangi is widely viewed as a unique document, its uniqueness resting less in the text, which is quite similar to those of other British colonial treaties, and more in the treaty's dual composition.[51] As Keith Sorrenson explains, the Maori text is not a mere translation of the treaty from the English text, but is rather, in one sense, another composition. Therefore, the Waitangi Treaty is as ambiguous in its meanings and stipulations as it is clear. The resultant ambiguities have sustained competing interpretations from its inception. As Andrew Sharp explains, "in Article 1 of the English language version, the Crown was granted 'sovereignty' by the Maori. In the Maori version (signed by all 13 of their leaders), the Crown had been granted only 'kawanatanga': a power to govern for strictly limited purposes."[52] In other words, there were conflicting understandings of sovereignty and of what was ceded. Predictably, the English version interprets Maori concessions broadly and the Maori interpret their concessions far more narrowly. According to the English version, "the Crown guaranteed the Maori, in exchange for sovereignty, the 'full exclusive and undisturbed possession of their Lands and Estates Forests and Fisheries and other Properties so long as it is their desire to do so.' In the Maori version, though, they were guaranteed 'te tino rangatiratanga' (full chieftainship; sovereignty) in their lands and habitations."[53]

Despite its provisions for protecting Maori land and self-government, for over one hundred years the New Zealand government and Crown regarded the treaty largely as dead letter. The British Crown did not entirely ignore the treaty, especially in the early years. However, it was eventually rendered impotent as local colonial governance was strengthened by passage of the New Zealand Constitution Act of 1852. With that Act, the British Parliament transferred constitutional authority from England to New Zealand's British settlers.[54] Over time, the colonists either ignored or interpreted the treaty in ways

[50] Australian Electoral Commission (AEC) Info Centre (2006).
[51] Sorrenson (1993: 29).
[52] Sharp (1997a: 428).
[53] Ibid.
[54] Armitage (1995: 142).

that advanced their interests and displaced Maori interests. Colonists' halfhearted efforts to include the Maori in New Zealand governance further revealed that they did not intend to include the Maori fully nor respect their cultural traditions. For example, although the 1852 legislation that granted the franchise to landowning males did not legally exclude Maori males, it did so in effect, because Maori communal lands were deemed not to satisfy the individual landownership requirements.

Barred from participating in national elections – and, to an even larger extent, unwilling to participate – the Maori demanded their own political autonomy by naming their own king, Potatau the First.[55] Open warfare soon broke out in 1860 between the two sides (known as either the "Maori Wars" or the "Pakeha Wars") and continued intermittently for seven years. In the end, the Maori were defeated and the government seized approximately 3 million acres of farmland as punishment. The Parliament also passed several pieces of legislation, all aimed at both addressing Maori grievances and enabling firmer government control over the Maori population. The Maori Representation Act of 1867, which reserved four seats in the Parliament for Maori representatives and established a separate Maori role, "was based neither on the Treaty of Waitangi nor on the principles of fair representation," but was a political compromise and a peace measure.[56] In addition to engineering Maori electoral participation, national policy making extended into other aspects of Maori social and economic life. The Native Department, which the government first established in 1861 to promote Maori assimilation through education and policing, was reconstituted in 1906 as a land management agency.[57] Its mission was to assist the Maori in consolidating and managing the lands they still possessed, while also encouraging Maori assimilation.

Although controversial throughout its 126-year history, the four reserved Maori seats endured, in part because New Zealand political and intellectual elites thought them temporary measures, lasting only until full Maori assimilation was achieved.[58] The envisioned

---

[55] Ibid. (143).
[56] Durie (1998: 97).
[57] Fleras and Elliott (1992: 198).
[58] It is important to note also that, even with the four seats, the Maori were still underrepresented. If the seats had been based on population, the Maori may have had fourteen or fifteen seats. Durie (1998: 97).

assimilation never arrived. Instead, the impetus for abolishing Maori reserved seats came in the wake of electoral reform. New Zealand's Royal Commission on the Electoral System (1985–6) recommended that New Zealand shift from a "first past the post" system to a "mixed-member proportional" (MMP) system. Judging that Maori had not been well served by separate seats and would be better served by a proportional list system, the commission called for the termination of separate seats. However, Maori defended their separate seats and were able to retain them, with modification, before the first MMP election in 1996. The 1993 Electoral Law, which authorized the MMP system, also modified the method by which the number of Maori representatives is determined. The fixed number of four, which was not based on the Maori roll (the number of Maori who choose to register on the Maori roll rather than the general roll), is now replaced by a number that is so based. After the first election under the new system in 1996, the number of Maori representatives increased steadily for several years, from five in 1996, to six in 1999, and to seven in 2002.[59]

The American government's approach to self-governance contrasts with that of Australia, Canada, and New Zealand. Native American self-governance has been powerfully shaped by the Constitution's recognition of Native American sovereignty in its treaty clause and in early Supreme Court decisions ("Cherokee Nation cases") that upheld that sovereignty while also assigning to the U.S. government a trust responsibility. In 1802, the federal government and State of Georgia agreed that, if Georgia relinquished its claims to western lands, the federal government would extinguish Native American land title in the state. But twenty-five years passed and the federal government still had not extinguished Native American title. So, disregarding Native American territorial autonomy within its boundaries and prompted by the discovery of gold on Cherokee lands, the Georgia legislature decided unilaterally to claim sovereignty and control over the Cherokee nation. With this usurpation of Cherokee political authority and other measures, the legislature hoped to force the Cherokees to accept a treaty of removal. The Cherokee nation sued the State of Georgia before the

[59] New Zealand Electoral Commission (2005); New Zealand Electoral Commission and the Ministry of Maori Development (n.d.).

U.S. Supreme Court (*Cherokee Nation v. Georgia*, 1831) on the grounds that it should be treated as a "foreign state."[60]

Chief Justice John Marshall disagreed in part with the Cherokees, deciding that the Cherokees were neither a foreign state nor a state, but rather "domestic dependent nations." Their relationship to the United States, he wrote, "resembles that of a ward to his guardian. They look to our government for protection; they rely upon its kindness and its power; appeal to it for relief of their wants; and address the President as their great father."[61] In the subsequent case of *Worcester v. Georgia* (1832), Marshall decided, in qualification of his earlier ruling, that "domestic dependent" status did not mean that the Cherokee nation should be stripped of all power and authority within its lands. Although the Cherokee nation enjoyed the "protection of the United States," it still remained a "distinct political" community over which the State of Georgia could not claim sovereignty. The Court ruled Georgia's laws to be unconstitutional. Only the federal government was permitted by the Constitution (Article 1, section 8) to interact politically with Native American tribes. Yet, as is well known, while the Supreme Court ruled in favor of the Cherokees' right to remain on their lands in Georgia, the issue was ultimately settled politically and militarily. The Andrew Jackson administration pressed on with its plans for removing Native Americans. In 1838, the Cherokee were forcibly moved west along the "Trail of Tears."

As scholars have observed, the central issues raised in the Cherokee cases endure and are reflected in subsequent policy making and thought regarding Native Americans.[62] The idea of Native American dependency had many meanings. It meant not only that Native American nations were "domestically dependent" because of their existence now within the same land mass claimed by the U.S. government, but also that Indians, dispossessed of land and means of living, were left materially dependent. It meant also that they were purportedly culturally dependent, in need of white guidance, tutelage, and civilization.

---

[60] They claimed that the Cherokee nation was "a foreign state, not owing allegiance to the United States, nor to any State of the Union, nor to any prince, potentate or State, other than their own." Mason (2000: 18).

[61] Ibid.

[62] Ibid. (22–39).

The trust relationship described by Marshall is institutionalized in the Bureau of Indian Affairs' responsibility, delegated by the U.S. Congress, to hold and dispense proceeds from Native American land ceded or sold to the U.S. government.[63] At the same time, because the U.S. federal government recognized Native American "nationhood," Native American sovereignty was retained.

Over the course of the nineteenth century, federal laws and court decisions steadily eroded the authority and power of tribal governments. In 1871, the Congress stopped entering into treaties with Native American nations altogether. Of even greater consequence for self-governance was the passage of the General Allotment Act of 1887 (the Dawes Act), which led to the dramatic decrease in Native American land ownership by distributing land to individual Native American families in fixed allotments. (The "surplus" land was sold to nonindigenous settlers.) The decrease in land possession significantly diminished the authority of Native American governments and reduced their economic self-sufficiency. As a result, the U.S. Bureau of Indian Affairs (BIA), in the form of agents and superintendents, became increasingly involved in, and often controlled, tribal governments. Federal policy turned dramatically again in 1934, with the passage of the Indian Reorganization Act (IRA). This Act allowed for the adoption of tribal constitutions that the U.S. government would recognize upon approval of the secretary of the interior.[64] However, many governance problems have emerged from these constitutions, mainly because these constitutions were themselves "boilerplates," not designed to address the particular needs of a given Native American nation. Since the 1970s, the federal government has officially promoted a policy of "self-determination," allowing tribal governments to assume most of the functions of their own government. Indeed, in key matters of governance – including membership, inheritance, taxation, property rights, and domestic relations – Native American law prevails. Although fundamental limits remain on tribal authority due to Congress's overriding plenary power, the Congress can and has over the last thirty years used its power to strengthen Native American self-government

[63] Cornell (1988: 48).
[64] Lemont (n.d.).

and economic self-sufficiency through greater reliance on tribal governments for the administration of federal programs and economic development projects.[65]

The Affective Dimension of Membership: Disappearance and Invisibility

The affective dimensions of national membership operate in at least two interrelated ways: how one is viewed and treated by others, and how one views and treats others. In all four of the countries examined here, state policies required indigenous people to alter fundamentally their ways of being and to conform to those mandated by the state before being granted entrance into the national political community. There was general agreement that indigenous people needed to change, even if there was deep skepticism about their ability to do so. But governments differed on the best ways to achieve indigenous "invisibility."

Assimilation policies were inherently contradictory. State officials wanted to keep indigenous people apart and "protected" from rapacious settlers and dishonest land surveyors, among others. They believed that relegating indigenous people to reservations (or reserves) would allow these inferior cultures to survive temporarily, before they either died off or were eventually assimilated. Yet when the reservation and separation policies did not lead to the envisioned assimilation (on its face, an unlikely outcome – how can separation result in assimilation?), government officials shifted policy to the termination of all legal distinctions and the introduction of "formal equality." Today the tables have turned yet again, as governments embrace, to greater and lesser extents, an asymmetrical notion of membership: Indigenous people are members of their own political communities, as well as of national communities. Yet such state recognition also places a burden on indigenous institutions and organizations to work at retaining and fortifying political allegiances if they are to achieve and maintain meaningful self-government.

Long-standing indigenous resistance to state-imposed assimilation and the emergence of indigenous rights movements in the 1960s are

---

[65] Aleinikoff (2002: ch. 5, 6).

the clearest evidence of competing understandings of membership and belonging. Among indigenous peoples, state assimilation policies bred deep resentments and suspicions, precisely because of the terms on which membership was presented. The methods devised by legislators, state officials, church authorities, and intellectual elites for achieving assimilation, as well as the racial ideas that justified it, were similar in all four countries.

Assimilation policies served two primary and connected purposes. One was to further the alienation of indigenous land, and the other was to make indigenous people more "white," thereby facilitating indigenous entry into the larger societies. The two are connected insofar as the acquisition of indigenous lands depended on the willingness of indigenous people to transform their cultures and their modes of land use to conform to settler standards. Of course, most lands were acquired through violent or otherwise coercive methods. Nonetheless, legislation that mandated the division of communal land into individual allotments had the dual effect of significantly reducing overall indigenous landholdings and of pushing forward individual landownership, with such ownership's attendant cultural mores.

Land allotment schemes became U.S. federal policy in 1887 with the passage of the Dawes Act, although similar schemes had been included in earlier treaties. Canada's Indian Act made individual landownership a requirement for enfranchisement. Similarly, New Zealand's Native Land Act of 1862 enabled the establishment of Native Land Courts, whose "main judicial tasks were to determine ownership and then to facilitate the individualisation of title," which led to the sale of land to white settlers.[66]

It is important to emphasize that assimilation was not merely a pretext for land acquisition. In one way, assimilation policies presumed the eventuality of land dispossession (by treaty, sale, war, fraud, or forced removal). The question of what would become of the people remained. Thus assimilation was valuable in and of itself because it could save purportedly "dying" and vanquished races. On this score, racial theories offered competing and shifting assessments of indigenous peoples' capabilities and prospects. On the one hand, missionaries, scientists, and state officials thought assimilation could be achieved for many,

[66] Durie (1998: 121).

although perhaps not for all. Their optimism was rooted in an Enlightenment vision of the malleability of human cultures and the certainty of human progress through progressive stages. Nineteenth-century American ethnologists, for example, believed that environmental conditions were largely to blame for purported Native American backwardness and lack of civilization. A change of environment, which included living conditions, education, and social organization, would result in Native American progress.[67] By the end of the nineteenth century, state officials, scientists, and intellectuals in all four countries were increasingly taking an opposite view, seeing government and other efforts as well-intentioned but futile efforts to delay, but not thwart, Aboriginal disappearance.[68] In the words of Canada's minister of Indian affairs, Clifford Sifton, speaking before Parliament in 1904: "I have no hesitation in saying – we may as well be frank – that the Indian cannot go out from school, making his own way and competing with the white man. . . . He has not the physical, mental or moral get-up to enable him to compete."[69] The pessimism of the "doomed race" theory challenged but never completely replaced assimilation's sanguinity, as its adherents judged Aboriginal progress toward "civilization" to have come far too slowly and incompletely, if at all.

Government agents and religious authorities used education, broadly conceived, to crush Aboriginal cultural values and to replace them with "white" ones. Religious missionaries administered most of the government-funded schools for indigenous peoples. Because the schools were usually a long distance from the reservations and reserves, the children who attended them were necessarily separated from their families and communities. The explicit tasks of these schools were to remake and "civilize" indigenous children. In Canada, indigenous residential schools were located in nearly every province and territory except the maritime provinces of New Brunswick and Prince Edward Island. In existence for 122 years (1874–1996), the schools enrolled approximately one hundred thousand children and were jointly operated with religious organizations until 1969, when the Canadian government assumed full responsibility for them.[70] Likewise, in the United

---

[67] Bieder (1986: 9).
[68] Dippie (1982); McGregor (1997).
[69] Armitage (1995: 104).
[70] Canada Indian and Northern Affairs (n.d.).

States, Native American schools were known as "contract schools" because they contracted religious missionaries to run them, although for a far shorter time (1879–1900) than in Canada. Although New Zealand's Native School Act of 1867 established state-financed and -administered schools and required them to provide instruction in English, the schools were not residential and hence did not separate Maori children from their families and communities.

State authorities also used child welfare policies as instruments of assimilation. In addition to placing indigenous children in residential schools under the care of school administrators, government agents also removed them, often forcibly, from their parents' care. State officials justified the removal of children by charging parental negligence, even though, using the logic of assimilation policies, simply raising children with indigenous values and ways might well have constituted negligence. Australia's twentieth-century policy of child removal was based in part on the belief that Aboriginal children, especially those who were "half-caste," would be better off living away from reserves, either in state-run orphanages or with white families. In the late 1930s, Australia's Aboriginal policies centered on "absorption," once it was clear that Aborigines, particularly "half-castes," were not dying off, as had been predicted.[71] Most policy makers still believed that "full-blooded" Aborigines were headed toward extinction. However, the number of half-castes appeared to be increasing. Speaking at the 1937 Conference of Commonwealth and State Aboriginal Authorities, A. O. Neville, commissioner of native affairs for the State of Western Australia, reasoned that they need not concern themselves with "full bloods" because "no matter what we do, they will die out."[72] In contrast, Neville and the other commissioners were more hopeful about addressing the half-caste problem, which could be solved by "absorption." The supposedly growing number of half-castes stoked fears of an Aboriginal presence for generations, undermining the policy makers' vision of a "white Australia."[73] Cultural assimilation and the literal "absorption" of half-breeds into the white population seemed a feasible and permanent solution to the "Aboriginal problem." Yet, as

---

[71] Chesterman and Galligan (1997: 151).
[72] McGregor (2004: 293).
[73] Idem (1997: 15).

Russell McGregor argues, the absorption vision was short-lived; during the post–World War II period, the conventional idea of assimilation was dominant among policy makers who focused on the formal political and social integration of Aboriginal peoples into the Australian polity, assuming their internalization of the majority's cultural norms and values.[74]

In all four countries, meaningful state-led policy reforms began in the 1950s and 1960s. The pressures for change were both domestic and international. Over the course of the twentieth century, indigenous organizations had advocated for both equal civil rights, and increasingly and more stridently, indigenous rights. Bureaucrats and politicians began to view past policies of assimilation as largely ineffective domestically and increasingly out of step with new international norms. Indigenous peoples were living in a materially impoverished and politically weak state of wardship, with very few being "assimilated" and the majority segregated and neglected. A growing number of political elites viewed these circumstances and the policies that led to them as affronts to domestic political ideals of equality and inclusiveness. For example, writing in support of the 1967 Referendum proposal that Aboriginal Australians be included in the national census, Prime Minister Harold Holt, Deputy Prime Minister John McEwan, and opposition leader Gough Whitlam explained, "Our personal sense of justice, our commonsense and our international reputation in a world in which racial issues are being highlighted every day require that we get rid of this outmoded provision" of excluding Aboriginal people from the census.[75]

Governments responded by proposing formal inclusion or integration. They defined inclusion to mean the dismantling of laws, procedures, and administrative institutions that excluded indigenous peoples from the formal rights and entitlements of citizenship. As earlier discussed, the Australian Commonwealth government extended the federal franchise to Aboriginal Australians in 1949, and over the following fifteen years the states also extended the franchise. Eventually, as Chesterman and Galligan document, Aboriginal came to mean, in law and policy, a description of descent rather than a category of wardship,

---

[74] McGregor (2004: 294–8).
[75] Neill (2002:1)

with its associated restrictions and regulations.[76] Similarly, the New Zealand government's 1960 Hunn Report announced the abandonment of assimilation and the adoption of integration, which meant the extension of general social services to the Maori and the dismantling of separate administrative units, such as the "Native Schools Division within the department of Education and the Maori land court."[77] Finally, integration also meant nurturing the sentiments of acceptance among the majority population that presumably accompany formal inclusion and equality. The expressed goal was to bring Aboriginal peoples in, to view them as equals, and to treat them like other citizens.

Indigenous groups responded critically to these moves toward formal equality. Government officials and indigenous leaders held opposing views. Indigenous groups, largely opposed to assimilation, welcomed government movement away from it. However, they thought the solution was self-determination and cultural acceptance, and not just formal inclusion. As important, they expected that their cultural rights and traditions would be respected by the government and the wider citizenry. Indigenous leaders claimed that their constituencies wanted neither to become nor to be treated just like everyone else.

Governments responded to these largely negative reactions with greater accommodation of indigenous claims and more deliberate efforts to include them in policy formulation. In short, contemporary policies of governments with respect to indigenous peoples and their participation in government bear the stamp of their contributions. Alan Cairns's observation of Canada's experience holds true for all four countries: "The elimination of difference was the official policy of the Canadian state when Indian influence on that policy was negligible. The present drive to recognize and reinforce difference is a product of Aboriginal input."[78] Ideas of multiculturalism today, while encompassing both Aboriginal and racial/ethnic minorities, differentiate between their claims, often giving deference (rhetorically, at least) to the former. Aboriginal groups claim their place as the original occupants – the "First Nations," in Canadian political parlance. As such, their

---

[76] Chesterman and Galligan (1997: 192).
[77] Armitage (1995: 146).
[78] Cairns (2000: 48).

concerns go far beyond the free expression of cultural identity and extend to political and economic self-determination. Further, indigenous struggles for cultural recognition and autonomy are properly viewed as the precursors and foundation of today's multiculturalism.

Generally, how indigenous people are viewed and treated by governments and fellow citizens has improved. For nearly all of the national histories, indigenous people were despised, pitied, patronized, ignored, romanticized, or in some other way regarded by governments and the wider public as outsiders or marginal to national life and politics. Today, the official embrace of multiculturalism, along with real political, legal, and economic gains, demonstrates a higher level of acceptance by the majority populations. On the other side, indigenous groups demand greater autonomy, while also acknowledging their greater social and political acceptance.

Conclusion

National histories are, of course, far fuller and more complex than what I have presented here. The purpose of this chapter is not to provide comprehensive accounts, but to outline the historical development of membership, so that contemporary demands for apology and change may be understood in that context.

As we have seen, there are broad historical patterns with common features. Government policies in all four countries have headed in the same direction, to varying degrees. On the status of citizenship, governments intended to exclude. Inclusion was granted only when indigenous peoples satisfied one or more requirements, such as individual landownership or English language acquisition. Only in the twentieth century did governments extend citizenship status to indigenous peoples without conditions. Their citizenship, as a legal matter, is settled, and apologies would seem to have little or no role in altering that status.

Self-government, and self-determination more broadly, has been the most contentious issue because it encompasses the specification of political jurisdiction, settlement of land claims, control over natural resources, and formulation of economic development plans. Here, the experiences of the four countries differ in significant ways. Since 1982, the Canadian Constitution has recognized Aboriginal right to self-government. Indigenous bands are slowly entering into agreements with federal and provincial governments to work out the legal, political, and economic particulars of these arrangements.[79] Similarly, in the United States the federal government's policy of self-determination, adopted in the 1970s, has gone some way toward strengthening tribal governments. Enormous challenges remain, however, to the full exercise of tribal authority in decision making, precisely because tribal leadership's decisions are often significantly affected by those made by the federal government, the Congress, and the courts. Nonetheless, as Joseph Kalt and Joseph Singer observe, the federal policy of self-determination has "proven to be the only policy that has shown concrete success in breaking debilitating economic dependence on federal spending programs and replenishing the social and cultural fabric."[80]

In New Zealand, separate Maori seats have survived recent electoral reforms. Judging from election results, Maori continue to exercise their option to vote on a separate Maori roll, increasing the number of Maori seats from five in 1996 to seven in 2002. Maori self-government is far less developed in terms of separate governance structures and Crown recognition. At present, the Waitangi Treaty claims process dominates most of the interactions between Maori and the Crown, leaving unknown what the Maori–Crown relationship will be after the claims process ends. Like other indigenous peoples, Maori desire autonomy. However, the nature and extent of that autonomy are still very much undecided.[81]

In Australia, Aboriginal self-government and its federal recognition seem a remote prospect. Aboriginal organizations appear divided in their goals of securing a treaty or gaining greater representation within government. Although these goals are not necessarily incompatible, a basic tension exists between them insofar as the first advances Aboriginal sovereignty and self-government and the latter advances full inclusion and participation in the national political process, including, perhaps, reserved seats.[82] The government of Prime Minister John Howard has judged the Australian government's extremely limited

---

[79] Frideres (1998: 386–7).
[80] Kalt and Singer (2004: 1).
[81] On the treaty claims process, see Ward (1999); on the future relationship between the Crown and Maori, see Coates and McHugh (1998).
[82] Parliament of New South Wales Legislative Council (1997).

effort to include Aboriginal voices in policy making and administration "a failure". His administration has been firmly committed to "main-streaming" and strongly against separate governance.

Overall, it is difficult to see how an apology would strongly and directly affect the main issues of self-government in any of the four countries. However, an apology can help a government to steer federal policy making in that direction or allow a government to emphasize its commitment to self-government by acknowledging the failures of past policies.

In all four countries, government policy has shifted perceptibly, although not completely, from its racist, intolerant, and paternalistic views of indigenous peoples to an official acceptance of multicultur-alism. Still, even with fundamental changes in state policy, the public remains alarmingly ignorant of the history, laws, and policies that have profoundly shaped Aboriginal experiences, grievances, and demands. Apologies, in their recounting of history and expression of regret about it, would seem to perform an educative role while also contributing to societal reconciliation.

3

To Apologize or Not to Apologize: National Histories and Official Apologies

Canadian political scientist Alan Cairns has described the history recounted in Canada's 1996 Royal Commission of Aboriginal People's Report as "a historical storehouse of mistreatment, deception, arrogance, dispossession, coercion, and abuses of power."[1] Many scholars, politicians, policy makers, and segments of the public in Australia, New Zealand, and the United States have reached similar conclusions about their national histories and treatment of indigenous people and other minority groups. Government apologies have followed in the wake of official disclosures in certain of our cases, but not all of them. What drives government to apologize or refuse to apologize and what drives groups to demand them? Why are apologies desirable?

This chapter examines state motivations for granting apologies and group motivations for demanding them. It contends that state officials will apologize when they ideologically support and seek to advance minority rights. This is not to suggest, however, that state officials will necessarily initiate the apologies, but rather that they are more likely to apologize when pressured. Aggrieved groups, on the other hand, insist and/or receive apologies, perceiving them as legitimatizing both their claims of historical mistreatment and present-day demands for rectification and self-determination. As state and group actors perceive them, apologies' efficacy in sustaining minority demands derives, in part, from their essential qualities. Apologies perform three tasks, with

[1] Cairns (2003: 78).

71

national histories and their reinterpretations necessarily at their center. First, apologies validate reinterpretations of history by formally acknowledging past actions and judging them unjust. Second, with history acknowledged and judged as unjust, apologies may strengthen history-centered explanations of minority disadvantage. Third, apologies advance reconsideration of the obligations and boundaries of membership in the national community.

As we shall see, it is precisely these qualities and the politics that apologies advance that explain why governments have refused to apologize. These political leaders neither support minority demands for self-determination or remedies for historical mistreatment nor do they judge that the historical record unquestionably supports these demands.

The 1998 Canadian Apology

The Canadian apology is an example of a government seeking to register its support of indigenous demands, including historical reinterpretation, while also responding to political pressures. The 1998 apology resulted from a report issued by the Royal Commission on Aboriginal Peoples (RCAP), a government commission. RCAP was itself a response to indigenous unrest. Prime Minister Brian Mulroney convened RCAP in 1991, judging in the wake of the 1990 Oka crisis – where the Mohawk and Quebec municipal, state, and federal governments were locked in an armed standoff over land – that the federal government had to do something.[2] Moreover, national political developments also contributed to political instability. The most recent round of constitutional debates left the basis of Aboriginal self-government in dispute: Did the right to self-government require entrenchment in the Constitution, as the government claimed, or was it inherent, predating the Constitution, as indigenous groups claimed? Also, indigenous leaders had been fundamentally opposed to the 1987 Meech Lake Accord, and an Aboriginal legislator had contributed directly to its defeat because the Accord ignored Aboriginal demands for autonomy and distinctness while recognizing those of Quebec.

[2] Dickason (1997: 319–22); Frideres (1998: 350–7).

Canadian politicians have conventionally used royal commissions "to change the direction" of past policies and "to raise the status or recognition of a people or marginalized group."[3] Both of these objectives were satisfied, in some measure, by RCAP. Designed "to investigate and report on the situation of Aboriginal peoples across the country," RCAP distinguished itself from previous twentieth-century government reviews of Canadian Aboriginal policies in several important ways.[4] First, it included both Aboriginal and non-Aboriginal members. Of the seven commissioners appointed, four were Aboriginal, including one of the cochairs, George Erasmus (former chief of the Assembly of First Nations). René Dussault, former judge of the Quebec Appeals Court, was the other cochair. Although Aboriginal leaders were consulted for the 1969 White Paper, which acknowledged the different and unequal past treatment of Aboriginals, their recommendations were neither incorporated nor evidently taken seriously.[5] The earlier Hawthorn Report (1966–7), which first introduced the concept of "citizens plus," did not include Aboriginals among its authors, although indigenous leadership favorably received the report's ideas. An even earlier parliamentary committee empaneled immediately after World War II to reexamine the Indian Act consulted the indigenous community widely, although its final provisions reflected very little of their input.[6] Second, it was the most expensive royal commission in Canadian history, beginning with an initial budget of CAN$42 million, which swelled to CAN$58 million. Approximately 3,500 individuals and organizations testified at public hearings held throughout the country, and hundreds of research reports were solicited.[7] Third, the report's twenty-year action plan goes further than previous reports in proposing Aboriginal self-government and the settlement of land claims.

The RCAP report did not explicitly recommend an apology. Instead, it offered a twenty-year plan accompanied by over four hundred

---

[3] Cairns (2000: 19).

[4] Dickason (1997: 397).

[5] Weaver (1981).

[6] Nichols (1998: 289–90).

[7] The report, in book form, consists of five volumes. A CD-ROM was also produced, which includes both the five volumes and the commissioned research reports. The production of the CD-ROM cost another CAN$27 million.

recommendations that comprehensively address the constitutional, political, economic, social, and cultural concerns of Aboriginal communities. RCAP went further than previous reports in proposing Aboriginal self-government and the settlement of land claims. According to the report, Aboriginal governance would be achieved through the addition of an Aboriginal branch of government working with existing municipal, provincial, and federal authorities in the provision of services. RCAP provided a bill of CAN$38 billion to be allocated to Aboriginal Affairs over a twenty-year period. (By way of comparison, in 2004, the Canadian federal government spent CAN$8.2 billion in Aboriginal programs out of a national budget of CAN$211 billion.)

The Canadian government responded to RCAP in 1998. Its response, *Gathering Strength: Canada's Aboriginal Action Plan*, included a formal apology that was publicly presented by Minister of Indian Affairs Jane Stewart to National Chief of the Assembly of First Nations Phil Fontaine. The "Statement of Reconciliation" acknowledged the deleterious effects of past government policies on Aboriginal peoples and specifically apologized for the mistreatment of Aboriginal peoples in the residential school system.[8] (The statement read in part, "The Government of Canada today formally expresses to all Aboriginal people in Canada our profound regret for past actions of the Federal government," and "To those of you who suffered this tragedy at residential schools, we are deeply sorry.") The government also established a CAN$350 million "healing" fund to assist victims of the residential school system and allotted CAN$250 million for Aboriginal economic development and governance initiatives.

Prime Minister Jean Chrétien did not attend the ceremony, claiming that he trusted his minister of Indian affairs, Jane Stewart, to represent

---

[8] As a Canadian government web page explains:

Residential Schools generally refers to a variety of institutions that existed over time, including: industrial schools, boarding schools, student residences, hostels, billets and residential schools. These schools were located in every province and territory, except New Brunswick and Prince Edward Island. . . . It is estimated that approximately 100,000 children attended these schools over the years in which they were operation (from 1874–1996). The Government operated nearly every school in partnership with various religious organizations until April 1, 1969, when the Government assumed full responsibility for the school system. Most residential schools ceased to operate by the mid-1970s, with only seven remaining open through the 1980s. The last federally school closed in 1996 (Canada Indian and Northern Affairs, n.d.).

her portfolio and his government ably. In deciding not to attend, but still supporting Minister Stewart, Chrétien was able to split the difference, as it were. His government signaled that it generally supported Aboriginal claims and was attentive to historical grievances, in keeping with policy statements that his party issued before the 1993 elections. (In the electoral document better known as the "Red Book," the party devoted one chapter to Aboriginal issues, outlining a process and policies in keeping with the general goals of Aboriginal leadership.) At the same time, he signaled that he did not fully support RCAP by withholding the full weight of the government's imprimatur, which only his presence could provide. According to press reports, he disagreed with certain of RCAP's recommendations – for example, the recommendation that a separate justice system be established for Aboriginal peoples. He also judged the RCAP recommendations to be too expensive.[9] Finally, he did not want his presence to be perceived as an admission of government guilt and thus introduce liability for sexual abuse at the residential schools.[10]

Aboriginal leadership responded to the apology with mixed reviews: Some openly welcomed it, others responded more tepidly, and some flatly rejected it, although many had called for an apology long before RCAP.[11] These varied responses can be attributed in part to who participated in the drafting of the document. Fontaine, head of the Assembly of First Nations, the largest and most powerful indigenous organization, worked closely with Minister Stewart. In fact, the government's *Gathering Strength* report parallels closely the content of *An Agenda for Action with First Nations*, which was developed in consultation with the Assembly of First Nations, and which was released shortly after *Gathering Strength*.[12] Not surprisingly, Fontaine described the apology and report as "the beginning of the empowerment of first peoples," although he later had to convince a number of his organization's members to accept the apology and money.[13]

Canadian government officials did not consult with the leaders of the Métis, urban Aboriginals, and the Inuit, and consequently those

[9] Speirs (1998).
[10] Winsor (1998).
[11] Anderssen and Greenspon (1998); Aubry (1998a); Steffenhagen (1998).
[12] Castellano (1999: 100).
[13] "Chiefs Asked to Accept Apology, Money" (1998: A6).

leaders were far less enthusiastic.[14] These groups disagreed with the apology's origins. Moreover, they judged the apology and the government's policy response to be insufficient, observing that for all the pomp and circumstance (including a peace pipe, a drum ceremony, and the printing of the "Statement of Reconciliation" on a scroll), Prime Minister Chrétien neither attended the ceremony nor signed the statement. These leaders charged that his absence diminished the apology's weight, deeming the apology and "healing fund" to be "too little, too late." Moreover, they maintained that the government's Action Plan ignored the main recommendations of the RCAP report.

Finally, the Canadian public supported the apology, although only 51 percent thought that the government was apologizing on their behalf. The rest, evidently, did not view the issue as one of collective guilt.[15] A number of newspaper editorials also endorsed the apology. The *Vancouver Sun*, for example, applauded the government's efforts, but called for "realistic objectives" on the government's part and greater attention to self-responsibility, accountability, and democratic governance on Aboriginals' part.[16] The national *Globe and Mail*'s editorial echoed RCAP's recommendation that the relationship between Aboriginals and the Canadian government be based on "mutual respect and understanding."[17]

The Abandonment of "False Assumptions"

Canadians – elites and populace – have not widely called the propriety of their government's apology into question. Nor have the debates about Canadian history been especially heated, although history is at the heart of the matter. The RCAP report condemns Canadian history as being founded on "false assumptions," identifying four at the base of Canada's historical treatment of Aboriginal peoples: (1) that "Aboriginal people are "inherently inferior" and incapable of self-governance; (2) that treaties and other agreements were entered into for reasons of expediency and were not viewed as binding "covenants of trust

---

[14] Aubry (1998a).
[15] "Apology to Natives Gets Wide Support in Poll" (1998).
[16] "A Path from Shame and Dependence" (1998: A18).
[17] "Resident Schools, National Scandal" (1998: A16).

and obligation," and as such could be ignored or trampled at will; (3) that wardship was appropriate for Aboriginal peoples, and thus their consent or involvement was unnecessary; and (4) that community and individual development for Aboriginals would be defined on non-Aboriginal terms. Indeed, these "false assumptions" are the making of a moral failure and bringing them to light would, in RCAP's words, "surely persuade the thoughtful reader that the false assumptions and abuses of power . . . are inconsistent with the morality of an enlightened nation."[18] This reinterpretation of Canadian history, in turn, justifies concerted commitments to advancing and strengthening Aboriginal autonomy. The reinterpretation also provides an explanation for present-day Aboriginal disadvantage as the result or legacy largely of state and private actions.

The RCAP report is not, of course, the Canadian government's first effort at altering indigenous policy. Indeed, the interactions between indigenous peoples and Canadian governments have been a defining feature and challenge of governance since European settlement. Nor was it the first policy report to rely on history in its rationale. But in contrast to the government's past efforts, the RCAP report is one of a few, if not the only, government findings to call for the strengthening of Aboriginal cultural, economic, and political autonomy, and not for its eventual abolition. This distinctiveness is most sharply revealed when contrasted with the failed 1969 White Paper, produced under Prime Minister Pierre Trudeau, a major policy initiative that preceded RCAP and the impetus for Aboriginal mobilization.[19]

Larger social and political developments in the 1960s led to greater visibility for Aboriginal issues and reassessments of Canadian history. Canada's 1967 centennial celebrations sparked interest in and critical examination of history, such that perceptions of the "Indian problem took shape within the framework of historical reassessment."[20] Increased public concern about poverty also focused attention on Aboriginal impoverishment, and the U.S. civil rights movement contributed to internal discussions among Canadians about their treatment of minorities. Still, enduring questions of national unity, specifically

---

[18] Royal Commission on Aboriginal Peoples (1997: Volume 1).
[19] Chrétien (1969); Weaver (1981).
[20] Weaver (1981: 13).

Quebec secession, dominated the political landscape.[21] Although the federal government took the political demands of Francophone Canadians far more seriously than those of Aboriginal Canadians, the demands were broadly similar. Both groups desired cultural, political, and economic autonomy and respect. Maintaining national unity was an overriding concern of the Trudeau administration, and it, along with Trudeau's personal aversion to "special rights" for groups, significantly shaped and is reflected in the White Paper.

The abolition of the Indian Act was the 1969 White Paper's signature recommendation. The White Paper presented history as having conferred a "special status" and "special treatment" that had been largely debilitating. ("This system – special legislation, a special land system, and a separate administration for the Indian people – continues to be the basis of present Indian policy. It has saved for the Indian people places they can call home, but has carried with it serious human and physical as well as administrative disabilities."[22]) Furthermore, the paper recognized indigenous grievances but judged that such grievances were to be neither directly repaired by the policy nor made the rationale for policy changes. Rather, according to the White Paper, what mattered most was that Aboriginals were treated differently in the past. The nature of this different treatment was less important. ("The treatment resulting from their different status has been often worse, sometimes equal and occasionally better than that accorded to their fellow citizens. What matters is that it has been different."[23])

The White Paper's call for the termination of Indian status and the introduction of formal equality made it decidedly forward-looking. It sought to make Indian status indistinguishable from that of other Canadians, and thus required that vestiges of past policies be abruptly cut off. Altering the terms of Indian membership did not mean attempting to approximate prior conditions of sovereignty, but rather looking toward the creation of one national community, in which Aboriginals would be fully invested as members. Although Trudeau and fellow policy makers viewed indigenous cultural values as important for individuals, such values could not be the basis of legally entrenched rights.

---

[21] Ibid.
[22] Chrétien (1969: 7).
[23] Ibid. (5).

Thus, Trudeau's answer to Aboriginal rights was "no." In his famous 1969 speech at the Vancouver Liberal Association dinner, Trudeau put his position this way: "Our answer is no. We can't recognize aboriginal rights because no society can be built on historical 'might-have beens.'"[24]

Most Aboriginal leaders disagreed with Trudeau, and their opposition led to the eventual withdrawal of the White Paper. What the White Paper referred to as "special rights" (especially land and treaty rights and certain protections of the Indian Act) were not seen by Aboriginals as "special rights" at all, but as poor substitutes for lost autonomy and land. In their view, history had been far more disastrous and differently injurious for Aboriginals than the White Paper argued. More debilitating than the "special system" was the dispossession that preceded it, of which the Paper made scant mention. It was to a historical "time zero" that Aboriginal leadership wished to return and reconstitute.

A historical time zero seems to be the basis of the RCAP report and apology, however. Yet, it still remains to be explained how the liberal government of Prime Minister Chrétien, the perceived keeper of the Trudeau flame within the Liberal Party, came to support not only apology but the direction of Aboriginal policy toward group rights, self-governance, and their historical justification.[25] The first changes in Liberal Party behavior, and presumably in attitudes toward Aboriginal rights, came in the immediate aftermath of the White Paper's release to the House of Commons and to the public. As mentioned, Aboriginal organizations mobilized against the White Paper, producing the counter "Red Paper." Although it was Chrétien, then a young minister of the Department of Indian Affairs and Northern Development, who initially defended the paper publicly, his defense was soon followed by reversal. By 1971, he was publicly advocating a "new ideology" toward indigenous affairs, which now included indigenous participation in policy making.[26] This ideological turnaround has, over the past thirty years, engendered significant, if incremental, policy and constitutional

---

[24] Weaver (1981:179).
[25] Regarding Chrétien and his followers as guardians of Trudeau's legacy, see Carty, Cross, and Young, (2000: 77)
[26] Weaver (1981: 186).

developments toward Aboriginal rights, self-governance, and participation in policy making.

The apology should be seen, then, as one more step along the road.
It helps to justify the policy changes proposed by the Canadian government. In the White Paper, history was to be avoided, not retrieved.
In the RCAP and government's report, the converse is true: The past,
prior to European settlement, provides an aspirational, although not
actual, blueprint for the future as the Canadian government recom-
mits itself to assisting in the development of Aboriginal economies and
governments.

New Zealand and the Queen's Apologies

The New Zealand apologies provide two more examples of a government seeking to register its support of Aboriginal demands for self-
determination, including acknowledgment of historical injustices, but
with several important differences. Unlike in Canada, the Crown's
apologies to Maori groups were prompted indirectly by the actions
of a government body, the Waitangi Tribunal, and by Maori mobilization. Moreover, these apologies accompanied the Crown settlements of a land claim and a breach-of-contract claim and focused on
specific historical periods or acts experienced by the Waikato Tainui
and Ngai Tahu peoples, respectively. The apologies did not include
either a general statement about New Zealand history or the general direction of government policy. Taken together, these differences
point to the government's intention to attempt to conclude negotiations with Maori groups, with apologies being part of that "full
and final" settlement process.[27] Rather than the Crown's apologies
marking the beginning of a "new relationship," as in Canada, they
accompany settlements that are intended, in some way, finally to close
the books.

New Zealand's Parliament established the Waitangi Tribunal,
through the Treaty of Waitangi Act (1975), to "hear 'claims' of 'prej-
udice' (that is, hurt, damage, and injustice) by any 'Maori' or 'group
of Maori' against 'acts or omissions' on the part of the Crown or

---

[27] Fleras and Spoonley (1999: 140).

its agents."[28] Parliament purposefully designed the Tribunal to be ineffective, establishing it as a way of avoiding Maori demands that the Treaty of Waitangi be made, by statute, part of New Zealand domestic law.[29] The general idea was to move Maori claims about the breach of treaty rights out of the political arena (the Parliament) to a quasilegal body.[30] By the mid-1970s, Maori strategies had shifted from declaring the treaty "a fraud" to making it the basis for claims of reparative justice.[31] Yet even with these implicit purposes for establishing the Tribunal, Parliament still had to be persuaded. The governing Labour Party's minister of Maori affairs, Matiu Rata, successfully steered the bill's passage "despite widespread ambivalence" within Parliament.[32] The Tribunal's perceived ineffectiveness was due to its limited powers. While the Tribunal (consisting of the chief judge of the Maori Land Court and two other members) could hear claims as they bore on "the meaning and effect of the 1840 Waitangi treaty" and make reports and recommendations about claim settlements to the executive; it could neither "legally enforce the treaty nor specify Treaty rights and request the Government to enforce them."[33] Moreover, the time frame of permissible claims constrained the Tribunal's power. Any claims against the Crown dating from 1840 to 1975 were excluded. The only claims that could be heard were those dating after the Tribunal's establishment in 1975.

In addition to these statutory limitations, the Tribunal initially received very little government support. The National Party government that succeeded the one-term Labour government was not supportive of the Tribunal, allowing it to remain underfunded and understaffed.[34] As a result, the Tribunal accomplished little in its first nine years of existence, hearing just fourteen claims.[35] The most important

---

[28] Ibid. (74).
[29] Ibid.
[30] Ibid. (296).
[31] Ibid. (448).
[32] Havemann (1995: 88).
[33] Sharp (1997b: 75).
[34] Ibid.
[35] Of these fourteen, "three had been 'dealt with', three had been withdrawn, three referred back to the claimants for further information and five were in the pipeline." Ibid. (76).

development (from the perspective of Maori demands) during this otherwise barren period was the appointment in 1983 of Maori judge E. T. J. Durie as the Tribunal's chair. Under Durie's leadership, the Tribunal produced several well-researched reports with thoughtful recommendations, signaling that the Tribunal was intent on being taken seriously by the government and society at large.[36] Durie clearly appreciated the Tribunal's ability to uncover and fortify Maori claims by reinterpreting New Zealand history "'from a Maori point of view.'"[37]

Maori leadership advocated reforms that would enhance the Tribunal's powers while also continuing to bring their claims before it, in spite of its limitations, because the Tribunal authorized, through statute, an outlet for their claims of Crown breaches of their treaty rights. In 1984, the again-governing Labour Party, responding to Maori reform demands and mindful of the Tribunal's budding reputation, moved to amend the Treaty of Waitangi Act.[38] Again, Labour's minister of Maori affairs, Karo Wetere, oversaw the successful passage of the amended act amid heated parliamentary debate about the potential costs – financial, social, and political – of land claims settlements and other compensatory measures.[39] The amended Treaty of Waitangi Act (1985) authorized the Tribunal to hear claims dating back to 1840 and enlarged the Tribunal "from three to seven members, of whom four were Maori."[40] The legislation also provided for greater administrative, research, and legal resources. The Labour government again amended the Treaty Act in December 1988, increasing the total membership to up to sixteen members (excluding the chair) and eliminating the Maori membership quota.[41] This larger Tribunal allowed for, among other things, multiple hearings.

The now thirty-two-year-old Tribunal has proven far more effective than the government intended. Although empowered initially only to hear claims and make recommendations, the Tribunal's fact-finding and dissemination of recommendations enormously assisted Maori demands. Moreover, because the Parliament assigned the Tribunal an

[36] Durie became chief justice of the Maori Land Court in 1981. Havemann (1995: 89); Sharp (1997b: 77).
[37] Oliver (2001: 10).
[38] Sharp (1997b: 79).
[39] Havemann (1995: 89); Sharp (1997b: 79); Ward (1999: 28–31).
[40] Havemann (1995: 89).
[41] Sharp (1997b: 81).

advisory role, the executive, Parliament, and eventually the courts were obligated to listen to the body's findings.[42] On the other hand, the Waitangi Tribunal's powers and influence have been noticeably constrained since the 1990s. Although the Tribunal was empowered, through the 1988 amendment to the Act and related 1989 legislation, "to require and not simply recommend, that the Crown return land and forests to claimants," it has exercised that power just once, in a 1998 recommendation.[43] Moreover, the government has returned to negotiating directly with groups (thereby electing to bypass the Tribunal), and the courts are increasingly asserting their authority as the ultimate interpreters of law.[44]

The Crown's 1995 and 1998 apologies to the Waikato Tainui and Ngai Tahu people, respectively, while not the direct results of the Waitangi Tribunal, were influenced by it in two critically important ways. First, since the early 1990s, governments, whether led by either the Labour or National parties, have returned to direct negotiations, as had been the practice before the Waitangi Tribunal. This return is in part a reaction both to the Tribunal's centrality (it receives large numbers of claims) and to its limitations(the reports are slowly produced, the claims are backlogged, and the Tribunal has chosen not to exercise all of its power). More importantly, the government simply wishes to reassert Crown sovereignty over the claims settlement process. Second, the Tribunal has played a crucial educative role, contributing directly to political and public acceptance of the apologies and settlements. Its 1984 Manukau Report and 1991–3 Ngai Tahu reports first introduced the general public to reinterpretations of said historical events, focusing on Crown misdeeds and framing them as breaches of the treaty.[45] As Andrew Sharp observes, when the Manukau Report was first released in 1984, the New Zealand public denied and dismissed its account of Crown transgressions. Yet, the 1995 apology and settlement, which referred directly to those same transgressions, did not raise public objection, suggesting the acceptance, among certain segments of the citizenry at least, of a new historical narrative.[46]

---

[42] Sharp (2001: 37).
[43] Sharp (1997b: 292); on the 1998 recommendation, see Waitangi Tribunal (n.d.).
[44] Sharp (1997b: 300); Fleras and Spoonley (1999: 22).
[45] Sharp (1997b: 300).
[46] Ibid.

The 1995 apology was included in the preamble of the Waikato-Tainui Settlement Bill. The preamble (written in both English and Maori) read, in part:

[The Crown and] its representatives and advisors acted unjustly and in breach of the Treaty of Waitangi. . . . The Crown acknowledges that subsequent confiscation of land and resources under the New Zealand Settlements Act . . . were wrongful. . . . The Crown expresses its profound regret and apologises unreservedly for the loss of lives because of the hostilities arising from the invasion, and at the devastation of property and social life which resulted.[47]

In addition to the apology, the Waikato-Tainui received a payment of NZ$170 million. In its 1998 apology to the Ngai Tahu, "the Crown conceded that had acted 'unconscionably' in repeated breach of the Treaty of Waitangi principles and expressed 'profound regret' for suffering caused by significantly impairing social, economic, and cultural development."[48] The government also paid NZ$170 million to the Ngai Tahu and provided an additional NZ$2.5 million to resolve thirty small private claims.[49]

New Zealand's History According to the Tribunal

As in Canada, the Waitangi Tribunal's work and the Crown's subsequent apologies have validated reinterpretations of New Zealand history. Unlike Canada's RCAP, the Waitangi Tribunal is empowered to provide both recommendations and limited binding judgments. As a "permanent commission of inquiry"[50] and not a court of law, the Tribunal hears claims, is empowered to subpoena witnesses and documents, and makes recommendations to the Crown.[51] These recommendations necessarily depend on the Tribunal's gathering and interpretation of historical evidence. More than using history to make these recommendations, it also provides a "new" history. This is because, as Giselle Byrnes argues, the Tribunal's governing legislation requires that

---

[47] Quoted in Alves (1999: 128–9).
[48] Fleras and Spoonley (1999: 135).
[49] Ibid.
[50] It is "permanent" as long as the New Zealand Parliament does not pass legislation to dismantle it.
[51] See Waitangi Tribunal (n.d.).

Crown culpability and Maori harms be identified.[52] Although "the Tribunal has never admitted that is engaged in writing (or rewriting) history," Brynes and others argue otherwise, precisely because it requires historical research, interpretation, and judgment to determine whether the Crown is responsible for alleged acts of commission or omission, whether it acted prejudicially against Maori interests, and whether the treaty was breached.[53] In keeping with its mandate to hear claims of Crown harms against the Maori, the Tribunal has, not surprisingly, presented a history of Maori loss and Crown culpability.[54]

In which ways these narratives should ultimately be regarded as examples of historical writing is of some dispute, among scholars, supporters, and detractors. Are they examples of a new public history, where history is made accessible to wider audiences? Or are such narratives examples of a postcolonial history, where the contemporary consequences of historical injustices are analyzed as thoroughly, if not more thoroughly, than historical reconstruction itself? Or are they examples of a "juridical history," where the past is represented "so as to make it available to legal and quasi-legal judgement in the present"? Or do they simply comprise a "grievance history," nakedly driven by the prospects of material compensation?[55] Two points are not in dispute, however. The first, and most obvious, is that throughout the world, debates about history and historical writing are usually contentious. New Zealand's experience is both universal and particular. The second is that the Tribunal has been enormously helpful in creating and disseminating Maori views of historical events and fortifying Maori claims for reparations and increasingly for dual sovereignty.

The BIA and Proposed Congressional Apology to Native Americans

The 2000 Bureau of Indian Affairs (BIA) apology and the pending congressional resolution apologies are both examples of elite-driven apologies that in their reinterpretations of history generally support Aboriginal demands for self-determination but do not endorse either

---

[52] Byrnes (2004: 2).
[53] Oliver (2001: 11).
[54] Sorrenson (1989); Sharp (2001: 41–8).
[55] Byrnes (2004: 1–29).

specific alterations in federal policy or land claims. Moreover, these apologies are not the results of direct pressures either from government commissions or grass-roots Native American organizations. Instead, the BIA apology was guided chiefly by moral concerns, whereas the pending congressional resolutions have been driven by electoral considerations.

Assistant Secretary of the U.S. Bureau of Indian Affairs Kevin Gover used the ceremony marking the BIA's 175th anniversary in September 2000 to apologize for the past policies and practices of the BIA: "On behalf of the Bureau of Indian Affairs, I extend this formal apology to Indian people for the historical conduct of this agency."[56] Although Gover is himself a Native American, that fact neither deterred him from making the apology nor diminished its value for those who attended the ceremony.[57] (The apology did not escape criticism, however. Hoopa leader Lyle Marshall judged the apology "inadequate because it came from the wrong person."[58]) According to Gover, he intended to show that his sentiments and those of his staff accorded with the audience's: "Just like you, when we think of these misdeeds and their tragic consequences, our hearts break and our grief is as pure and complete as yours."[59] In a telephone interview with the author, Gover stated that he was guided largely by his own moral sensibilities and those of his staff.[60] He said that he thought it was simply the right thing to do. Although he and his staff were aware of the Canadian government apology and it figured in their thinking, he emphasized that they were driven by their own consciences and desire to signal to Native Americans that the BIA had changed in fundamental ways. (And as mentioned in Chapter 1, neither the Congress nor the president encouraged or ordered Gover to apologize.)

Gover's apology, like that of the Canadian and New Zealand governments, advances historical reinterpretations that fundamentally buttress Aboriginal claims. The apology rejects the simple view that the agency's past policies and practices were necessary, if unfortunate, components of national settlement and expansion or that they were

[56] Gover (2000).
[57] Kelley (2000); Stout (2000).
[58] Tsosie (2006: 186).
[59] Gover (2000).
[60] Author's telephone interview with Kevin Gover, December 6, 2000.

great "civilizing" missions. Rather, the apology judges the BIA to have committed acts of profound brutality resulting in incalculable human suffering and loss. Furthermore, the apology, in highlighting Native American suffering and loss at the U.S. government's hand, partly justifies and affirms present-day government policies promoting Native American self-determination. Gover wanted to reassure his audience that the BIA, now staffed mostly by Native Americans, works with Native American peoples, not against them, broadly speaking (the known and alleged cases of significant BIA fiduciary mismanagement notwithstanding).[61] The larger, if mostly inattentive, national audience was to gain a greater awareness of past government actions against Native Americans. One result would perhaps have been a better understanding, if not support, of Native American claims and causes.

Electoral considerations, and not morals, were the principal motivations behind the proposed (and still pending) congressional apology to Native Americans. In May 2004, Senator Sam Brownback (R-KS), along with Senator Ben Nighthorse Campbell (R-CO) and Senator Daniel Inouye (D-HI), introduced a Senate Joint Resolution, and in June 2004, Representative Jo Ann Davis (R-VA) introduced its companion, House Joint Resolution 98, "To acknowledge a long history of official depredations and ill-conceived policies by the United States Government regarding Indian Tribes and offer an apology to all Native Peoples on behalf of the United States." Brownback, one of the resolution's original sponsors, stated that a desire for intergroup reconciliation prompted the bill. The "depth of anger" that he felt on visits to Kansas reservations as a newly elected senator surprised him: "I didn't have personal relationships with Native Americans.... The bitterness caught me by surprise."[62] Despite Brownback's disavowal of electoral motives, the press viewed the apology resolution as a bipartisan attempt to affect several 2004 senatorial races and the presidential election. Describing the resolution as "refreshing," a *New York Times* editorial also observed that the resolution indicated growing Native

---

[61] There was no mention, for example, of the 1996 class action suit (*Cobell*) filed by individual Native Americans, which alleged "wholesale mismanagement" by the BIA of "Individual Indian Money (IIM) trust accounts – totaling billions of dollars." Buck (2006: 100).

[62] Mollison (2004b).

American electoral strength.[63] Although they constitute 1.5 percent of the nation's population, Native Americans are 16 percent of the electorate in Alaska and important members of the electorate in the Dakotas and the western states of Arizona, New Mexico, and Nevada. Moreover, casino revenues are an important source of influence for Native Americans, enabling them to make substantial campaign contributions.

That the Senate continues to act on the Resolution after the elections suggests that other considerations, besides electoral, may explain the senators' actions. However, the evidence supporting this claim is weak. In April 2005, the Senate's sponsors again introduced the Resolution and it was referred to the Committee on Indian Affairs, cochaired by senators John McCain (R-AZ) and Byron Dorgan (R-ND). In May 2005, the Committee held hearings; testimony was given by Tex Hall, president of the National Congress of American Indians; Edward K. Thomas, president of the Central Council of Alaska's Tlingit and Haida Indian Tribes; and Dr. Negiel Bigpond of the Euchee Tribe. There has been no further action on this Resolution since and none is forthcoming. This outcome is predictable, however. Without mobilized Native American constituencies or media attention and in the face of larger and more pressing partisan concerns, the senators will likely allow the bill to sit in committee indefinitely. In his study of congressional treatment of Native American policy, Charles C. Turner finds that "greater salience," as measured by media coverage and group mobilization, increases the chances "of Indian bills being reported by committee, of these bills being voted on by the chamber, and the pro-Indian outcome being victorious."[64]

That the apology will be in legislative form and, if ever passed, be endorsed by members of the majority population makes it more similar to Canada's and New Zealand's apologies than to Gover's. But the Resolution, should it pass, stands alone. It does not allow for making or settling claims against the U.S. government. Furthermore, in its comprehensive recounting of American history, the Resolution is more like the Canadian apology than either the New Zealand or Gover apology, which focus on specific historic episodes or one federal

---

[63] "The Long Trail to Apology" (2004: A18).
[64] Turner (2005: 132).

agency, respectively. The Resolution begins with a brief description of life before European settlement up to the present, with mention of all of the atrocities and sacrifices in between, including the Trail of Tears and the massacres at Sand Creek in 1864 and Wounded Knee in 1890. It is also, at points, a testament to understatement, describing "extermination, termination, forced removal and relocation, the outlawing of traditional religions, and the destruction of sacred places," as "ill-conceived Federal policies." Nonetheless, as a *New York Times* editorial observes, the Resolution "pulls few rhetorical punches about the genocidal wounds American Indians suffered," and the apology itself "would have been received as fighting words at the Capitol in the Indian war era."[65] This Resolution could contribute, as Gover hoped his apology would, to a greater public awareness about and support of Native American claims.

The 1993 Apology Resolution to Native Hawaiians

The 1993 Congressional Resolution is an example of an apology resulting from the shared political goals of an organized constituency and members of the political elite. As with the other apologies, historical reinterpretation is at the center. The Hawaii sovereignty movement and Hawaii's U.S. senators pursued and successfully achieved the apology resolution as a corrective to an official report that denied that the United States was responsible for the overthrow of the Hawaiian kingdom. Correcting the historical record was not the only reason that the apology was pursued, but it was one of the most important. The political demands of Native Hawaiians for self-determination and sovereignty stood to be notably strengthened if the U.S. government acknowledged that it had overthrown a sovereign kingdom. The 1993 apology Resolution includes such an acknowledgment.

The origins of the push for the apology partly rest in the findings of a government report. In December 1980, Congress empaneled the Native Hawaiians Study Commission (NHSC) to "conduct a study of the culture, needs, and concerns of the Native Hawaiians."[66] Although the report was wide-ranging, most important for our purposes was its

---

[65] "The Long Trail to Apology" (2004: A18).
[66] DiAlto (2002: 29).

determination that the U.S. government bore no responsibility for the overthrow of the sovereign Hawaiian kingdom. It said that although Americans had participated in the overthrow, they had not acted as government agents and that therefore the United States was neither morally nor legally obligated to pay reparations to Hawaiians. Similarly, although the commission's report offered policy recommendations for improving the collective conditions of Native Hawaiians, it did not recommend an apology, thereby disconnecting present-day political disadvantage from historical disempowerment. Notably, several members dissented from the 1983 final report's historical interpretation of the overthrow and outlined their dissent in a separate volume.[67]

The commission's report and dissent energized the Hawaiian sovereignty movement by keeping the issues – the historical record and, therefore, an apology – unresolved. Shortly after being elected to the Senate in 1990, Senator Daniel Akaka (D-HA) first introduced the Joint Resolution (cosponsored by Hawaii's senior senator, Daniel Inouye) calling for an apology. In arguing for the resolution, Akaka stressed two points: first, that the U.S. government must acknowledge and apologize for its role in the Hawaiian kingdom's overthrow; second, that because certain provisions of the Hawaii Admission Act (1959) implicitly established a trust relationship, with fiduciary obligations, between the federal government and Native Hawaiians, Congress must now formally declare it as such.[68] After four unsuccessful attempts in three Congresses, the Resolution was finally passed in October 1993, when Senator Akaka removed the statements about a trust relationship and instead focused on Hawaiian history and reconciliation. Fellow senators resisted the declaration of a trust relationship precisely because, among other things, it would have buttressed Hawaiian sovereignty claims. In his opposing remarks, Senator Slade Gorton (R-WA) argued that the "logical consequences of this resolution would be independence."[69] President Bill Clinton signed the Resolution into law as Public Law 103–150 in November 1993. Although the trust relationship

---

[67] Ibid. (30).

[68] "Apology for the Overthrow of the Kingdom of Hawaii" (1990).

[69] "100th Anniversary of the Overthrow of the Hawaiian Kingdom" (1993: S14479).

declaration was removed, the Resolution still fortified sovereignty claims because it affirmed U.S. involvement in the overthrow of a sovereign kingdom. For a subset of self-government movements, a first step in reclaiming sovereignty is to establish prior sovereignty.

The 2005 U.S. Senate Apology on Lynching

The 2005 Senate apology on lynching shares three important similarities with and differs in three important ways from the BIA 2000 apology and the pending congressional apology to Native Americans. First, like the BIA apology, the Senate's 2005 Resolution apologizes for the actions of a specific institution – in this case, the Senate's failure to pass antilynching legislation. Second, similar to the BIA's apology, the target audience of the Senate's apology was a limited one: the (deceased) victims of lynchings and the living descendants of lynching victims. Third, like the pending congressional apology, it disallows any claims being brought against the Senate for its failure. Although this prohibition is not explicitly stated (as in the Native American apology Resolution), it is strongly implied in the Resolution's narrow language and in its careful avoidance of any reference to reparations. There are two interrelated differences: (1) The Senate apology, unlike both apologies to Native Americans, was driven by organized group pressures, and not only by political elites; and (2), the Senate passed the lynching resolution. That the congressional Native American Resolution continues to languish in the Senate Committee on Indian Affairs is due in some measure to the absence of mobilized pressure and the low salience of Native American issues.

In June 2005, the U.S. Senate apologized for having in the past failed to pass antilynching legislation. Between 1920 and 1940, the House thrice passed such legislation, and seven presidents petitioned for it between 1890 and 1952, but the filibustering of southern senators always prevented a vote on the issue. Lynchings and mob violence directly precipitated the creation of the National Association for the Advancement of Colored People (NAACP) in 1909. Securing passage of a federal antilynching law was one of the organization's chief objectives for over thirty years. Of an estimated 4,742 people lynched in the United States between 1882 and 1968, the majority were African

Americans, but scholars think that the number is higher because many lynchings went unreported. Also, early activists, the keepers of the public record, were divided in their definition of lynching, with arguments centering on whether community support for a killing was the defining difference between a lynching and a racial murder.[70]

The two cosponsors of the bill, Democrat Mary Landrieu of Louisiana and Republican George Allen of Virginia, were prompted to act by organized pressure and by political ambition, to varying degrees. Along with all other senators, they were pushed by a loosely constituted group, the Committee for a Formal Apology, composed of lynching victims' relatives, politicians, and other concerned persons. The committee lobbied by sending each member a book containing "postcards" of lynchings.[71] (Beginning in the late nineteenth century, photographs of lynchings had been used as postcards.) As for personal ambition, Allen was reportedly considering a run for the presidency in 2008. He thought his cosponsorship of the bill would help his reputation with white moderate Republicans, many of whom are uncomfortable with the image of a racially intolerant party. In the past, Allen had been criticized for displaying a noose in his law office and a Confederate flag at his home.[72] While governor of Virginia, Allen decreed a Confederate History Month.[73] As for African American voters, their views about Allen were unlikely to change. Allen received a grade of "F" from the NAACP Washington Bureau, based on his voting record on civil rights and related issues during the 108th Congress (2003–4). Landrieu, in contrast, received a grade of "A."[74]

Despite the Resolution's subject, the procedure leading to its passage aimed to downplay, not highlight, its significance. Senate Majority Leader Bill Frist (R-TN) vetoed both a roll-call vote and a floor debate on the Resolution, which would have been held during regular business hours on a day other than Monday, ensuring that most senators would be in attendance. Instead, Frist decided on a voice-call vote to be taken after business hours on a Monday evening, in direct opposition to the desires of Landrieu and the Resolution's advocates.[75]

70 Waldrep (2000).
71 Allen et al. (2000).
72 Stolberg (2005a).
73 Thomas-Lester (2005).
74 NAACP Washington Bureau (2004).
75 Shepard (2005).

The Resolution's language is clear and narrow, stating in part that the Senate "apologizes to the victims of lynching" for its "failure to enact anti-lynching legislation," and that the Senate "expresses the deepest sympathies and most solemn regrets" to the descendants of lynching victims.

Australia's Refusal to Apologize

The Australian federal government, which refuses to issue an apology to its indigenous peoples, is an example of a government that does not seek to support or advance Aboriginal claims for autonomy and self-determination. Although the federal government has generally agreed that historical harms were committed against Aboriginal peoples, the government has also challenged both the historical facts and the propriety of suggested remedies, including apology and future policy making. Instead, the government proposes a policy of "practical reconciliation" that presumes symmetrical citizenship (and not Aboriginal rights) and that does not endorse an apology. Australian history is neither a "storehouse" of abuses for which the government must apologize, nor is it the source of all Aboriginal disadvantage for which the government must now make amends.

In the early 1990s, heads of several Australian government agencies, child welfare advocates, and Aboriginal organizations began to call for a national investigation into the state policy of removing "half-caste" Aboriginal children from their parents' care and placing them in orphanages, in group homes, and with individual white families.[76] The policy, in place from 1910 to 1970, was based partly on the belief that "full-blood" Aborigines were a vanishing race but that "half-caste" children could be saved. In response to pressure from nongovernmental groups, the Labor government's Attorney General Michael Lavarch authorized the Human Rights and Equal Opportunity Commission (HREOC) to conduct an inquiry and produce a report, which was to include recommendations on compensation "for people affected by separation."[77]

Related political developments allowed the HREOC to conduct its inquiry within a relatively receptive political environment. Since the

[76] McGregor (1997).
[77] Human Rights and Equal Opportunity Commission (1997: 18).

1960s, Aboriginal issues have remained visible on the political landscape, and legislative action and monumental judicial decision making
in the 1990s increased this visibility further. In 1991, the Parliament,
with cross-party support, passed the Council for Aboriginal Reconciliation Act, setting in motion a formal process of reconciliation. The
Parliament charged the Council, whose members included both Aboriginal and non-Aboriginal Australians, with identifying – through
consultations at all levels of government and nationwide town-hall
meetings – the legislative, administrative, and social changes needed to
secure meaningful and lasting reconciliation between Aboriginal and
non-Aboriginal Australians.[78] The Council was to submit to the Commonwealth Parliament formal documents of reconciliation by 2001,
the centenary of Australian federation. As important, in its 1992 decision *Mabo v. Queensland*, the High Court of Australia overturned the
principle of *terra nullius*, which had effectively banned native title since
English settlement.[79]

The HREOC's report, *Bringing Them Home: National Inquiry
into the Separation of Aboriginal and Torres Strait Islander Children
from Their Families* (hereafter *BTH* report), formally introduced (or
"tabled") in May 1997, concluded "with confidence that between one
in three and one in ten Indigenous children were forcibly removed
from their families and communities" from approximately 1910 until
1970.[80] Because Aboriginal policies were governed at the state rather
than the federal level, each state enacted "protective" legislation that
permitted state officials to remove Aboriginal children "without having to establish to a court's satisfaction" that the children were so
badly neglected as to require removal.[81] Although governments prac-
ticed the policy of Aboriginal child removal nationwide, the regional
location and concentration, the treatment of the removed children, and
the comprehensiveness of state administrative records varied.

---

[78] Council for Aboriginal Reconciliation (2000).
[79] The Crown's concept of *terra nullius* (empty land) had decreed the British the first
    legal occupants of the land and the Crown the first sovereign. Stephenson (1995);
    Brennan (1998).
[80] Human Rights and Equal Opportunity Commission (1997: 37). It is important to note
    here that the number "one in ten" has come under fierce attack by the conservative
    right. For a summary and rebuttal of conservative claims, see Manne (2001).
[81] Legg (2002: 411).

The *BTH* report concluded that the government's policy of child removal violated the values of domestic laws and breached several international laws. In the cases of Aboriginal children and their families, the *BTH* report found that states often "removed the safeguard of judicial scrutiny," resulting in the "deprivation of liberty," "abolition of parental rights," "abuses of power," and "breach of guardianship obligations" on the part of state officials.[82] Among the international laws and conventions it said had been breached were the United Nations Charter (1945), the Universal Declaration of Human Rights (1948), the Intervention Convention on the Elimination of All Forms of Racial Discrimination (CERD) (1965), and the Convention on the Prevention and Punishment for the Crime of Genocide (Genocide Convention) (1948). Of these alleged violations, the most controversial is the charge of genocide. According to the inquiry, the removal of children from their families met the Genocide Convention's criteria of "forcibly transferring children of [a] group to another group with the intention of destroying the group (regardless of the extent to which that intention was achieved)."[83]

The *BTH* report offered fifty-four recommendations, each with sub-recommendations. The recommendations for acknowledgment and apology were derived from international law and from the submissions of nongovernmental organizations, including Aboriginal groups. According to the Aboriginal and Torres Strait Islander Commission (ATSIC), "The prospect of apologies to indigenous peoples has been raised on many occasions. There is no uniform view about reparations but there is a consistent view of indigenous peoples as to the necessity for apologies."[84] The van Boven Principles ("Basic Principles and Guidelines on the Right to Reparation for Victims of Gross Violations of Human Rights and Humanitarian Law") – specifically principle 15, which concerns "satisfaction and guarantees of non-repetition" – also figured prominently in the recommendation's rationale.[85] Principle

---

[82] Human Rights and Equal Opportunity Commission (1997: 252).
[83] Gardiner-Garden (1999: 11).
[84] Human Rights and Equal Opportunity Commission (1997: 285).
[85] The van Boven Principles are named after Professor Theo van Boven, who was authorized in 1989 by the UN Sub-Commission on Prevention of Discrimination and Protection of Minorities to conduct a study "concerning the right to restitution, compensation, and rehabilitation for victims of gross violations of human rights and fundamental freedoms." Legg (2002: 419).

15 calls for, among other things, "verification of the facts and full and-public disclosure of the truth," "commemorations and paying tribute to the victims," and most relevant to the topic at hand, "apology, including public acknowledgement of the facts and acceptance of responsibility."[86] *BTH* called for an apology from Australia's state parliaments and Commonwealth Parliament, state police forces, and churches and other nongovernmental agencies "for the past laws, policies and practices of forcible removal."[87]

The reactions of state officials, Aboriginal leaders, intellectuals, and the general public to the report's apology recommendations coalesced around two interconnected and enduring issues. First, all sides debated the necessity of the apology for the larger and ongoing project of reconciliation, as legislatively enabled by Parliament. Second, they argued about the report's assessment of the child removal policy – about its outcomes in particular, and about the nature of Australian history more broadly. Whether one considered an apology appropriate largely hinged on his or her views of the policy, of Australian history, and of reconciliation.

Nearly all of the state parliaments, along with state police forces and many churches and nongovernmental agencies, issued formal apologies as recommended. The reasons for apologizing given by the Anglican diocese of Sydney also reflect the reasons given by others. They thought an apology essential to ensure that the reconciliation process be taken seriously and advanced.[88] Indeed, the Parliament of New South Wales explicitly linked its apology to "its commitment to the goals and processes of reconciliation in New South Wales and throughout Australia."[89] Only the state parliament and police forces of the Northern Territory (NT) and the Commonwealth (federal) Parliament did not offer apologies. Although there was considerable debate in the Northern Territory Parliament, in the end there was not enough support because lawmakers maintained that neither the NT Parliament nor its police force was "a party to the removal of children."[90] Instead, the NT Parliament argued that the responsibility for such an apology lay

---

[86] Boven (1996).
[87] Senate Legal and Constitutional References Committee (2000: 109).
[88] Ibid. (126).
[89] Ibid. (130).
[90] Ibid. (137).

with the Commonwealth Parliament. It is important to note that part of the NT Parliament's claim is based on the historical jurisdictional relationship between the Northern Territory and Commonwealth governments. Specifically, in 1911 the Northern Territory came under the jurisdiction of the Commonwealth government, whereas prior to that, beginning in 1863, it had been governed by the laws of South Australia.

Prime Minister John Howard has steadfastly refused to apologize formally, although in August 1999 he introduced a motion ("Motion of Reconciliation") in the House of Representatives. The motion, although expressing "deep and sincere regret that Indigenous Australians suffered injustices under the practices of past generations," did not use the words "apology" or "apologize," unlike those offered by the other state parliaments. Nor did it specifically apologize to the "stolen generations." Yet, similar to the other parliamentary motions, Prime Minister Howard's "Motion of Reconciliation" also expressed its commitment to the reconciliation process ("reaffirms its wholehearted commitment to the cause of reconciliation"). Nevertheless, Howard's motion has been judged unsatisfactory by a large plurality (although not a majority) of Australians, by the HREOC, and by a Senate committee. In a 1997 poll taken immediately after the report was tabled, 65 percent of the 2,065 Australians polled agreed with the recommendation that there be parliamentary apologies. By 1999, however, a majority (57 percent) were against government apologies to Aboriginal people.[91] In 2000, the Senate Legal and Constitutional References Committee deemed that Howard's motion did not constitute a formal apology because it did not refer specifically to the "stolen generations."[92]

Prime Minister Howard has offered several reasons for refusing to apologize in a way that would be widely judged as satisfactory. Some of his reasons are directly tied to the *BTH* report itself – its findings and recommendations. The most important reasons, however, extend beyond the report, to his ideological views and understandings of Australian history and of reconciliation.

Relating specifically to the report, Howard's government has maintained that the policy of child removal did not violate either domestic

---

[91] Newspoll, Saulwick & Muller and Mackay (2000).
[92] Senate Legal and Constitutional References Committee (2000: 128).

or international laws and that it should be judged by the standards – moral as well as legal – of its time, not by those of today. Similarly, in his view the policy did not constitute "a gross violation of human rights and humanitarian law," and thus is not now subject to its principles.

The *BTH* report's charge of genocide is even more controversial. According to *BTH*, between one in ten and one in three Aboriginal children had been separated from their families, most often forcibly or under duress.[93] Government policy was expressly designed to assimilate the children and to remove them permanently from their families and cultures. That intent, according to the *BTH*, was genocidal, in keeping with the definition of genocide as the "destruction of the essential foundations of the life of national groups."[94] In the federal government's view, both the state and federal governments' explicit desire to assimilate "half-caste" Aboriginal children into Australian society by removing them from their families does not itself signal genocidal intent. The Howard government rejected the *BTH*'s methodology and argued that no more than 10 percent of Aboriginal children had been removed.[95] Finally, the government argued that the van Boven principles do not have formal standing in international law and hence are without force.[96] Thus, by disqualifying the sources and rationale from which the apology recommendation was derived, the prime minister deemed an apology improper. In his view, the policy, which left the majority of Aboriginal children unaffected, was lawful at the time and beneficent in intent, not malevolent and certainly not genocidal. According to the Howard government, conservative historians, and journalists, there were no "stolen generations," and an apology was not due.[97]

Howard, early on at least, also questioned the legality of a Commonwealth apology, suggesting that it would expose the federal government to legal liability.[98] On that issue, however, government counsel contradicted him. In 2000, the presiding judge of one of the first test cases of

---

93 Macintyre and Clark (2003: 154).
94 Human Rights and Equal Opportunity Commission (1997: 271).
95 Herron (2000: 5–18).
96 Legg (2000: 423–4).
97 Herron (2000); Manne (2001); Macintryre and Clark (2003).
98 Gordon and Harvey (1997); Senate Legal and Constitutional References Committee (2000: 113).

the stolen generations (*Cubillo v. Commonwealth*) commented on the legality of a formal federal apology, although the issue had not been raised in the case. Judge Maurice O'Loughlin observed that such an apology would be covered by absolute parliamentary privilege.[99] It is important to add that Howard's opposition to apology was matched by his government's opposition to compensation. In 2000, the government clearly indicated that it would not provide a "statutory scheme of compensation" as recommended by *BTH*.[100] Alleged victims would have to pursue lawsuits if they desired compensation. (The aforementioned test case, *Cubillo v. Commonwealth*, was unsuccessful.[101])

The "Black Armband View" of History and Apologies

Howard's aversion to making a formal apology is driven by his views of Aboriginal rights and his related views of Australian history and of reconciliation, and not only or even primarily by his disagreements with the *BTH* report. Aboriginal rights are based, in significant measure, on Aboriginal experiences, as a group, of dispossession and conquest. For Howard, rights derive from membership in one national political community, of which Aboriginal Australians are now formally full members. Australian history is, in Howard's words, "the story of all of our people and it is the story for all our people. It is owned by no-one."[102] Australian history is also more than "a disgraceful record of imperialism, exploitation and racism," which he refers to as the "black armband view" of history. (Black armbands have been worn by Aboriginal activists to express solidarity and mourning for their losses.) Australian history, he has said, is also one of prideful achievements.[103] Because the *BTH* report seemed to him to express more of the black armband view, an apology would plainly endorse that view

---

[99] Ibid. (2000: 113–14).

[100] Herron (2000: 40).

[101] In *Cubillo v. Commonwealth* (2000), Judge Maurice O'Loughlin decided that the plaintiffs had not been wrongly imprisoned; that they had not been "victims of a breach of statutory duty by the Director of Native Affairs (for whom the respondent was alleged to be vicariously liable)[;] and that they had not suffered loss by reason of breaches of duties of care and fiduciary duties owed by the Commonwealth." Clarke (2001: 228).

[102] McKenna (1997–8).

[103] Howard (1997).

and related claims of Aboriginal rights. In fact, even before the apology issue emerged, Howard spoke out frequently against negative presentations of Australian history. Along with other politicians, he has been drawn into and become a contributor to ongoing public debates about history. These debates began in 1988 with the bicentennial celebration of Australia's founding and have made historians into public figures and political actors. Just as importantly, political parties have used their ideological orientations to shape their competing views of history and their specific policy prescriptions.[104]

The bicentennial celebration sparked critical public reexamination of Australia's founding. Although most white Australians felt positively about the celebration, Aboriginal Australians did not and registered their disapproval in public protests, describing the celebration as a "farce" and "hypocrisy."[105] At the same time, historians, clearly associated with the two main political parties – Labor and the Coalition (Liberal) – publicly staked out competing views of Australian history, which may be broadly described as denunciatory or celebratory in tone.[106] In 1993, the historian Geoffrey Blainey, associated with the Liberal Party, publicly accused fellow historian Manning Clark, associated with the Labor Party, of presiding over the 1988 bicentenary with a "gloomy view."[107] Blainey, who coined the phrase "black armband," describes it thusly: "The black armband view of history might well represent the swing of the pendulum from a position that has been too favourable, too congratulatory, to an opposite extreme that is even more unreal and decidedly jaundiced."[108] For his part, Clark expressed views that were decidedly more critical. In a 1988 article titled "The Beginning of Wisdom," Clark proclaimed that Australians were "ready to face the truth" about their past – that is, that the arrival of the British had ushered in "three great evils: violence against Aborigines, violence against convict laborers, and violence against the land itself."[109]

---

[104] McKenna (1997–8).
[105] "Black Power on the March" (1988), quoted in Attwood and Markus (1999: 315).
[106] Macintyre and Clark (2003: ch. 6).
[107] In Blainey's words, "My friend and undergraduate teacher Manning Clark, who was almost the official historian in 1988, had done much to spread the gloomy view and also the compassionate view with powerful prose and Old Testament phrases." McKenna (1997–8: 2).
[108] Ibid. (3).
[109] Ibid. (4).

To be sure, the close relationship between politics and historical narratives did not begin in 1988 and is not limited to public intellectuals, political parties, and electoral politics. For most of Australian history, conventional narratives largely supported the claims of white Australians to the land and the foundations of Australian jurisprudence. Landownership was essentially decided by conquest and settlement. Australian jurisprudence from 1788 until the monumental 1992 High Court decision in *Mabo vs. Queensland* had presumed Australia to be an empty land (*terra nullius*) as far as Aboriginal rights to ownership were concerned. British settlement had itself extinguished all native land claims.

Moreover, Australian national identity and collective self-perception have also been buttressed by traditional narratives. Australia views itself as a democratic country forged nobly by Britain's castoffs, having been founded as a penal colony. Australians have attached great value to the notion of a "fair go" – that everyone has a fair chance in his or her individual and collective pursuits. There is little room or incentive, then, for seeing the settlers and their actions as less than noble. Until recently, the treatment of Aboriginal Australians had not vitiated or sullied Australian self-perceptions of being a "fair go" people. Indeed, reflecting on recent flare-ups in Australia's history battles, historian David Day remarked, "It's about the legitimacy of our occupation. We have this idea of ourselves as mates, citizens, and yet the reality of our history is very different: of a people who are always ready to go to war and have claimed the place largely through conquest."[110]

Traditional narratives identified Aboriginal Australians as outsiders to the national community and justified their exclusion by pointing to a supposed cultural and racial inferiority. Finally, historical narratives and anthropological writings, especially of the early twentieth century, contributed significantly to the view that Aboriginal traditions, and Aboriginal peoples themselves, were disappearing through death or eventual assimilation, thereby making Aboriginal political autonomy impossible.[111] If these views had prevailed, white Australians would never have been compelled to reorder Australian governance

---

[110] Fickling (2003: 19).
[111] McGregor (1997).

fundamentally in order to recognize and accommodate Aboriginal autonomy – or to take Aboriginal aspirations seriously at all.

The 1988 celebration publicly disclosed a contested shift well under way in Australian scholarship, begun in the late 1960s: Traditional historical narratives were being displaced (although not necessarily replaced) by new narratives. There are several intertwined reasons for this shift. First, both Aboriginal mobilization and white interest in and support of Aboriginal issues increased. Recall that the 1967 Referendum, approved by 90.7 percent of voters, authorized the inclusion of Aborigines in the federal census and empowered the federal government to enact "special laws" for Aboriginal people. Second, greater mobilization and coalition building were affected by larger international developments, most notably the Vietnam War, decolonization in Africa and Asia, and the U.S. civil rights movement. Third, a new generation of scholars, many future "new historians," were beginning their professional careers in a charged political and social atmosphere. Aboriginal peoples were also involved through their deliberate efforts to tell their own personal histories (largely through published memoirs) and to document collective histories and traditions.[112] White historians have incorporated Aboriginal documents and oral histories into their scholarship.[113]

The new histories turned much of the old history on its head, using new sources and reinterpreting old ones. Just as conventional narratives both buttressed and reflected certain political claims, so do the new histories. Most significant in this regard is the influence of the new narrative's basic ideas of "violent conflict" and subsequent "dispossession," which lend legitimacy to the idea of prior possession.[114] The High Court's rejection of the *terra nullius* doctrine in 1992 drew directly from and cited new historical thinking and writing.[115] In important ways, then, the *Mabo* decision and the *BTH* report starkly revealed how radically the direction of public policies could change – and was seemingly required to change – once reinterpretations of history were taken seriously.

---

[112] See, for example, Reynolds (1999); Attwood and Foster (2003: 3–9).
[113] See, for example, Rose (2003).
[114] Attwood and Foster (2003: 3–8).
[115] McKenna (1997–8); Ray (2003: 14).

Howard's election in 1996 put a brake on all of this. Shortly thereafter, he spoke against this manifest power of historical reinterpretation, remarking, "One of the more insidious developments in Australian political life over the past decade or so has been the attempt to rewrite Australian history in the service of a partisan political cause."[116] He viewed this development as insidious not only because history was being used for political purposes, but, more importantly, because he judged the interpretations flawed. After all, both Howard and conservative historians use history to support their political views. A partisan political cause to which Howard was no doubt referring was the Aboriginal cause and, by extension, the defeated Labor government of Paul Keating, who had championed that cause. The stakes, partisan and otherwise, attached to Australian history were raised higher still with the subsequent release of the *BTH* report, its charge of genocide, and its recommendation for apology. The "history wars" continue to rage over the occurrence and extent of "frontier massacres" during early settlement and over the proper exhibits and accompanying descriptions at the national museum.[117] Through it all, Howard's views have remained firm and consistent. He rejects Aboriginal rights and the "black armband view" of history on which such rights partly rest.

Howard's refusal to apologize, then, is rooted in his ideological views of political life and interpretations of Australian history. These views, in turn, shape his understanding of which direction reconciliation should go. It is important to note that Howard has not always simplistically defended the traditional historical narratives. He agrees with the new history's most basic and general point: that white Australians treated Aboriginal Australians badly and unjustly. (In his words, "Now of course we treated Aborigines very, very badly in the past...."[118]) However, although Howard acknowledges past injustices, he judges prideful achievements to outweigh them: Pride in, and not guilt about, Australia's past should be history's main lesson; moreover, the acknowledgment of past wrongdoing requires neither an apology nor compensation. Although he recognizes a legacy of disadvantage, just how much current disadvantage can be attributed to historical mistreatment

---

[116] Macintyre and Clark (2003: 137).
[117] Ibid.; Manne (2003); Attwood and Foster (2003).
[118] McKenna (1997–8: 6).

is in his view an open and ultimately pointless question. Rather, Howard regards the proper response as one that "commits to a practical programme of action that will remove the enduring legacies of disadvantage," and not one "that apportions blame and guilt for historic wrongs."[119] Howard's program of reconciliation is discussed more fully in Chapter 4. Most important for our purposes here is the fact that Howard's concept of practical reconciliation focuses on the future rather than the past, treats citizens as individuals and not members of groups, and does not require an apology for its fulfillment.

No Apology for American Slavery

The effort to secure a congressional apology resolution for slavery is an example of an elite-driven effort that, although motivated largely by moral concerns, failed because it did not receive sufficient congressional support. Nor was it a response to group mobilization. The effort also provides proof of how contentious public discussions about slavery and Jim Crow segregation still are. Certainly much of the attention garnered by calls to apologize for slavery is due to the public's association of apology with monetary reparations. That issue has received even more scholarly and public attention. Neither the calls for reparations nor for apology are the topics of government commissions, although since 1989, Representative John Conyers (D-MI) has annually drafted a bill requesting the establishment of a commission to study slavery and reparations. The most recent call for a congressional apology for slavery came from within the Congress itself, not from an outside organized group, thereby distinguishing it from the 2005 Senate apology about antilynching legislation.

On June 12, 1997, Representative Tony Hall (D-OH) introduced House Concurrent Resolution 96, which "apologizes to African-Americans whose ancestors suffered as slaves under the Constitution and laws of the United States until 1865."[120] The bipartisan resolution had twenty cosponsors: thirteen Democrats and seven Republicans. As a concurrent resolution, it was not "legislative in character," but was used, as such resolutions are, to express principles and opinions. It was referred to the House Committee on the Judiciary, where it stayed.

[119] Howard (1997).
[120] Hall (1997).

The following week, on June 18, 1997, Hall was given five minutes on the floor to make the case for the resolution. According to Hall, apologizing is "the right thing to do." Congress, as an institution, bore responsibility, he argued. ("The laws we passed ignored, even encouraged slavery."[121]) Because congressional apologies are rare, they are "special," according to Hall. The resolution simply read, in its entirety: "Resolved by the House of Representatives that the Congress apologizes to African-Americans whose ancestors suffered as slaves under the Constitution and laws of the United States until 1865."[122]

In newspaper reports, Hall explained that the apology issue was one of morality. However, in spoken remarks, Hall also linked the apology issue to President Clinton's recent commencement address at the University of California at San Diego, where he announced his intention to initiate formally a "dialogue on race."[123] On June 13, 1997, the day after Hall introduced the apology resolution, President Clinton established through executive order the President's Initiative on Race (PIR) and authorized the creation of an advisory board to examine "race, racism, and the potential for racial reconciliation in America using a process of study, constructive dialogue, and action."[124] Although the board was a racially diverse group, its credibility was deeply compromised from the start by the absence of Native Americans.[125]

Like Australia's HREOC and Canada's RCAP, the PIR advisory board traveled widely, hosting "eight public meetings in five states and the District of Columbia"; individual board members participated in "approximately 300 meetings with a wide cross section of communities and constituencies."[126] The PIR advisory board also stressed the importance of understanding history and its relationship to current problems: "A critical component for a constructive and honest dialogue about race and racism is a greater public awareness of the history of oppression, conquest, and private and government – sanctioned discrimination and their present-day consequences."[127]

---

[121] U.S. House of Representatives (1997: H3890). Available online at http://thomas. loc.gov.

[122] Hall (1997).

[123] Williams (2003: 312).

[124] Advisory Board of the President's Initiative on Race (1998).

[125] Williams (2003: 315).

[126] Ibid.

[127] Advisory Board of the President's Initiative on Race (1998: 35).

The report offered recommendations on several important and big issues, ranging from civil rights enforcement, education, and poverty to criminal justice and immigration. Given the breadth and complexity of the topics, the recommendations were general and largely unobjectionable. Who could disagree with the recommendation that income inequality be examined more closely or that the effectiveness of antipoverty programs be evaluated or that public education be improved?

It also provided a list of "Ten Things Every American Should Do to Promote Racial Reconciliation."[128] The recommendations focus on behaviors (attending cultural events, getting involved in the community, starting a community group, and so on) that encourage greater civic participation, with the expressed purpose of promoting interactions between people of different racial and ethnic groups. The PIR's recommendations that promote social involvement are similar to those made by Australia's HREOC and Council of Aboriginal Reconciliation reports. In Australia, "sorry days," "sorry books," and local grassroots organizations dedicated to reconciliation were the outcomes. Indeed, such local efforts were judged to be the clear successes of the whole reconciliation process.

Notably, however, the PIR report did not recommend an apology. Moreover, unlike the commissions in Australia, Canada, and New Zealand, which saw their tasks as setting the historical record straight in addition to making policy recommendations, the PIR simply reported its findings. Stressing the points of agreement and common concern about a range of issues, the PIR report reads like the transcript of a national "conversation." Given the advisory board's broad charge and President Clinton's penchant for discussion, the initiative and its final report were largely dismissed as more of the same. The brewing Monica Lewinsky scandal also worked to overshadow the PIR's efforts.[129]

As for Representative Hall's apology, Clinton first indicated that he might support it, but then backed away, explaining in August 1997 that he would await the advisory board's view. Back in June, Clinton had been quoted as saying: "An apology, under the right circumstances, those things can be quite important. Surely every American knows that

---

[128] Ibid. (102–4).
[129] Williams (2003: 322–8).

slavery was wrong, and that we paid a terrible price for it and that we had to keep repairing that."[130] However, Clinton did not specifically charge the advisory board with examining the apology issue or with making a recommendation about it.

By August 1997, Hall acknowledged that his concurrent resolution had received very little support in the House, thereby making it impossible to secure Senate support or White House attention. Whereas in other countries the apology issue raged on for months and sometimes years, within two months the slavery apology issue was dead, at least as a congressional matter. But Hall resurrected it again three years later in June 2000, again in the form of a House Concurrent Resolution. This time, the Resolution called for "acknowledging the fundamental injustice, cruelty, brutality, and inhumanity of slavery in the United States and the 13 American colonies, and for other purposes." This time the Resolution also called for "a commission to examine the institution of slavery and subsequent racial and economic discrimination against African-Americans," a school curriculum that includes a standardized discussion of slavery, and the establishment of a national museum and memorial regarding slavery and African American history. As before, the Resolution died.[131]

Conclusion

Apologies and demands for them have both long-term and immediate sources. Their long-term sources are the earlier efforts of group mobilization and legislative and policy reforms discussed earlier in this chapter. The immediate sources rest with political actors – political elites and organized groups – and their motivations. In instances where apologies are given, either the support of the political elite and organized pressures both were present or political elite support stood alone. The Canadian, New Zealand, BIA, congressional, and senatorial apologies fall into this category. However, political elite support was not always a guarantee of success, as the Congressional Resolution for American Indians and Representative Hall's Concurrent Resolution on slavery demonstrate. The configuration of power (partisan and institutional) within the U.S. Congress combined with the perceived salience of the

---

[130] Holmes (1997: A15).
[131] U.S. Congress (2000).

issue matters. In any event, without political elite support, an apology is impossible. With such support, it is possible, but not guaranteed.

Political elites who ideologically support indigenous claims and want to advance group demands offer apologies. They are guided also by a sense of history's moral obligation, by feelings of guilt, and by ideas about justice. The moral dimensions of their support are revealed in remarks preceding the apologies. For example, Australia's Prime Minister Keating stated in 1993 that the country had to get things "right with the Aborigines." Indeed, evidence suggests that political elites themselves believe that such feelings are important in explaining changes in policy direction. For example, a study of U.S. Native American policy development in the 1970s found that congressional legislators and their staffs believed that feelings of guilt and fairness (among other things) motivated their support of pro–Native American policies.[132]

Organized pressures are also powerful motivators for political elites, who respond to them to gain political and sometimes electoral advantage. The political advantages are broad, indicating a willingness on the part of political elites to recognize, confront, and act on basic and enduring issues of indigenous political and material life. Indigenous groups and their supporters have largely managed to keep indigenous issues on the national political radar since the 1960s in ways that demand responses (however uneven in force and form) from central authorities. Electoral incentives are most clearly evident (but ultimately inconsequential) in the proposed 2004 congressional apology to Native Americans.

Indigenous and other minority groups are motivated to reach their political and material goals of political and economic autonomy while also emphasizing what they perceive to be the righteousness of their cause. That is, their desired goals are explained and justified by their historical experiences of dispossession and marginalization. Getting lawmakers and society at large not only to reexamine national histories critically but to render moral judgments about them is central to advancing Aboriginal rights. Apologies contribute directly to these tasks.

Finally, historians are also important background players in apology politics, as they are helping to rewrite histories. In Canada and

[132] Gross (1989: 77).

New Zealand, they have served on RCAP and the Waitangi Tribunal respectively, contributing directly to the background materials, as in Canada, and to the official reports, as in New Zealand. In Australia, historians have been more prominent still, associating themselves publicly and contributing directly to the historical views espoused by politicians (and being publicly associated with those views). In all of these cases, it is fair to say, at the risk of oversimplification, that these historians are motivated both by the "pursuit of truth" and their own viewpoints.

In addition to identifying the relevant political actors and their motivations, this chapter argued that apologies themselves perform three tasks that make them especially effective in fortifying and furthering Aboriginal claims. First, nearly all of the apologies ratified new understandings of historical events and rendered moral judgments about them. Canada's RCAP report, in reexamining that country's past, calls for the abandonment of "false assumptions" that it said had guided government policies in the past. The Canadian government's apology did not challenge RCAP's version of history, but rather expressed its "profound regrets" about that history. Similarly, the New Zealand government and the queen's apology also validated the view that the Crown's invasion and subsequent confiscation of Waikato-Tainui land was "wrong" and "unlawful." Conventional accounts had largely judged the invasion and confiscation lawful.

The Hawaiian apology Resolution, in a slight twist, did not endorse the historical reinterpretation produced by the NHSC. Instead, the resolution explicitly assigned the U.S. government partial responsibility for the 1893 overthrow of the Hawaiian kingdom, thus contradicting the NHSC report, which, in its denial of U.S. government involvement, did not deviate from standard accounts.[133] Finally, the Senate and BIA apologies, the pending congressional apology resolution, and the unsuccessful slavery apology openly acknowledge historical wrongs

---

[133] The 1993 resolution reads in part:

> Whereas, on January 14, 1893, John L. Stevens (hereafter referred to in this Resolution as the "United States Minister"), the United States Minister assigned to the sovereign and independent Kingdom of Hawaii, conspired with a small group of non-Hawaiian residents of the Kingdom of Hawaii, including citizens of the United States, to overthrow the indigenous and lawful Government of Hawaii. ("100th Anniversary of the Overthrow of the Hawaiian Kingdom" (1993: S14479).

and contain informative descriptions of them. In contrast to all others, Australian Prime Minister Howard refused to apologize precisely because he was unwilling to endorse either the *BTH* report's description and explanation of the child removal policy or the "new historians'" views of Australian history.

Second, nearly all of the apologies contend that current disadvantage is, in some measure, attributable to past mistreatment. The Canadian government openly makes the connection in its 1998 *Gathering Strength* report and apology; it states that the government must "find ways to deal with the negative impacts that certain historical decisions continue to have in our society today." The Hawaii apology also links the present-day disadvantages of Native Hawaiians to the enduring impact of economic and social upheavals a century earlier.[134] Kevin Gover, author of the BIA apology, directly linked "the rampant alcoholism, drug abuse, and domestic violence that plague Indian country" with federal policies.[135] Similarly, the proposed congressional apology contends that federal policies are partly to blame for the "severe social ills and economic troubles in many Native communities today."[136] Likewise, the Queen's apology implied a legacy of hardship for New Zealand's Waikato-Tainui by acknowledging the "devastation of property and social life which resulted" from the Crown's actions.[137]

In contrast, the U.S. Senate apology Resolution on lynchings did not propose that lynchings led to or are connected with current social and economic disparities between whites and African Americans. Rather, the Resolution commented only on the lynching phenomenon and the Senate's decades-long failure to pass federal antilynching legislation. Prime Minister Howard has acknowledged that Aboriginal peoples were badly treated and recognizes that some portion of present-day disparities is attributable to historical mistreatment. However, Howard has deliberately not weighed events of the past more heavily, asserting

---

[134] The 1993 resolution reads in part: "...the long-range economic and social changes in Hawaii over the nineteenth and early twentieth centuries have been devastating to the population and to the health and well-being of the Hawaiian people..." (ibid.).

[135] Kevin Gover, Assistant Secretary for Indian Affairs, Department of the Interior, remarks at the Ceremony Acknowledging the 175th Anniversary of the Establishment of the Bureau of Indian Affairs, September 8, 2000.

[136] S.J. Resolution 15, "To acknowledge a long history of official depredations and ill-conceived policies by the United States Government regarding Indian tribes and offer an apology to all Native Peoples on behalf of the United States," April 19, 2005.

[137] Alves (1999: 128).

instead that recent and present-day actions, by both former Labor governments and Aboriginal peoples themselves, are also responsible for Aboriginal hardship.

Third, certain of the apologies propose a new course of government action, and nearly all identify societal reconciliation as a goal. The Canadian government confirms its commitment to the further strengthening of Aboriginal self-governance and to more cooperative relationships between indigenous nations and governments. Similarly, the BIA apology explicitly pledges that the BIA will help Native Americans, not wage war on them, both literally and figuratively, since the BIA's bureaucratic predecessor was the War Department. A number of the apologies simply vow that past actions will not be repeated in the future and express hope that the gesture will contribute to reconciliation among citizens.

Prime Minister Howard's refusal to apologize does not mean that he has no views either about a future course of action or about reconciliation. He is committed to formal equality, which means that there is and will be only one body of laws and political institutions governing all Australian citizens, including Aboriginal peoples. His conceptualization of reconciliation does not require that his administration apologize.

In sum, political actors use apologies (or nonapologies) to express support for and advance the ideas and policies they favor. Once an apology is given, political actors use it as proof that the government recognizes its obligations to mend current disadvantages, because they are the result, in part, of past government actions and policies. Finally, political actors use apologies as platforms for announcing new policy directions and promoting societal reconciliation. Even in the Australian case, the demands for apology and Howard's refusal to apologize set in motion the same dynamics as successful apologies, if in the opposite direction. Howard will not apologize because he rejects Aboriginal rights and attendant historical interpretations, does not judge history to be the main source of present-day hardships, and does not want to go in the direction of Aboriginal self-governance.

In the next chapter, we shall see whether apologies have observable effects on legal status, political arrangements, and collective sentiments.

4

Beyond Sentiment? Apologies and Their Effects

Popular views of apologies and most scholarship focus logically on their emotional dimensions. The hope is that apologies will contribute to societal reconciliation, dampening animosities and fostering feelings of national unity. This book takes a wider view of apologies and of reconciliation itself, arguing that apologies assist also in altering the terms of national membership. Reconciliation often includes more than enhanced collective sentiments, extending to the redistribution of political authority and economic resources. Political actors use apologies to advance claims because apologies underscore a state's obligations – moral, political, and sometimes legal – to indigenous people, including the redesign of government policies in ways that largely conform to indigenous objectives. Apology and the attendant historical discussion further these objectives because indigenous arguments rest on historical claims of mistreatment as well as broken treaties and agreements. As Rebecca Tsosie asks in the case of Native Americans, "Why should Congress continue to respect its historic bargain with Native peoples if the citizens of the United States begin to doubt the existence or validity of those agreements?"[1] Revisiting history and apologizing for aspects of it contribute to the needed justifications in all of our cases.

The central question, whether and in which ways are apologies effective, remains to be answered. This chapter seeks to answer that question, assessing in each instance of apology its effects on the legal,

---

[1] Tsosie (2006: 203).

political, and affective dimensions of membership and belonging. In cases where state officials declined to apologize, the chapter examines how the absence of apology affects the prospects for affective reconciliation and the direction of federal policies. Here, the expectation is that the absence of apology and accompanying diminishment of historical justifications will advance political objectives and policies that run counter to indigenous demands.

Canada

The Canadian government's apology did not at all affect the legal status of Aboriginal peoples as Canadian citizens. However, the apology affirmed the government's commitment to Aboriginal self-governance, contributing less to actual changes in policy than to fortifying self-government as the ultimate policy objective, shared by both government and Aboriginal leadership. Public support of the apology and muted dissent against historical narratives that emphasize historical injustices suggest that Canadians are prepared to support the direction of federal policies and to embrace collective sentiments of empathy.

The Canadian government identified dealing with the past, both learning from and apologizing for it, as starting points for Canada's renewed Aboriginal policy. The disadvantaged position of Aboriginal peoples today is attributed, in some unstated measure, to their historical treatment. In the words of the government's 1998 "Statement of Reconciliation," "Our purpose is not to rewrite history but, rather, to learn from our past and to find ways to deal with the negative impacts that certain historical decisions continue to have in our society today."

The government's responses to RCAP, both in rhetoric and in practice, have fallen noticeably short of RCAP's recommendations while still affirming Aboriginal self-governance. (RCAP recommended, for example, that the Canadian government establish a separate Aboriginal parliament.) In its initial policy statement, *Gathering Strength*, the government committed itself to discussions and consultations but not to negotiations with Aboriginal peoples. It also committed itself to working on the achievement of Aboriginal self-governance, "within the context of the Treaty relationship." In an important way, government policy is heading in the direction of self-governance and self-sufficiency first set out in the 1970s. Indeed, as Parliament's own research shows, many of the self-governance initiatives classified as *Gathering Strength* initiatives had been under way before the 1998 apology.[2] The negotiations between the Canadian government and Aboriginal groups (First Nations) are complex and organized into three stages: the "framework agreement" is the first stage, "agreement-in-principle" the second, and "final agreement" the third. According to government sources, between 1998 and early 2005 the federal government entered into approximately eleven "final agreements" with eight First Nations; fifteen "agreements-in-principle" with eleven First Nations, and three "framework agreements."[3] These are in addition to the 1975 James Bay and Northern Québec Agreement with the Cree band, the 1986 Sechelt Indian Band Self-Government Act, and a 1993 umbrella final agreement with seven Yukon First Nations.[4]

Since 1998, the Canadian government has misstepped along, but not strayed from the self-governance path. For example, the 2002 attempt by former Federal Indian Affairs Minister Robert Nault, under former Prime Minister Jean Chrétien, to replace the Indian Act with the First Nations Governance Act appeared to contradict the spirit, if not the letter, of the RCAP report. According to First Nation organizations, Nault did not consult with them in designing the scheme. It is for this reason that they organized widely and protested to have it defeated. An editorial in the *Toronto Star* also denounced Nault's unilateral approach. Aboriginal leadership agreed with the bill's purpose, expressing dissatisfaction with the Indian Act and its restrictions on decision making within bands.[5] The bill allowed indigenous bands to establish their own code of financial management.[6] However, they felt that they had not been equal partners in the bill's drafting. Rather, the minister acted as other ministers had in the past: He came to them with a formulated policy and expected Aboriginal peoples simply to accept it. Aboriginal resistance was key to the bill's defeat and abandonment of the

---

[2] Hurley and Wherrett (2000: 5).
[3] Canada Indian and Northern Affairs (n.d.).
[4] Hurley and Wherrett (2000: 2).
[5] The bill was intended to change electoral laws and financial management within bands. As the legislation was written, if its codes were not established within two years and approved by at least 25 percent of the band population, the rules would be imposed directly by the federal government.
[6] Murray (2003).

accompanying Indian Act review process, which itself cost CAN$10 million.[7]

Moreover, the Liberal Party government of Paul Martin, which took office in 2003, appeared to take a page out of Australian Prime Minister John Howard's book on practical reconciliation. At the April 2004 Canada–Aboriginal Peoples Roundtable, over which Prime Minister Martin presided, Martin announced his intention to get results in four key policy areas: economic development, education, health, and housing. According to Martin, policy must be results-oriented. The current CAN$8 billion in government expenditures should produce better outcomes. His results orientation was similar to Howard's practical reconciliation. But unlike Howard, who pushed practical reconciliation forward while sidelining Aboriginal self-governance or even involvement, as evidenced by the abolition of the Aboriginal and Torres Strait Islander Commission (ATSIC), Martin could not go nearly that far. Whatever his emphasis on specific policy areas, he also identified Aboriginal self-government as the ultimate goal and did not dispute the historical origins of federal obligation. Martin operated within the constraints of Aboriginal policy making in Canada, the legal and political leverage that Aboriginal groups exert, and the Liberal Party's expressed commitment to Aboriginal rights.

In late 2005, shortly before the Liberal Party was toppled by the Conservative Party in January 2006 elections, Martin, together with ten provincial premiers and Aboriginal leaders, signed the Kelowna Accord. The Accord, reached after eighteen months of negotiation, committed CAN$5.1 billion over five years for federal programs aimed at improving the basic living conditions and health and education outcomes of Aboriginal peoples. The Accord's life, however, was short-lived; the current prime minister, Stephen Harper of the Conservative Party, has largely ditched the Accord, judging it to be both the result of last-minute election-driven bargaining and economically infeasible. Instead, his party has replaced the Accord's CAN$1 billion a year commitment to new expenditures with a $225 million a year commitment.[8] Using his position as former prime minister as a bully pulpit, Martin has decried the abandonment of the Accord as "immoral," arguing

---

[7] Bailey (2004).
[8] Aubry (2006).

that "Kelowna is essentially about narrowing and eliminating gaps in health care and education, housing and clear water. You're either for that or you're against it. . . . "[9] As we have seen, in advocating for Aboriginal issues in Canada and elsewhere, state officials often invoke morality in the absence of or in addition to other means. For their part, Prime Minister Harper and his minister of Indian Affairs, Jim Prentice, have stressed poverty alleviation and greater inclusion within Canadian society, not Aboriginal governance, as their priorities. However, the priority of poverty alleviation, at least, is not incompatible with Aboriginal autonomy, as the experiences of a number of U.S. Native American tribal governments demonstrate.

Public opinion polls taken before and after the government's 1998 "Statement of Reconciliation" show that the Canadian public was widely supportive of the apology itself and the direction of the government's Aboriginal policies. In a poll conducted by the Angus Reid Group for the government in December 1997 (a month before the government's apology), non-Aboriginal Canadians were asked whether they would support or oppose an apology. Specifically, the question read, "Do you support or oppose the government making an apology to all Aboriginal Peoples?" A substantial majority (75 percent) said they supported it, 22 percent said they were opposed, and 3 percent responded that they weren't sure. However, only a slight majority (51 percent) thought that the government was apologizing on their behalf.[10] The poll also revealed that Canadians did not believe a "quick fix" existed for Aboriginal issues, but were generally supportive of the government's policy agenda. Thus the government released its January 1998 "Statement of Reconciliation" and *Gathering Strength* report knowing that both were generally supported by the majority of Canadians.

Moreover, according to press reports, surveys conducted earlier in the 1990s showed that "almost half of Canadians believe aboriginals have an equal or better standard of living than the average citizen and 40 percent believe natives have only themselves to blame for their problems."[11] These earlier polls, taken before the 1996 release of the RCAP

---

[9] Thompson (2006).
[10] Aubry (1998b).
[11] "Apology to Natives Gets Wide Support in Poll" (1998, p. A12).

report, provide an admittedly imprecise baseline of Canadian attitudes, suggesting that the RCAP report may have had some positive effects in educating Canadians toward a more sympathetic view of Aboriginal claims. Perhaps after exposure to the RCAP report, Canadians were both open to an apology and accommodating of activist federal policy making.

Aboriginal organizations also commissioned their own survey to gauge attitudes toward Aboriginal issues. Between November 27 and December 5, 1998 (eleven months after the apology and the *Gathering Strength* report), Environics Research Group conducted a national survey of 1,500 adult Canadians for the Assembly of First Nations. This poll did not ask direct questions about the government reports, either the RCAP report or *Gathering Strength*, but focused instead on federal policy in general. The results generally bode well for reconciliation's success in Canada: "[A] plurality (37 percent) say that the federal government should devote either a lot more (16 percent) or somewhat more (21 percent) attention to the issues and concerns of First Nations. One-third (33 percent) say the federal government should be paying the same level of attention." A majority (53 percent) reported that "their level of support ... remained relatively unchanged over the past two years."[12] Considered in tandem with the existing support for government policy, this finding suggests that the RCAP report and other developments simply affirm public sentiment. However, 21 percent answered that over the past two years they had become supportive, thereby suggesting that the RCAP report likely had the desired effects. As important, these results suggest that the RCAP report did not immediately generate a negative backlash. In a related response, the majority (58 percent) recognized and accepted that efforts will require significant government expenditures over a long period of time. Finally, 67 percent answered that they "knew too little about the issues and challenges" facing Aboriginal peoples. This result may perhaps be interpreted in two opposing ways. One way is that the educative functions of the RCAP report and other government reports have been less effective than expected. Alternatively, the result may indicate that these efforts have been effective, alerting Canadians that Aboriginal issues are more complex and varied than they had previously appreciated.

[12] Environics Research Group (1998: 1–2).

In addition to offering its general apology, the government apologized specifically to the victims of sexual and physical abuse at the residential schools administered by various church denominations under government auspices. In 1998, the government established the Aboriginal Healing Foundation to handle these issues. Not surprisingly, neither the apology nor the "healing fund" was enough. (Commenting on the healing fund amount, Henry Daniels, president of the Congress of Aboriginal Peoples, observed, "I don't want to trivialize the $350 million but that's far less than the money than [the government] gave to a helicopter company not to build helicopters."[13] In 1993, the Chrétien government paid a CAN$500 million penalty to cancel a helicopter contract.) Aboriginal people sued both the government and the churches. In June 2001, the government established a new department, Indian Residential Schools Resolution Canada, to handle the abuse claims.

The government also sued churches as a way of sharing both culpability and compensation costs. The churches maintained that the lawsuits would bankrupt them. At first, the government and churches entered into cost-sharing agreements. For example, in March 2003, federal authorities and the Anglican Church of Canada finalized a CAN$25 million plan, according to which the church would pay 30 percent of compensation, up to a maximum of CAN$25 million. The government would assume the remaining 70 percent.[14] However, in April 2006, a final agreement was reached among the Assembly of First Nations, churches, and the government. Mediated by former Supreme Court justice Frank Iacobucci, the settlement, totaling approximately CAN$2 billion, provides each of the approximate eighty thousand claimants with a flat payment of CAN$10,000 plus CAN$3,000 for each year that he or she attended the schools.[15] Prior to the settlement, approximately 2,676 claimants had their claims resolved either through alternate dispute resolution (ADR) and/or litigation, totaling over CAN$100 million.[16]

The Canadian public is apparently prepared to bear the costs because they have judged their government to be partially responsible.

---

[13] Speirs (1998).
[14] Mofina (2002).
[15] Editorial (2006).
[16] Indian Residential Schools Resolution Canada (n.d.).

In summarizing the results of a March 2001 government-commissioned survey, researchers found that most Canadians thought their government bore some responsibility, although not primary responsibility. They also expected that their government, in assuming its responsibility, would, in the researchers' words, "deal fairly and generously with victims of a very serious crime."[17] At the same time, a plurality (48 percent) doubted that many of the claims were true. Moreover, a majority (78 percent) considered "support groups and counseling" to be the "most effective responses" to abuse, whereas only 31 percent considered financial compensation to be such.

Finally, the final 2006 settlement, while welcomed by residential school survivors, has also ignited demands for an official apology from Prime Minister Harper. Although the Chrétien government apologized directly for residential school abuse, survivors maintain that an apology from the prime minister himself is still required. The financial settlement is not enough. Here, survivors desire the moral evaluation of wrongdoing that an apology provides, lest the settlement be viewed simply as a payment.[18]

New Zealand

The Crown's apologies alone did not at all effect the legal status of the Maori as New Zealand citizens and appears to have had minimal direct effects on Aboriginal policy making or on political debates about reconciliation. Rather, the significance of the apologies rests in their reliance on the Waitangi Tribunal's historical research and the influence of such research on legal settlements. Here, the apologies' effects are more constrained and conventional, lending closure and meaning to monetary and material settlements.

In contrast, the Waitangi Tribunal's proceedings have affected New Zealand politics enormously. Although the Treaty of Waitangi had been largely ignored in law and policy for most of New Zealand's history, it is no longer. The Tribunal has contributed to "a fundamental paradigm shift or revolution in official discourse" and government practice, in which treaty principles now exert considerable influence.[19] Much of

[17] Pollara Research and Earnscliffe Research and Communications (2001).
[18] "Ex-Students Want Apology for Residential School Abuse" (2006).
[19] Havemann (1995: 73).

the political contention turns, as it always has, on the interpretation of treaty principles and what that interpretation requires. In this sense, New Zealand politics resembles that of Australia insofar as historical reinterpretation is at stake. But whereas in Australia apology served as a main (but not sole) catalyst for this historical debate, in New Zealand the catalyst is the Waitangi Tribunal.

Support for the Waitangi Tribunal, as for apology in Australia, essentially means support for Aboriginal rights; such support has specific implications for the direction of state policy and the vision of New Zealand's history. In the run-up to the 2005 national elections, the opposition National Party's candidate, Don Brash, effectively used the Waitangi Tribunal as a wedge issue, reviving a moribund party and nearly winning the election. In his arguments against the Tribunal, Brash sounded like Australia's Prime Minister Howard. In a January 2004 speech delivered to the Orewa Rotary Club, Brash spoke out forcefully against the treaty claims process, which he labeled the "treaty grievance industry," and the ways in which the Treaty of Waitangi, through its principles, is incorporated into domestic legislation. He judges the treaty process divisive. While acknowledging the alienation of Maori land as well as their historical and current disadvantage, Brash does not think that the treaty is a blueprint for the future. He opposes race-specific policies or preferences and calls instead for New Zealanders to see themselves as one people. The treaty, in his view, does not confer "greater civil, political or democratic rights for Maori than for any other New Zealander."[20] Rather, he says, the treaty should be seen as a "launching pad for the creation of one sovereign nation," and not for two sovereign nations. Brash, like Howard today and Canada's Pierre Trudeau in the 1960s, desires a formal equality. Yet it is unlikely that existing institutional arrangements dedicated to fostering Maori economic, political, and cultural autonomy can be either easily or fully dismantled.

Whatever the improbability of overturning Maori policy as Brash has advocated, his remarks were well received by white New Zealanders (who are also referred to as *Pakeha*). In a February 2004 Herald-DigiPoll survey of 642 Pakeha, 75 percent responded affirmatively when asked, "Do you support Dr. Brash's proposals to remove racial distinctions from Government services?" Although none of the

[20] Brash (2004).

questions asked specifically about the Waitangi Tribunal settlements, they did ask whether the Maori had "the right to special treatment." The majority (76 percent) did not think that the Maori had such a right.[21]

Not surprisingly, the Maori responded negatively to Brash's remarks, although they acknowledge that he has said what many Pakeha think but would not admit: "70 percent of Maori polled think that the Treaty should be part of New Zealand law." There was support in theory for the principle of needs-based assistance – only 31 percent believe that the government should treat the Maori differently from other New Zealanders. But at the same time, there was strong support for specialist Maori schools (78 percent) and health services (79 percent), and separate Maori parliamentary seats and consultation with Maori by district councils (77 percent).[22]

Although the National Party very narrowly lost the election, Brash's arguments against the Waitangi Tribunal (and the public support they seemed to enjoy) caused the ruling Labour Party to call for a national inquiry into several of New Zealand's basic constitutional issues, including the role of the Treaty of Waitangi.[23] Labour also enacted legislation in 2004 that grants ownership of New Zealand's shore and seabed to the Crown, in response to fears that successful Maori land claims would result in restricted public access.[24] Labour's backing of this legislation contributed, in some measure, to the strong showing of the newly formed Maori Party that won seats among the reserved Maori seats previously held by Labour.

Based on public opinion polls showing polarization on Maori issues, the Waitangi Tribunal has not produced a reconciled political community. White New Zealanders and the Maori are far apart on key issues regarding the treaty and its obligations. Maori do not think that they are receiving special treatment. Rather, they believe that "Maori-targeted funding and measures to reduce inequality are part of the Crown's treaty obligations."[25] White New Zealanders, in contrast, view Maori-targeted programs as "special treatment" and appear to be growing tired of it all. In commenting on a recent book about the

---

[21] "What's Eating Pakeha?" (2004).
[22] Taylor (2004); "The Race Debate: Maori Say Paychecks Are Part of Treaty" (2004).
[23] "Brash's Race Card Trumps Labour Treaty of Waitangi Policy" (2005).
[24] "Maori Warn of Battle over Water" (2006).
[25] "The Race Debate: Maori Say Paychecks Are Part of Treaty" (2004).

Treaty of Waitangi, one reviewer noted in 2004 that the book's author "fails to observe that the treaty has come to be seen by many as a one-way street, a document that enables Maori to claim and receive apologies and compensation from a largely Pakeha government without reciprocation, let alone thanks." The reviewer continues, "It does not matter whether the claims are justified – as most of them are. Pakeha are required to carry a moral burden."[26] It is true that the Waitangi Tribunal has very directly contributed to informing both state officials and the public about Crown actions and Maori losses. It has also contributed indirectly to major land and monetary settlements between the Crown and Maori groups, allowing recipients to exert meaningful control over their economic, political, and social lives. The resentments expressed by the reviewer reveal that a key issue appears to be not one of disapproval because of the Waitangi Tribunal's failures, but one of exhaustion because of its successes, which are based on historical and moral claims.

The U.S. Congressional Apology to Native Hawaiians and the BIA Apology

The Congressional Apology Resolution to Native Hawaiians had no effect on the legal status of Native Hawaiians as U.S. citizens. However, it did directly buttress senators' efforts, ultimately unsuccessful, to confer on Native Hawaiians the same legal standing as Native Americans and Native Alaskans. The apology's effects on collective sentiments appear to be minimal. In 2001, the Hawaii Advisory Committee's report judged the apology to be largely ineffective, noting that "however symbolic, the Apology Resolution does not remedy the effects annexation has had on the people of Hawai'i."[27]

Although that assessment was likely true in regard to the apology's emotional impact, it was premature in regard to the apology's political effects. Beginning in 2000, Hawaii's senators Daniel Akaka and Daniel Inouye drafted legislation that sought federal recognition of Native Hawaiians as native peoples, providing them with a separate governing body that would negotiate directly with the U.S. federal government

---

[26] Temple (2004).
[27] Hawaii Advisory Committee to the U.S. Commission on Civil Rights (2001: 19).

over the disposition of land and other resources now owned by the U.S. government. In June 2006, the legislation, the Native Hawaiian Government Reorganization Act (known as the Akaka bill), failed to receive the sixty votes necessary to bring the bill to a Senate floor debate. The final count was fifty-six favoring debate and forty-one against, with Republicans casting all of the "no" votes.[28] The future of the bill is uncertain, as Senator Akaka has not indicated an intention to abandon it. Although the apology resolution itself did not account for this legislation, its admission that a sovereign government (Hawaii) was overthrown by another sovereign government (the United States) supports Native Hawaiian claims of prior sovereignty and recognizes their standing as Hawaii's indigenous peoples. These two premises are at the heart of the Akaka bill.

Given the nature of the 2000 Bureau of Indian Affairs (BIA) apology, it is not surprising that it had no effect on the legal status of Native Americans or relations between tribes and the federal government. Its effects on collective sentiments are split. It was quite meaningful for its intended audience of Native Americans. Press and scholarly accounts describe open displays of emotion, with Assistant Secretary Kevin Gover receiving a standing ovation.[29] However, the apology's effects on reconciliation more broadly are negligible, in large part because very few citizens knew (or know) anything about it. It was not widely reported or commented upon. The "hidden history" of BIA policies and practices were all starkly recounted in Gover's speech. However, unlike the cases of Australia, Canada, and New Zealand, this history still remains hidden or, more precisely, ignored, with the apology (or public debates about one) not contributing to wider societal knowledge. Societal reconciliation presumes and requires broad awareness of historical injustices and an acknowledgment of government's role in perpetrating those injustices.

Australia

The Australian government's refusal to apologize, which polls show the majority of Australians support, has not only meant that Aboriginal

[28] Magin (2006).
[29] Buck (2006).

efforts to strengthen Aboriginal rights have gone unsupported, but have been actively opposed. Moreover, and seemingly incongruously, Australians have indicated in polls that they support "reconciliation," but oppose apology in achieving it. Instead, Prime Minister Howard's government has implemented his practical reconciliation program, which does not derive its justification from remedying historical injustices and that does not seek to advance Aboriginal rights and autonomy. Unlike in other instances where apology is presumed to be a prerequisite for reconciliation, for Howard, the opposite is true. Not only is an apology not required for his idea of reconciliation, it would be largely antithetical to it.

The developments of the 1990s in Australia – most notably the *Mabo v. Queensland* decision, the establishment of the Council for Aboriginal Reconciliation (CAR), and the Human Rights and Equal Opportunity Commission (HREOC) and its *Bringing Them Home* report – all energized Aboriginal demands for a rethinking of citizenship rights. There is some talk of a treaty, but most Australian Aboriginal activists describe self-determination and sovereignty as an issue of empowerment and autonomy; they seek some meaningful involvement of Aboriginal people in government decision making and some measure of self-governance.[30] Most demands for self-government fall far short of the powers already possessed and aspired to by tribal governments in Canada and the United States, for example.

The Howard government has responded to all demands with his "practical reconciliation" policy. "Practical reconciliation," as its name implies, is not limited to affective attachments. Rather, it focuses on policy making that will concretely address Aboriginal disadvantages in education, employment, health, and housing. The policy's emphasis on practicality sets it squarely against the symbolism and abstractness of apology and "indigenous rights." It also sets the Liberal

---

[30] ATSIC Chair Geoff Clark called for a treaty at the CAR's Corroborree 2000 event. Also, under Clark's leadership, ATSIC supported the establishment of a National Treaty Support Group, which convened a national treaty conference in August 2002. Pratt (2003: 21, n.45). On the other hand, Dr. William Jonas, the Aboriginal and Torres Strait Islander Social Justice commissioner within the HREOC, argues that "self-determination" is increasingly being defined as greater representation within the body politic, but in ways that go beyond the formal equality endorsed by Prime Minister Howard.

Party's approach to Aboriginal issues against those pursued by previous Labor governments, which conservatives have judged to be mostly symbolic and hence ineffective. Howard's idea of practical reconciliation acknowledges past injustices in a general way, but does not make the remedy of specific harms (such as land dispossession) the basis for his policy. Instead, his vision of reconciliation is decidedly forward-looking, resulting in a society in which "all Australians [work] together under one set of laws to which all are accountable and from which all are entitled to an equal dispensation of justice."[31] As for apology specifically, Howard has long held that this understanding of reconciliation does not require one.

Howard's practical reconciliation confirms that policies can and obviously do change without apologies. However, as this book has argued, a key reason that Aboriginal groups desire an apology is to influence the content and direction of policy, not simply to instigate policy changes. Proponents view the apology as embracing a particular understanding of Australian history and endorsing a specific policy direction. The apology is a tactic in their broader strategy. Likewise, Howard's refusal to apologize is also a tactic. He envisions a formal equality for Aboriginal Australians where they are beholden to the same laws and political institutions as other Australians. Howard perceives an apology, with its attendant meanings, to be at odds with his vision of Australia's past and of its future. Moreover, by late 2003, Howard considered the apology issue solved insofar as "people no longer ask me for an apology."[32] According to press accounts, he attributed the lack of asking as evidence of the government's improved relationship with Aboriginal communities.

The ideological basis and tactical utility of Howard's refusal were not lost on Aboriginal leadership and Howard's opponents. They have responded, at times, by minimizing the importance of an apology (from Howard, at least) for reconciliation's progress. They stopped asking because they recognized the futility of the request, not because they no longer considered an apology important. Instead, they vowed to wait for the next prime minister. According to Audrey Kinnear, a cochair of the National Sorry Day Committee, "John Howard had his chance

---

[31] Howard (2000).
[32] Riley (2003a: 1).

and he has shown he hasn't got the heart to do it. So, we'll wait till we get another Prime Minister, who has a heart."[33] More often, however, they have judged Howard's reconciliation, in the absence of an apology, morally empty. The apology and reexamination of Australian history provide Aboriginal issues with great moral weight and Aboriginal leadership with political leverage. Howard's refusal to apologize marginalizes moral reflection on what is "justly due" in light of Australian history. In Howard's words, "National reconciliation calls for more than recognition of the damaging impact on people's lives of the mistaken practices of the past. It also calls for a clear focus on the future."[34] Aboriginal leaders and their supporters want that moral reflection to remain at the center.

Practical reconciliation narrows the scope of Aboriginal policy making, focusing on employment, health, education, and housing. How it has fared since 2001 depends on what is being measured and who is doing the measuring. Not surprisingly, the government argues that its policy is producing the desired results. In its official response to the CAR's Final Report and in parliamentary debates, the Commonwealth points to increased government expenditures and government policy initiatives as proof of practical reconciliation's existence. For example, "in the 2001–02 budget, $75 million was allocated for extra housing," and for housing repairs and replacements, and the government has introduced an indigenous employment policy designed to increase small business ownership and create job networks among Aboriginal Australians.[35]

Aboriginal leaders, along with opposition party leaders and government officials, have criticized practical reconciliation, both on its own terms and on their understanding of reconciliation. They oppose the policy's narrowness, but not the four issue areas on which it focuses. They too agree that Aboriginal employment, health, housing, and education require Commonwealth attention. Yet they judge that on these issues the government has not done enough. In a report issued by the Senate Legal and Constitutional References Committee report titled "Reconciliation: Off Track," the same socioeconomic indicators that

---

[33] Riley (2003b: 4).
[34] Howard (2000: 89).
[35] Australian Commonwealth Government (2002: 10–14).

the Commonwealth points to as proof of progress are interpreted by the committee to show that much more work is needed.[36] Several statistical studies also conclude that Howard's practical reconciliation has fared no better in improving income, health, and education outcomes for Aboriginal Australians than the policies of the previous Labor government.[37]

As important, the Senate committee and others judge reconciliation "off track" because of the Howard government's policy constrictions. By restricting reconciliation to four policy areas, Howard's practical reconciliation has effectively squeezed out discussion of larger issues, such as Aboriginal rights, customary law, native title, and treaties, as well as discussion of symbolic ones, such as an apology. As Aboriginal leaders see it, by foreclosing serious discussion about indigenous rights and claims to land, practical reconciliation neutralizes the moral and political force of Aboriginal demands. After all, they base their demands on their status as Australia's Aboriginal people, a status to which certain rights are presumed to attach and certain assumptions to hold. The most fundamental assumption is that of self-determination, or some approximation of it. Practical reconciliation, in the words of Dr. William Jonas, Aboriginal and Torres Strait Islander social justice commissioner, makes indigenous rights "merely desirable or aspirational" as the basis for addressing Aboriginal disadvantage, but says that they "are not connected to the real issues at hand."[38]

In contrast, their understanding of reconciliation is far broader than Howard's. It means taking Aboriginal political, economic, and cultural aspirations seriously. It also means that reconciliation requires a Commonwealth apology. On this view, reconciliation does not mean that Aboriginal Australians reconcile themselves to formal inclusion, as practical reconciliation demands. Howard's practical reconciliation resembles the 1969 White Paper of Canada's Prime Minister Trudeau in its thrust and desired outcomes. Like Trudeau, Howard desires a formal equality and symmetrical citizenship, where Aboriginal Australians are, in effect, treated just like everyone else. They would have neither special claims to land nor special rights to political autonomy.

---

[36] Senate Legal and Constitutional References Committee (2003: 125).
[37] Altman and Hunter (2003); Hunter and Schwab (2003).
[38] Jonas (2000: ch. 2, 16).

Their disadvantage will be tackled through the government channels and policy levers used for other similarly, if not identically, disadvantaged segments of Australian society. In Canada, Jean Chrétien, then minister of Indian Affairs, expected that the White Paper would start a discussion with Aboriginal leadership. However, Aboriginal leaders expected to participate in the paper's formulation, not simply be handed the finished product. When Aboriginal groups rejected the White Paper, the Trudeau government responded with what has over the last thirty years amounted to a full reversal of policy making.

Australian groups are unlikely to overturn practical reconciliation. Prime Minister Howard is popular and powerful, having been reelected in October 2004 to a historic fourth term, making him Australia's second-longest serving prime minister.[39] As important is the political strength of Aboriginal groups themselves and government responsiveness to their demands. As expected, given Howard's views about Aboriginal rights and Australian history, his administration has been not merely unresponsive; it has been combative. At this point, Aboriginal leaders are resigned to working with Howard on issues of mutual concern. As Aboriginal leader Patrick Dodson wrote in December 2004, "We have agreed to work on what we have in common rather than what we may still disagree about, in search of a common good."[40]

If an apology is inconsequential to, indeed antithetical to, Howard's policy of practical reconciliation, how has the apology (or, more precisely, the nonapology) influenced the affective dimensions of reconciliation? Has the nonapology worsened reconciliation's prospects? The evidence is mixed. Polls and surveys show that white Australians also decouple apology from reconciliation, supporting reconciliation but opposing an apology. In a Newspoll survey of thirteen hundred people nationwide, conducted for the CAR in March 2000, 81 percent of those polled characterized the reconciliation process as "quite important" (44 percent) or "very important" (37 percent).[41] Grass-roots organizations dedicated to reconciliation, which were

---

39 Robert Menzies is the longest-standing Australian prime minister, having served twice, in 1939–41 and in 1949–66.
40 Dodson (2004).
41 Newspoll Market Research (2000). Specifically, the question was posed as follows:

In 1991, Federal parliament voted to establish an organization called the Council for Aboriginal Reconciliation. The Council's aim is to assist the process of reconciliation between Aboriginal

established under the auspices of the CAR, continued to exist after CAR's formal dissolution in December 2000. These local reconciliation groups and their activities are widely seen as having contributed to the success of the People's Walk for Reconciliation across the Sydney Harbor Bridge in May 2000, for example. Approximately 250,000 Australians participated. This ongoing public commitment led politicians to characterize reconciliation as a "people's movement" and not merely a public policy label or state-generated activity. It is important to note that many of these local groups complained that they did not receive enough support from the Howard government.[42]

Apology, on the other hand, is not widely supported. The same 2000 Newspoll survey found that 57 percent disagreed with the statement, "On behalf of the community, governments should apologise to Aboriginal people for what's happened in the past." Forty percent agreed. Moreover, 63 percent agreed with the statement, "Australians today were not responsible for what happened to Aboriginal people in the past, so today's governments should not have to apologise for it." Nearly 80 percent agreed that "Everyone should stop talking about the way Aboriginal people were treated in the past, and just get on with the future." Taken together, these results show clearly that apology is widely viewed as an inappropriate government gesture. It is especially undesirable when the apology is construed as attaching responsibility for past wrongs to Australians today. Australian society, the public believes, should just "get on with things."[43]

The strong aversion to an apology might suggest that Australians have a benign view of their national history. But that interpretation would be wrong: "A large majority (84 percent) agree that 'In the past Aboriginal people were treated harshly and unfairly.'" A smaller majority (around 60 percent) also agree that the nation should formally acknowledge "Aboriginal people as the original owners of traditional lands and waters," and "that Australia was occupied without the consent of Aboriginal people."[44] Thus, although Australians recognize an

---

people and the wider community. Overall, do you think a process of reconciliation between Aboriginal people and other Australians is...?

[42] Senate Legal and Constitutional References Committee (2003: 7–9).
[43] Newspoll Market Research (2000).
[44] Ibid.

unjust past, they do not think that the current government or citizens should apologize for it. Taken together, these surveys suggest that non-Aboriginal Australians are unwilling to apologize in part because they do not feel responsible for Aboriginal historical mistreatment. Further research supports this observation. Researchers in two studies found that Australians who perceive in-group advantages over Aboriginal Australians and feel guilty about it or those who feel responsible for Aboriginal disadvantage and feel guilty about it are likely to support a government apology.[45]

Moreover, in these responses, the views of both Howard and Aboriginal peoples are partially supported. Howard's continued resistance to apologizing is endorsed, as is Aboriginal insistence on the unjustness of their historical treatment and displacement. Yet where Howard criticizes the "black armband view" of Australian history, Australians believe their harsh view to be the more accurate one. Where Aboriginal Australians view apology as an entirely appropriate response to this history, the majority of Australians think otherwise.

There are a number of important exceptions to this big picture. First, Aboriginal respondents see clear links between Australian history, apology, and reconciliation. They view the government's acknowledgment of historical injustices as commanding an apology, which in turn would advance reconciliation. In a qualitative study of Aboriginal communities nationwide, researchers found that most interpreted an apology not as an admission of personal responsibility, but as an acknowledgment of past wrongs and an expression of sorrow about those wrongs.[46] Thus it follows that if white Australians recognize historical injustices, they should be prepared to apologize for them. An acknowledgment of past wrongs, and the consequent expression of sorrow, would mark an important step toward reconciliation. Second, although the majority of Australians polled oppose an apology, a sizable plurality (40 percent) support it.

The rationale for the Howard government's policy of practical reconciliation is the remedying of Aboriginal disadvantage. A large majority of Australians, Aboriginal and non-Aboriginal, support some notion of reconciliation. The question is, do they support Howard's?

[45] McGarty et al. (2005).
[46] Irving Saulwick & Associates (2000: 8)

In one way, the answer is apparently yes, given Howard's political successes, both legislatively and electorally. Yet the Newspoll data suggest that a slight majority of white Australians question the very existence of Aboriginal disadvantage, the object of practical reconciliation's efforts. When asked whether Aboriginal people, compared to other groups, were disadvantaged or not, 52 percent answered "not disadvantaged," 41 percent "disadvantaged," and 7 percent "neither/don't know." To the question of living conditions, 52 percent answered that Aboriginal people are "worse off" than other Australians, whereas 41 percent answered "better or same." Moreover, according to those polled, the sources of Aboriginal disadvantage rest in themselves and not in the past. Forty-seven percent agree that "Aboriginal people have mainly themselves to blame for their current disadvantage," whereas 38 percent think that "disadvantage experienced by Aboriginal people today is mainly a result of the way they were treated in the past." Fifteen percent answered "neither/don't know."

The reality of Aboriginal disadvantage, as measured by government and nongovernmental agencies, belies these public perceptions. Indeed, the Newspoll authors are led to comment as follows:

If it is a statistical fact that Aboriginal and Torres Strait Islander people are the poorest, unhealthiest, least-employed, worst-housed and most imprisoned Australians, but only half the community believes Aboriginal people are generally worse off than other Australians (and only around 30 percent believe they are "a lot" worse off), then there is a significant gap between the facts and what people believe about the position of Aboriginal people.[47]

Howard's policy appears out ahead of one-half of public opinion, at least in recognizing Aboriginal disadvantage. However, there is also agreement between Howard and the majority, who agree that the past should have no bearing on the present and future, as either an explanation for Aboriginal disadvantage or something for which apologies should be made. As important, they also agree with Howard that "getting on with things" means the "mainstreaming" of Aboriginal issues and not support of Aboriginal demands for self-determination, including native title and customary law.

---

[47] Newspoll Market Research (2000).

U.S. Apology for Slavery

In the United States, there has been neither an apology nor reparations for slavery, although there has been public discussion about both. As we have seen, a substantial plurality of Australian citizens and the majority of Canadians have supported apology. But in the United States, apology and reparations are extremely polarizing issues, thus making significant changes in public policies to address African American disadvantage and racial reconciliation, using these devices, highly unlikely. As Michael Dawson and Rovana Popoff observe, the difference in opinion between African Americans and whites "is about as large as one is likely to see in American public opinion surveys," with gaps growing to "truly enormous proportions."[48] In a 2000 survey of 831 African Americans and 724 whites, Dawson and Popoff found that 79 percent of African Americans supported a government apology for slavery, whereas 21 percent did not. In nearly exact proportion, whites responded otherwise, with 70 percent opposed to a government apology and 30 percent in favor. Likewise, when asked whether the federal government should pay monetary compensation to African American descendants of slaves, 67 percent responded in the affirmative and 33 percent in the negative.

In contrast, the vast majority of whites were against reparations, with 96 percent answering in the negative and 4 percent in the affirmative. Two other polls commissioned by the Foundation for Ethnic Understanding in 1997 and 2001 revealed similar differences of opinion.[49] However, the results are still somewhat surprising because the survey was limited to Jews and African Americans. The expectation was that Jews would be more likely than other white Americans to endorse apology and reparations. This expectation was confirmed, although neither reparations nor apology was approved by a clear majority. Of the five hundred Jews interviewed, 58 percent were opposed to reparations and were nearly evenly split on apology, with 46 percent in favor and 45 percent opposed.

It should be mentioned that the Senate's 2005 apology for its failure to pass antilynching legislation did not generate much opposition,

[48] Dawson and Popoff (2004: 58).
[49] Watson (2001).

judging from press reports. The absence of public opposition can likely be explained by the narrow focus of the apology itself. As earlier discussed, the apology simply expressed regret for the Senate's actions. It did not refer to reparations for lynching victims' families.

Dawson and Popoff attribute their observed gaps in support for apology and reparations to differences in perceptions about whether and when blacks will achieve racial equality: "A majority of Whites – 60 percent – believe Blacks have either achieved, or will soon achieve, racial equality. An even stronger majority, over three-quarters of Blacks, believe the opposite – that Blacks will either not achieve racial equality during their lifetimes, or not at all within the United States."[50] As in Australia, there are significant differences in group perceptions: A large plurality of Australians polled think that Aborigines are doing better than they are, in part because of the purported "special treatment" they receive. In the United States, whites and African Americans recognize the existence of the African American working and middle classes, which argues against wholesale group marginality and disadvantage. In other words, circumstances are neither uniformly nor universally bad for African Americans, so neither an apology nor reparations are needed. Theories of social psychology posit that perceptions of social inequities can lead first to feelings of responsibility (individual and collective) for and guilt about them, and then to desires (individual and collective) to endorse remedies.[51] The differences in perceptions between white and black Americans about the existence of racial inequities makes societal or political elite support for apology and reparations improbable any time in the foreseeable future.

Although apology and reparations will not be catalysts for racial reconciliation in the United States, the reparations debate and lawsuits have contributed to the reexamination of history, as in Australia, Canada, and New Zealand, which in the long run should prove beneficial. Historian David Brion Davis, for one, sees the reparations debate as helping finally to debunk the "myth of the lost cause" the "Confederacy's ideological victory after the Civil War."[52] Although the South lost

---

[50] Dawson and Popoff (2004: 59); see also Bobo, Dawson, and Johnson (2001).
[51] Mallet and Swim (2004).
[52] Davis (2001: 1).

the Civil War, it won the subsequent national debate about the meaning of the war and even about the meaning of slavery. Similarly, historian Ira Berlin adds reparations to a long list of factors contributing to renewed interest in slavery and its role in American history.[53] More specifically, new historical research generated by lawsuits and state legislation seeks to reveal that predecessors of several modern corporations were involved in slavery. For example, in September 2002 a group of lawyers filed a class-action lawsuit against the FleetBoston Financial Corporation, Aetna Incorporated, and CSX Corporation, charging that those companies had used slave labor to enrich themselves unjustly.[54] Using the legal instrument of discovery, attorney Deadria Farmer-Paellman forced Aetna to open the company archives, where she found its slave policies. In March 2000, the company formally apologized for having provided slave masters with insurance on the lives of their slaves.[55] In 2002, the California Department of Insurance documented the "slavery era" insurance policies of recent insurers whose "predecessor corporations" insured slaves. The report provides a list of the names of slaves and their owners, where they lived, and when and which company insured them.[56] These lawsuits have no chance of succeeding given the expiration of the statute of limitations and the absence of surviving slaves.[57]

This research joins a larger reexamination of slavery currently under way (and widely commented upon) in American historiography.[58] For example, several books directly challenge the "lost cause's" central tenet that the South did not secede to preserve slavery and forthrightly examine the slaveholding practices of the nation's Founding Fathers.[59] To be sure, slavery, the Civil War, and Jim Crow segregation are staples of American historiography, subject to frequent reexamination. The point is that recent historical works, although not a direct result

[53] Berlin (2001).
[54] Fears (2002); Ogletree (2002); Reed (2002).
[55] Lewin (2001).
[56] California Department of Insurance, Slavery Era Insurance Registry (2002).
[57] Waldmeir (2001).
[58] Berlin (2001); Davis (2001); Wood (2003); Fredrickson (2004).
[59] On challenges to the "Lost Cause" see Blight (2001); Dew (2001): Gallagher and Nolan ( ); On the Founding Fathers, see Wiencek (2003): Gordon-Reed (1997).

of the reparations debate, contribute to it by providing a fuller historical record. Nevertheless, it is highly doubtful that either new historical
facts or new interpretations of old ones would be able to close the huge
chasm between white and African American opinion on government
apology and reparations; such opinions are based, in part, on perceptions of the existence and degree of present-day racial inequality.

Conclusion

This book's central argument is that apologies are given and desired
because they help to alter the terms of membership. Concretely, lawmakers can use them to change citizen status and political arrangements
and influence affective attachments. Apologies are useful to government and group strategies to alter membership because they fortify historical and moral justifications for these changes. However, the strate-
gic effectiveness of apologies relies upon ideological commitments to
group rights (held both by political elites and group members) and the
force of feelings of guilt and fairness. Broadly speaking, apologies have
had some of the expected effects on the three dimensions of national
membership, to varying degrees.

Not surprisingly, apologies have had no effect on the legal status of
citizenship. Aboriginal support of a notion of asymmetrical citizenship
presumes that they maintain their existing status as legal citizens of
their respective states.

Apologies' effects on political arrangements are more varied across
our cases. The Canadian government's apology is consistent with
the federal government's continuing commitment to Aboriginal self-
governance, having embraced it as an appropriate response to
disadvantage created by past federal actions and to Aboriginal
demands. The apology identifies historical mistreatment and dispossession as the source of much present-day disadvantage. An apology also
strengthens rectification of land and resources lost along with meaningful Aboriginal involvement in shaping a collective future. Given that
Canadian federal policy making had been heading in that direction
since the 1970s, it would be an overstatement to suggest that either
the RCAP report or an apology alone strongly accounts for this policy
trend. The prevailing commitment to self-governance appears now to

be entrenched enough to withstand efforts to contract the scope of federal policy initiatives. Prime Minister Martin's emphasis on four policy areas closely resembled Australian Prime Minister Howard's practical reconciliation program. However, Martin, unlike Howard, advanced his initiatives alongside self-governance agreements, not in place of them. The same appears to be true of the plans of the current prime minister, Harper, although he, even more than Martin, intends to take a far more measured and slower approach to self-governance.

By contrast, Prime Minister Howard's practical reconciliation policy does not propose a shift either toward full-fledged Aboriginal self-government or even toward autonomy, but rather displays a firm commitment to the status quo ante. When Howard dismantled ATSIC in 2004, he abolished the one federal agency explicitly designed to serve as a representative body for Aboriginal citizens. Since ATSIC was established in 1990, its effectiveness had been deeply compromised by its two competing tasks of administering federal programs while also advocating for Aboriginal interests, but instead of trying to fix this design flaw, Howard simply terminated the agency. He judged this "experiment" in Aboriginal self-governance to have been a "failure" not worth retaining and altering. Overall, Howard's refusal to apologize demonstrates how prospects for recognition of Aboriginal rights, specifically self-governance, are correspondingly diminished.

The 1993 Hawaiian apology resolution did not lead directly to the institutional changes desired by its advocates, but it has not been inconsequential either. Most advocates, state and federal officials, and elected politicians viewed the apology resolution as a first step in the reconciliation process. More important, the resolution fortifies the basic assumptions behind Native Hawaiian sovereignty claims: that they are a distinct people who were once governed by their own sovereign kingdom before it was overthrown by foreign civilians assisted by U.S. government officials.

In New Zealand, the Queen's apologies have been consequential mostly because they accompanied land claims settlements and compensation packages that were themselves enormously consequential. The 1996 apology to the Tainui peoples for the Waikato confiscation accompanied NZ$170 million in monetary compensation, plus "the return to Tainui ownership of some 15,000 hectares of land, including the Onewhero Forest, and land with tenants (for example, the

University of Waikato)." Similarly, the Queen's 1998 apology to the Ngai Tahu accompanied a package valued at NZ$170 million, which included pastoral and forest lands along with license fees for those lands, "the title to certain precious sites[,] and the title to certain reserves."[60] These settlements will almost certainly improve the political, social, and economic prospects of the respective groups.

By contrast, in the United States the 2000 BIA apology has had no significant effects on federal policy making, just as the pending congressional apology cannot be expected to influence policy. At best, both underscore the federal government's stated commitment to Native American self-determination. Moreover, the pending congressional resolution, through a disclaimer, explicitly disallows making or settling any claims against the United States. Neither the Senate apology for lynching nor the two failed slavery apologies refer to protecting the political rights of African Americans. There is no mention of voting rights, for example. However, Representative Tony Hall, in advocating an apology for slavery, asserted that it would somehow strengthen American democracy.

In nearly all of the cases, the apologies have generated public discussion about national histories and public reflection on reconciliation. Whether and to what extent apologies have themselves advanced emotional reconciliation is a different matter. In Canada virtually all public opinion polls showed strong support both for the government's apology (before and after it was given) and for the attendant policy reforms. Canadians apparently viewed apology as a means of achieving affective reconciliation. Moreover, the government's (if not the prime minister's) direct apology to victims of the residential school system and the financial settling of claims demonstrate good intentions, contrition, and advance reconciliation. By contrast, the majority of Australians did not see such a causal link. Although most supported the government's formal reconciliation process and thought reconciliation with Aboriginal Australians a worthy goal, a majority did not support a governmental apology itself. These views suggest that "reconciliation," whether in Howard's or some other form, does not require an apology for its achievement. In realpolitik, it meant that Howard's practical reconciliation policy enjoyed majority support, notwithstanding the sizable

[60] Ward (1999: 54, 57).

plurality of Australians who did see a causal relationship between apology and affective reconciliation. (Recall also that unlike the Canadian government, the Commonwealth government neither directly apologized to the "stolen generations" nor provided any compensation schemes. The majority of Australians supported the Howard government in these decisions.) The Australian public has been divided not only on apology but also on the meaning of reconciliation.

Although there is no direct evidence of the effects of the Queen's apologies on New Zealand reconciliation, it is clear that the Waitangi Tribunal itself is today a source of growing resentment among white New Zealanders. Recent opinion polls show that there is considerable support for a reevaluation both of the Tribunal and of the place of the Treaty of Waitangi in political and legal processes. On the other side, the majority of Maori continue to support the Tribunal and desire that the treaty's current place in politics and law be preserved or even strengthened. The effects on reconciliation of the 2000 BIA apology or the proposed congressional resolution appear to be null, in part because so few Americans know about them and because so little appears to be at stake. The same may not be said of the 1993 Hawaii apology Resolution precisely because it has helped to put the issue of Native Hawaiian sovereignty before the U.S. Congress. Although the 1993 Resolution was apparently widely supported in Hawaii and received considerable support within the Senate (it passed by a margin of twenty-one votes, sixty-five to thirty-four), the recently defeated bill recognizing Native Hawaiian sovereignty was more divisive.[61]

It is difficult to see how an apology for U.S. slavery could ever lead to emotional reconciliation, because the idea of even offering an apology is itself so explosive. Although apology and reparations for slavery are deeply divisive issues among the American public, such polarization need not be permanent. It is possible that a historical commission could lay the groundwork for such an apology. The Canadian experience supports this possibility and the Australian argues against it.

[61] Murphy (2005).

5

The Weight of History and the Value of Apologies

This book has argued that political actors use apologies to advance group rights based on historical claims. Apologies can be strategically effective as well as emotionally satisfying. Yet, when compared with material reparations, apologies are often judged "cheap talk." This presumed trade-off between apologies and reparations does not easily hold up, however. Apologies sometimes accompany reparations, and vice versa. The political actors and certain of their motivations (such as guilt and the desire to rectify past wrongs) are often the same. Nevertheless, under particular circumstances, such as those of historical injustices, political actors may marshal apologies and reparations to serve different purposes. Apologies potentially "open the books," whereas reparations close them. On this view, apologies can potentially be as consequential and as "costly" as reparations, although in different ways. Whereas reparations are lump-sum payments and settlements, apologies help to justify government policies designed to redistribute political authority and economic resources substantially over the long term.

As we shall see, the one shared and seemingly unqualified benefit of apologies and reparations, according to some, is a reexamination of the historical record. Yet, political actors, as our cases show, judge the importance of history differently, at least as it relates to indigenous claims. Whether the historical record is now regarded as more "truthful" does not subsequently mean that the content or direction of government policies on indigenous issues is self-evident. Rather, political actors weigh the historical record and its legacy differently in light of their prior political views about citizenship in general and indigenous claims in particular. Assessments of history's moral obligations are also derived in part from these views. In general, support for indigenous claims and responsiveness to group demands result in historical rationales being taken more seriously. Conversely, nonsupport of indigenous claims results in historical justifications being treated less seriously. This chapter begins with a comparative analysis of reparations and apologies, identifying their different purposes and, more specifically, how reparations do not address claims about political membership and how apologies do. It then returns to an examination of how and why political actors weigh the historical record as they do. Finally, the chapter concludes by assessing the role and value of symbolic politics for racial minorities and less powerful groups.

Apologies versus Reparations

Reparations most commonly refer to material compensation, usually monetary, for past wrongs. Over the course of the twentieth century, the idea has expanded from reparations for war to reparations for governmental or corporate wrongdoing.[1] Although, as John Torpey argues, apologies, memorials, and other forms of "communicative history" may be part of what he calls a "field of reparations politics," the defining characteristic of reparations is compensation.[2] Such compensation may be viewed as "forward-looking and utilitarian," especially when contrasted with restitution, which is "backward-looking and rights based."[3] Reparations are forward-looking insofar as material compensation is not meant to restore fully what was lost, but is instead intended to be useful to the injured parties going forward. In this way, monetary reparations are similar to apologies: Both seek to alter the future in some way. Yet, where reparations provide concrete or tangible benefits to individual members of a claimant group, apologies provide symbolic and diffuse benefits to an aggrieved group as a whole. If viewed as a payoff, reparations may be seen as "closing the books," whereas apologies may be viewed as the beginning of a "new

---

[1] Torpey (2006: 43).
[2] Ibid. (49–51).
[3] Elster (2004: 174).

conversation." A reparations settlement says, we've settled our debt, whereas an apology says, now that you've apologized, what are you going to do next to rectify the matter? It is precisely because reparations provide direct material compensation that they are commonly judged to be more beneficial than apologies. However, it may well also be that reparations and apologies cannot be directly compared. Official apologies (and not those apologies that themselves accompany reparations payments) perform different tasks.

Because reparations claims are based on compensation for wrongful acts, they are often pursued legally through tort litigation.[4] However, lawsuits against governments usually fail because courts grant governments sovereign immunity, rule that too much time has passed, or find that the government bears no direct responsibility. For example, in May 2005, the U.S. Supreme Court declined to hear a case brought on behalf of the African American victims of the 1921 Tulsa, Oklahoma, race riot, one of the worst in the country's history. Victims' groups petitioned the Supreme Court to take the case after the Tenth Circuit Court of Appeals ruled that the statute of limitation had expired. Similarly, although a Japanese district court ruled in a historic 1998 decision that the Japanese government compensate three former Korean "comfort women," the decision was short-lived.[5] The following year, a regional high court overturned the favorable ruling, leading the women to appeal to Japan's Supreme Court for assistance in securing compensation. In March 2003, the Japanese Supreme Court upheld the regional court's decision, thereby extinguishing any possibility of remedy from the Japanese government.[6] The Supreme Court's decision is in keeping with decisions of Japanese lower courts that have ruled, in approximately fifty cases, that "compensation can be paid only to states or the 20-year limit for compensation had expired."[7] As Roy Brooks observes, slavery-redress litigation has been unable to surmount "procedural barriers to sovereign immunity" and statutes of limitations, such that these cases "are dismissed before the judge has had an opportunity to consider the merits of the claims at trial."[8]

[4] Brooks (2004: 98).
[5] Watts (1998).
[6] Green (2003).
[7] Ibid. (15).
[8] Brooks (2004: 99).

Most successful reparations claims against governments have been achieved through legislation. German reparations after World War II to the state of Israel and surviving Jews are probably the most well known and serve, in their wake, as an exemplar of successful reparations. More recently, reparations have also been secured the wake of political transitions from authoritarian to democratic rule. In Argentina, for example, the National Congress passed legislation granting pensions to the spouses and children of disappeared persons and monetary awards to victims of arbitrary detention under military rule.[9] It would appear, then, that reparations are the products of extraordinary political moments (such as the end of a war or the wake of political transitions) in keeping with their origins in war cessation. However, reparations have been secured during "normal times." In the United States, for example, the 1988 Civil Liberties Act awarded individual Japanese-American internees $20,000 and apology nearly forty years after World War II.[10] Similarly, the Florida state legislature established in 1993 a $2 million fund to compensate the estimated eleven survivors of the 1923 Rosewood massacre. The legislation also "allowed individual property claims up to $150,000, as well as a modest education fund for descendants of the town residents."[11]

Reparations claims against private corporations have recently had a high rate of success, although this was not always the case. Lawsuits seeking compensation for Holocaust-related crimes have long failed. As legal scholar Michael Bazyler observes, the estimated twelve lawsuits against private entities for Holocaust-related World War II crimes filed by victims between 1945 and 1995 were summarily dismissed.[12] However, since 1995 nearly all such lawsuits have been successful, totaling settlement payouts of over U.S.$8 billion.[13] Similarly, Armenian insurance claimants, using these recent Holocaust cases as a model, successfully settled with the New York Life Insurance Company for U.S.$20 million in January 2004. On the other hand, numerous lawsuits against Japanese corporations for their use of slave labor during World War II have failed, and lawsuits against multinationals for

---

[9] Guembe (2006).
[10] Hatamiya (1993).
[11] Brophy (2002:111).
[12] Bazyler (2002: 11–12).
[13] Ibid. (12).

profiteering during apartheid and against German corporations during colonial rule in Namibia, for example, are still pending.[14] Bazyler attributes the recent successes and emerging lawsuits to several factors. The most important is the use of U.S. courts and American legal methods of discovery and class action suits to pursue transnational litigation against multinational corporations, many of which do substantial business in the United States. As important, over the past twenty years U.S. courts have grown receptive to human rights law to such an extent that they will today hear such cases "even if (1) the acts complained of did not occur in the United States and (2) the plaintiff is not American."[15]

All together, these cases demonstrate that reparation claims, whether successful or not, have been viewed and treated as settlements. They have not usually been connected explicitly, as have most official apologies, to justifications for alterations in future state policy. As expected, they are remedial responses to claimed injuries. Official apologies, in contrast, can mark the reinvigoration of ongoing national conversations about the future direction of policy making. It is unsurprising that the effects of apologies would be diffuse, abstract, and clearly symbolic in ways that reparations are not. However, these differences invite reassessments of the dismissive evaluation that apologies are useless – so much empty or cheap talk. This discussion underscores the book's argument that apologies can play a distinct role in advancing political claims.

So, apologies differ from reparations in that political actors use them to advance political argument rather than reducing it to a reparations settlement. It can be argued, however, that reparations settlements neither resolve issues quickly nor completely. Holocaust claims clearly show that reparations payments need not mean finality or the shutting down of public reflection on genocide and racism. Indeed, such ongoing reflection has provided a broader context for Holocaust reparations themselves, ensuring that they continue to be viewed as justly warranted decades after World War II. But, at bottom, legal and political contests over reparations follow a tort model, where the fight centers on specifying the harm(s), identifying the appropriate beneficiaries and perpetrators, and devising acceptable compensation schemes. Indeed,

[14] "Germany Urges Herero to Drop Lawsuit" (2004).
[15] Bazyler (2002: 13).

it is precisely because of this core purpose that recipients often insist
that reparations be accompanied by apologies, so that they will not
be viewed simply as payoffs. Apologies, or least our subset, emphasize
moral acknowledgment of wrongdoing and assist in ongoing negotiation over group rights and political autonomy. Considering, for example, whether a reparations model is appropriate for Native Americans,
William Bradford argues that "reparations would fail to advance, and
might even frustrate, important objectives, particularly the reacquisi-
tion of the capacity to self-determine on ancestral lands."[16] Bradford
judges apology to be more consistent with the ultimate goals of self-
governance.[17]

Weighing History and Apologies

Apologies, like reparations, draw attention to history. All sides agree
on the basic proposition that history cannot be ignored. That is where
the agreement largely ends. As the book has argued, political elites and
organized groups judge history's weight differently when determining the proper direction of policy policies. The reasons for this vari-
ation rest in the motivations of political actors – specifically, whether
they are sympathetic to indigenous claims and responsive to indigenous demands. Such sympathy and responsiveness, in turn, derive
largely from ideological views about citizenship and group rights. It
is important to emphasize, however, that in the case of political elites,
such meaningful ideological differentiation, along ideological-partisan
lines, is a relatively new phenomenon. Prior to the mid-twentieth century, most political elites in Australia, Canada, New Zealand, and the
United States were largely indifferent, and more often actively hostile,
to indigenous claims. With some notable exceptions in each country,
political elites were largely united in their support for assimilation policies and other state actions designed to marginalize indigenous claims
and political standing. Now that ideological differentiation and partisanship matters to a greater degree, it is evident in support (or lack of
support) for indigenous claims, in attendant assessments of history's
significance, and in the judgment of an official apology's propriety.

---

[16] Bradford (2005: 6).
[17] Ibid. (28).

Those politicians who are supportive of group claims are more likely to consider historical injustices to be a salient political issue requiring policy attention and rectification of some sort. Conversely, those political elites who advocate for individual rights, not group rights, do not think rectification of historical injustices should directly and boldly shape policy formulation. These evaluations of history's significance are tied to their stances on moral obligation and guilt. Those who agree that historical injustices partly account for current disadvantage and diminished group autonomy identify moral obligation and guilt as motivations in their support of apology. On the other hand, those politicians who do not think contemporary disadvantage is mostly attributable to historical injustices and do not consider diminished group autonomy to be a bad thing also do not think that history assigns either a moral obligation to restore or to feel guilty. An apology, therefore, is not necessary.

Demands for recognition of indigenous rights are widely supported by indigenous peoples. Acknowledgment of historical injustices and interpretations of national histories that focus on these injustices are central to their demands, precisely because the ultimate goal is the restoration of meaningful cultural, economic, and political autonomy. This is not to suggest, however, that there are not important differences in viewpoints and strategy. In Australia, for example, some leaders have called forcefully for a treaty, whereas others have called for de facto autonomy of Aboriginal institutions while maintaining beneficial arrangements with Australian governments. These two views are not incompatible, and most differences are those of emphasis.[18] An apology, in its moral acknowledgment of wrongdoing, is a first step toward the desired objectives of self-governance, economic self-sufficiency, and cultural autonomy.[19]

As mentioned earlier, discernible differences in political elite approaches to indigenous claims, along partisan lines, began in the latter half of the twentieth century. Since the 1970s, Australia's Labor Party has presented "itself as the most sympathetic" to Aboriginal Australians.[20] Beginning with Prime Minister Gough Whitlam's government (1973–5), the Labor Party "has become identified with

[18] Martin (2001); Behrendt (2003: 118–31).
[19] Ibid. (115–16).
[20] Bennett (1999: 61).

multiculturalism, with reorientation toward Asia, with republicanism, with equal opportunity programs, and with the full range of liberal attitudes on race relations." The championing of these issues, as James Jupp points out, marks "an almost complete reversal of traditional labor party attitudes," with the exception of Labor's continued focus on class.[21] That Labor has identified itself with protecting and advancing Aboriginal rights also requires that the historical origins and abrogation of these rights be acknowledged. An apology, then, is in keeping with Labor's expressed support of policies designed to advance Aboriginal rights. Finally, Labor Party politicians and affiliated intellectuals have openly expressed concern and discomfort with what they regard as the moral burden of Aboriginal mistreatment.

Similarly, New Zealand's Waitangi Tribunal has been instrumental in promoting a view of New Zealand's history that supports Maori claims. Although the one-term governing Labour Party (1972–5) desired to respond to Maori demands for justice, they also wanted to sidetrack Maori efforts to have the Treaty of Waitangi made part of domestic law. The establishment of a quasilegal body dedicated to hearing claims of historical injustice seemed to satisfy the Labour government's dual objectives: to hear out Maori grievances while also ensuring that the treaty not become domestic law. The Waitangi Tribunal has been far more successful than these political elites initially envisioned. As scholars observe, the Tribunal's power in directing attention to the past and future derives from its governing legislation, which requires that the Tribunal identify Crown faults and provide recommendations for remedy. Moreover, as Giselle Byrnes argues, the Tribunal's influence on understandings of New Zealand's history has gone much further than simply referring to history to satisfy its statutory charge. The Tribunal has "become an important 'voice' of the Treaty in recent years," bringing the nineteenth-century Treaty of Waitangi to bear directly on the current politics of Maori self-determination and economic issues of land and resource redistribution.[22] But whereas in Canada apology was used to signal a renewed commitment to indigenous goals of self-government, New Zealand's apologies accompanied land settlements and thus helped to provide meaning to the settlements.

[21] Jupp (1995: 213).
[22] Byrnes (2004: 3).

The apology offered by Canada's Liberal Party of Prime Minister Jean Chrétien seems to contradict my theory that ideological orientation largely dictates the stance on indigenous claims and hence on apology. Under Prime Minister Pierre Trudeau, the Liberal Party strongly resisted indigenous group rights, consistent with traditional liberal views on the primacy of individual rights. Recall that Trudeau had attempted through the now infamous 1969 White Paper to terminate universally all special treatment of indigenous peoples, including the Indian Act, and to introduce a policy of formal equality. Trudeau and policy makers believed that "that past could be closed off in some fashion so as to reorient the Indian world view to 'the future.'"[23] Yet, the Liberal Party's withdrawal of the Paper two years later and its sustained support of Aboriginal rights ever since have shown its form of liberalism to be capacious, indeed. In an important way, the Liberal Party, over the past thirty years, has responded to a radically transformed political landscape regarding indigenous rights. It is also a landscape partly of its making. As Sally Weaver observes, "Nativism, significantly enhanced by the policy, became firmly fixed on special rights, the basic Indian orientation which the White Paper had been designed to change."[24]

The Liberal Party has seemingly adjusted its ideological orientation to encompass indigenous rights and historical grievances in ways that seem to extend beyond Trudeau's defense of language rights, for example. In the case of Quebec, Trudeau stressed that Quebec's promotion of French language and culture was justified because "the state's obligation [is] to serve the individual interests of its citizens, who in this case happen to be largely French-speaking."[25] But, at the same time, Trudeau resisted Quebec's attempts to secure "special status, and rights" based on French culture.[26] The current position of the Liberal Party provides further proof of the party's ability to reinvent itself as required. Although such flexibility would seem to be a basic principle of political life, Canadian political scientists have judged the Liberal Party to be especially adept at it, to the dismay of some.[27]

[23] Weaver (1981: 196).
[24] Ibid. (189).
[25] Christian and Campbell (1990: 70).
[26] Weaver (1981: 53–6).
[27] Clarkson (2005).

Here, then, political interests and ideology appear to go hand in hand, with core liberal commitments leading the way until it makes more political sense to bend them. Today, Canada's Liberal Party is broadly supportive of indigenous claims and demands for self-government and mindful of historical grievances. Its apology to Aboriginal peoples is in keeping with this stance.

Political elites who are not in favor of indigenous group rights and instead advocate formal equality do not think that the rectification of historical injustices (such as restoration of meaningful autonomy and recognition of a right to self-determination) should guide current legislation and policy making. For example, when referring to Aboriginal rights, Trudeau held to the view that "no society can be built on historical 'might-have-beens.'"[28] Trudeau's sentiments have been faithfully reflected in the ideas and policies of Australia's Prime Minister John Howard and the defeated Don Brash of New Zealand. For Howard and Brash, indigenous group rights and the rectification of historical injustices should not and indeed cannot be the foundation for unified national sovereignty. Howard's insistence that all Australians be governed by the same laws and institutions means that Aboriginal peoples do not have distinct rights to be protected and promoted by the state. Although Howard recognizes that Aboriginal peoples have been badly treated, such recognition does not now require distinct policies or remedies; instead, their disadvantages should be addressed through existing state institutions. They should not be addressed by autonomous Aboriginal institutions, precisely because significant Aboriginal autonomy has no place in a unified nation-state.

In short, history carries very little weight when contemplating current and future policy making. Indeed, it may further be said that it is not only that history carries very little weight, but that whatever weight it does carry is discounted because Howard and others do not attribute current disadvantage wholly or even primarily to historical injustices, attributing it instead to the behaviors of Aboriginal peoples themselves and the enabling policies of opposition parties (such as Labor). Having rejected recognition of Aboriginal group rights, disqualified redress and restoration as the proper goal of policy, and discounted the lingering

---

[28] Weaver (1981: 55).

deleterious effects of historical injustices, Howard and likeminded Australians see no need for an apology.

Symbolic Politics and Political Membership

The issue of who could and should be full citizens has been profoundly troublesome for over two hundred years in Australia, Canada, New Zealand, and the United States. Indigenous peoples and African Americans have had the peculiar experiences of being the glaring exceptions to the otherwise happy stories of democratic rights, individual freedoms, and self-direction. The established rules governing the proper relationships between government and citizenry did not apply to these groups. They did not apply because indigenous peoples were not citizens but wards, locked out of the newly constituting nations and unable to live as independent nations. African Americans were slaves and then rendered second-class citizens whose political rights and civil liberties were nullified. These groups in turn have pressed their claims, demanding just and not always equal treatment, fairness, respect, and liberty. They have used different methods to achieve various objectives. Of what value are "apology politics" in advancing the goal of an altered, binational membership in the case of indigenous peoples or strengthened national membership in the case of African Americans?

In this book, I have taken the uncontroversial view that all politics have symbolic dimensions, and that symbolism contributes to achieving more concrete ends. However uncontroversial, symbolic politics in general and apologies, with their focus on historical injustices, typically raise two related criticisms. The first is that minority groups are overly reliant on symbolic politics. Symbolic politics is variously defined, but usually includes representational actions, discourse, and symbols themselves, all of which are invested with meanings. The worry, then, is that symbolic politics, both as a dimension of political action itself (such as protests) and as outcomes, is largely empty and incommensurate with either the depth of the problems or scale of the demands. These worries have merit, and empirical evidence both supports and undermines them.

As is well known, mass mobilization in the form of protest marches and such have, at critical historical junctures, been the appropriate form of political action precisely because of their broadly participatory nature, which allows for public demonstration of grievances and desires.[29] Public protests supporting the U.S. civil rights movement come immediately to mind. Marching peacefully in demonstrations, for example, allowed participants to signify both their agreement with the movement's nonviolence philosophy and their profound dissatisfaction with racial subordination. (To be sure, these actions were more than symbolic rituals because participation meant not attending school or working and, according to law enforcement officials, by protesting the participants were breaking the law.) Moreover, these efforts were effective, contributing to concrete gains in legislation and public policy. It is also true that factors other than public demonstrations account for such alterations, both big and small, in policy and law. In an example of "big" changes, the U.S. civil rights movement's success turned not only on mass protest, but also on economic, political, and social factors, such as the decline of cotton's importance to the southern and national economy, African American migration, and the corresponding strength of the African American vote in the North, and the creation of dense social networks in the South, for example.[30] For relatively smaller reforms, Radha Jhappan finds, for example, that symbolic strategies used by Canadian indigenous peoples, such as public protests, are more effective when they are employed in land and resource disputes than when they are used to affect larger policy issues.[31] Thus symbolic gestures are here effective because they are attached to concrete and urgent issues (land and resources) that usually involve third parties, not only the government.[32] The main point is that symbolic politics is inseparable both from other forms of political action and broader economic, political, and social developments.

The politically weaker use whatever tactics are necessary, including symbolic ones, to protect and advance their interests. In one sense, then, the criticism that minority groups rely too heavily on symbolic politics seems unfair in light of their relative political and economic powerlessness and, in our cases, small-to-tiny demographic size. Nonetheless,

---

[29] As Sidney Tarrow warns, "But we must be wary of turning mass politics into no more than a form of political theatre, a set of symbol-laden performances whose efficacy lies largely in their power to move specific audiences." Tarrow (1994: 119).

[30] McAdam (1999).

[31] Jhappan (1990).

[32] Ibid. (34–5).

there is no gainsaying the fact that in the absence of substantial economic, legal, and social resources, symbolic politics stands in as a lesser substitute. It is also true that symbolic politics can often seem to be a diversion, directing energies and attention away from more substantial matters or as "curtains" obscuring the real political actors and political processes working behind them or, just as often, in plain view. Finally, the incremental pace of change and relative inattention to minority issues, excepting major upheavals, argues strongly against assigning too much hope to symbolic politics in effecting sudden and radical change. As Philip Klinkner and Rogers Smith argue, for example, real racial progress for African Americans has only come in the wake of wars.[33]

The second worry is that the focus on apologies and historical injustices more broadly promotes a "victim's mentality" instead of a politics of citizenship or simply a more group positive identity. It is true that members of minority groups, when accounting for their current disadvantage, often emphasize historical mistreatment. Tim Schouls, in examining public testimonies of Aboriginal peoples before the Canada's RCAP, found not surprisingly that historical mistreatment figured prominently.[34] It is also true that support for apologies among majority populations is largely derived from feelings of guilt. As earlier discussed, recent research shows that non-Aboriginal Australians who feel guilty about in-group advantage over Aboriginal people are much more likely to support apologies.[35] Guilt about in-group advantage, rather than the mere perception of such advantage, is a strong predictor of support for apology. Taken together, then, the focus on historical injustices and offers of apology seems to turn neatly on the dyad of victim and victimizer.

However, whether the desire to assert a victim's identity is all there is to the focus on historical injustices is another matter. As our cases show, the emphasis on historical injustices has tended to support two related

---

[33] Klinkner and Smith (1999). Under war conditions, an organized African American leadership can leverage African American military valor and the evident contradiction between racial subordination and American values to win political concessions from political elites. Klinkner and Smith also discuss the "white backlash" that soon follows such concessions.

[34] Schouls (2003: 62).

[35] McGarty et al. (2005).

but distinct types of identity politics. The first is internally focused, where various groups with particular historical experiences and different cultures, languages, and material circumstances all lay claim to a shared history of mistreatment and resistance. The second type is externally focused, where the demands for a differentiated citizenship and self-governance are based on claims of a nonextinguished sovereignty, native title, and international indigenous rights. Here, the emphasis is on a status that antedates and is independent of the establishment of the respective states. In other words, in these cases, the focus on historical injustice supports not only a victim status but also one of a self-directed actor. In a similar way, researchers have found that the strongest predictor of support among African Americans for apology and reparations is among those who express prior support for "institutionalized Black autonomy."[36] In an indirect way, at least, these findings seem to suggest that the assertion of group agency and autonomy is at least as important in the focus on historical injustices as the mere claiming of a victim status.

The proposition that political elites and aggrieved groups employ apologies in ongoing efforts to change the meanings and workings of national membership has been this book's central theoretical proposition. We have seen that political elites who recognize group claims are responsive to minority demands and feel morally obligated to address historical injustices are more likely to apologize. Apologies, in turn, help to further the goals now shared by political elites and indigenous peoples of self-governance, economic self-sufficiency, and cultural autonomy. I have argued also that prior ideas about group rights and citizenship drive their evaluation of history's injustices and not vice versa. In other words, the sheer retelling of historical injustices is not enough to sway the argument, precisely because such facts must be interpreted. In the end, antecedent political ideas provide the lens through which the measure of historical facts is taken and considered.

---

[36] As Dawson and Popoff write: "the strongest predictor of support for Black and Japanese Americans receiving apologies and reparations is support for institutionalized Black autonomy" (italics in original). Dawson and Popoff (2004:78). They also tested the direction of causality and found that "Support for Black community control leads to greater support for an apology for slavery, but the reverse is not true." Ibid. (84).

At the same time, the reexamination of the historical record is still worthwhile, even with different and competing interpretations of its meanings. In the countries examined here, as in many others, the masking, denial, and nonacknowledgment of past injustices have been crucial in justifying government inaction toward remedy, in sustaining societal indifference (at best), and in fostering violence and exclusion (at worst). Moreover, dominant historical accounts, which rendered minority and indigenous groups almost invisible, both reflected and further contributed to the impotence of their political claims and argument. At the very least, light is shed on the darker sides of national histories.

Further, reexamination of the historical record may contribute to reconciliation in ways more lasting than heretofore appreciated, the possibility of backlash notwithstanding. Citizens may support minority demands for social and political change without thinking very much about historical injustices. Indeed, the U.S. civil rights movement altered the American political landscape profoundly, without requiring deep or prolonged engagement with history. Arguably, this proves that historical reinterpretations are not necessary to achieve deep political and social change. Still, thirty years after the civil rights movement, inequalities persist, as do battles over the past (for example, the Confederate battle flag controversies), and both are viewed as legacies of an unsettled past. As we know, in Australia, Canada, and New Zealand, history's centrality is even clearer. Support of indigenous demands for self-determination requires engagement with history as their claims are made intelligible by it. Indigenous peoples worldwide ground their demands for distinct rights in what they consider their status as "original occupants."[37] In any case, we expect there to be disagreement, sometimes deep, about history and its obligations – moral, political, and otherwise. In the end, I think that such historical disagreement can benefit society as a whole, if, as in some of our cases, it serves to further a national conversation about the meanings and boundaries of citizenship and membership.

[37] According to the draft *Declaration on the Rights of Indigenous Peoples* (1998), "Indigenous communities, peoples and nations are those which, having a historical continuity with pre-invasion and pre-colonial societies that developed on their territories, consider themselves distinct from other sectors of the societies now prevailing in those territories."

Of course, history and critical reexaminations of it are often not used in beneficial ways. History can be and is marshaled to support deeply chauvinistic nationalist narratives that politicians and citizens alike use in turn to justify and fuel exclusion and violence. This truth pertains as much to the past actions of governments and citizens in our cases as it does for numerous other countries today. Alternatively, the absence of open discussion about or reexamination of history from all sides is also undesirable. Here, the Palestinian–Israeli conflict and the Turkish denial of the Armenian genocide are both instructive. Many observers of the Israeli–Palestinian conflict recognize the need for greater (although not necessarily complete) agreement on the historical record and on the legitimacy of Palestinian grievances and concerns that arise from that record. In the case of the Armenian genocide, the Turkish government's denial of its occurrence remains strong, if currently embattled, thereby ensuring conflict and arguably endangering Turkey's chances of entering the European Union.

In the end, the power of historical interpretations and apology derives from human actions; such interpretations and apologies are not themselves independent forces. The ideas held by and motivations of political actors matter. For some, efforts to create greater political, social, and economic equality and to foster reconciliation require not only reckoning with the past but apologizing for it. For others, the opposite is true. The focus on history and rendering moral judgments about it impedes progress. "Apology politics" turns on our competing views about group rights, political community, and moral obligation, and on our perceptions about why history matters at all.

Appendix

Twentieth- and Twenty-First-Century Public Apologies

TABLE A.1. *Typology of Twentieth- and Twenty-First-Century Apologies, Based on Person(s), Group(s) or Institution(s) Offering the Apology*

Person(s), Group(s) or Institution(s) Offering the Apology	Number of Apologies
Heads of State/Government Officials	44
Governments	8
Religious Institutions	12
Organized Groups or Individual Citizens	5
Nongovernmental Organizations and Institutions	1
Private Institutions	2
Total	72

Heads of State and Government Officials

February 17, 1965: Japanese Foreign Minister Shinna Etsusaburo announces at Kimpo airport, upon his arrival at South Korea, that he "wished to express his 'sincere regret' for an 'unfortunate period' in relations between the two countries for which he felt deep remorse."[1]

---

[1] Yoshibumi (1999: 194). Scholars maintain that this apology helped to finalize the normalization talks between Japan and Korea, which had been under protracted negotiations for thirteen years. Yet, scholars also note the relative weakness of the apology, which referred to Japanese colonial rule in Korea as the "unfortunate period" or "unhappy period." As importantly, these scholars note that although the Japanese

December 14, 1970: West German Chancellor Willy Brandt kneels before a memorial for the dead of the Warsaw ghetto. Brandt expressed sorrow and German responsibility for the Holocaust. As Brandt explained, "I wanted on behalf of our people to ask for pardon for the terrible crime that was carried out in Germany's misused name."[2]

1972: Japanese Prime Minister Kakuei Tanaka tells visiting Chinese Premier Chou En-lai that "Japan realizes her heavy responsibility in causing enormous damage to the Chinese people in the past through the war."[3]

February 19, 1976: President Gerald Ford says the internment of Japanese Americans was "wrong" and officially revokes President Franklin Roosevelt's exclusion order.[4]

1984: Alluding to World War II, Japanese Emperor Hirohito tells the visiting South Korean president that "it is regrettable that there was an unfortunate period in this century."[5]

October 23, 1985: In an address to the United Nations, Japanese Prime Minister Yasuhiro Nakasone apologizes for Japan's role in World War II.[6]

April 1990: Soviet President Mikhail Gorbachev admits the Soviet Union was responsible for the 1940 massacre of Polish prisoners of war at the Katyn Forest. The government issued an official statement in which the Soviet Union expressed "profound regret over the Katyn tragedy," describing it as "one of the gravest crimes of Stalinism."[7]

December 4, 1991: Japanese Foreign Minister Michio Watanabe expresses "deep remorse" for the wartime suffering that followed Japan's attack on Pearl Harbor.[8]

---

agreed to an economic package consisting of U.S.$300 million in grants, U.S.$200 million in credits, and donations from the Japanese private sector totaling U.S.$100 million, they did not call these payments, "reparations." Instead, the Japanese government framed the payments in terms of "economic cooperation," with no direct connection to colonialism. Yoshibumi (1999: 183–201); Dudden (2005).

[2] "The Leaders' Apologies" (1993).
[3] Shriver (1995: 135).
[4] Ibid. (165).
[5] Ibid. (135).
[6] Tavuchis (1991: 106).
[7] Bohlen (1992: A1).
[8] Asada (1997: 182).

December 1992: Australian Prime Minister Paul Keating acknowledges wrongs done to Aborigines. ("We took the traditional lands and smashed the traditional way of life. We committed the murders."[9])

August 15, 1993: Japanese Prime Minister Morihiro Hosokawa publicly states that World War II was a mistake and an act of aggression.[10]

August 23, 1993: Hosokawa uses his first parliamentary policy address to convey "a feeling of deep remorse and apologies for the fact that our country's past acts of aggression and colonial rule caused unbearable suffering and sorrow for so many people."[11]

August 29, 1993: South African President F. W. de Klerk apologizes for apartheid.[12]

August 31,1993: Nelson Mandela apologizes for atrocities allegedly committed by the African National Congress against suspected enemies.[13]

September 20, 1993: Hosokawa, during meeting with British Prime Minister John Major, apologizes for suffering caused by Japan during World War II. ("I took this opportunity to express my deep remorse as well as to apologise for the fact that Japan's past actions had inflicted deep wounds on many people, including the former prisoners of war."[14])

October 12, 1993: Russian President Boris Yeltsin apologizes for the internment of six hundred thousand Japanese prisoners of war in Siberia after World War II.[15]

August 1994: After laying a wreath at a memorial for the failed Warsaw uprising, German President Roman Herzog remarks, "I ask for forgiveness for what has been done too you by Germans."[16]

March 1995: Lithuanian President Algirdas Brazauskas asks the Israeli Knesset for forgiveness for Lithuania's deeds in the

[9] "The Leaders' Apologies" (1993).
[10] Field (1995: 405).
[11] Berger (1993: 13).
[12] "The Leaders' Apologies" (1993).
[13] "Who's Sorry Now?" (1993).
[14] "The Leaders' Apologies" (1993).
[15] Ibid.
[16] Murphy (1994).

Holocaust: "I, the president of Lithuania, bow my head in memory of the more than 200,000 Lithuanian Jews who perished. I ask your forgiveness for the deeds of those Lithuanians who cruelly killed, shot, expelled and plundered the Jews."[17]

July 1995: Japanese Prime Minister Tomiichi Murayama apologizes to the roughly two hundred thousand women who Japanese forces put into brothels to serve as sex slaves or "comfort women" and sets up a private Asian women's fund to deal with reparations. The fund is "an expression on the part of the people of Japan to these women."[18]

July 16, 1995: On the fifty-third anniversary of the roundup of thirteen thousand Parisian Jews, French President Jacques Chirac apologizes for the help that the Vichy government gave the Nazis in deporting 320,000 French Jews to death camps.[19]

August 15, 1995: On the fiftieth anniversary of Japan's surrender, Prime Minister Murayama issues a statement of "heartfelt apologies" for Japan's aggression.[20] On the same day as Murayama's statement, the National Diet adopts a "Resolution to Renew the Determination for Peace on the Basis of Lessons Learned from History."[21]

January 15, 1997: Swiss President Jean-Pascal Delamuraz apologizes for deriding as "blackmailers" the Jewish organizations seeking compensation for Holocaust survivors whose assets were held by Swiss banks.[22]

May 16, 1997: President Bill Clinton holds a White House ceremony to apologize for the forty-eight-year Tuskegee Syphilis Study by the U.S. Public Health Service that withheld from African American subjects medical treatment for the disease. Five of the eight remaining survivors attended the White House ceremony.[23] (In 1974, the U.S. government settled a suit by the survivors for $10 million.)

---

[17] Bushinsky (1995).
[18] "Cold Comfort: Japan" (1996); Mitchell (1998: 46).
[19] "France Admits Role in Deporting Jews, Country Shares Responsibility for 'Criminal Folly'" (1995).
[20] Thornton (1995).
[21] Mukae (1996).
[22] Swardson (1997).
[23] Pells (1997).

June 1997: British Prime Minister Tony Blair expresses regret for English indifference to the plight of the Irish people during the Potato Famine of the 1840s.[24]

October 1997: King Harald apologizes for Norwegian injustices committed against the Sami when he opened the Norwegian Sami Parliament: "The Norwegian state is founded on the territory of two peoples – the Norwegians and the Sami. The history of the Sami is closely entwined with that of the Norwegians. Today we deplore the injustices committed in the past against the Sami People by the Norwegian state through harsh policies of Norwegian-ization."[25]

October 14, 1997: Queen Elizabeth pays silent homage and contrition in recognition of the 1912 Amritsar massacre during which thousands of unarmed Indian civilians were killed by British colonial troops.[26]

January 1998: Japanese Prime Minister Ryutara Hashiomoto offers his "heartfelt apology" to the British government and expresses "deep remorse" for Japan's treatment of British prisoners of war during World War II.[27]

March 1998: During his visit to Uganda, President Clinton repents for American participation in the African slave trade: "European Americans received the fruits of the slave trade. And we were wrong in that."[28]

March 26, 1998: President Clinton apologizes for U.S. inaction during the 1994 Rwanda genocide.[29]

October 1998: Japanese Emperor Akihito and Prime Minister Keizo Obuchi apologize to South Korean President Kim Dae Jung for Japan's occupation of the Korean Peninsula from 1910 to 1945.[30]

October 1998: Argentinian President Carlos Menem expresses regret over the Falklands War.[31]

---

[24] Lyall (1997).
[25] Dow and Gardiner-Garden (1998: 13).
[26] Burns (1997); Weisman (1997).
[27] Mitchell (1998: 47).
[28] R. Cohen (1998).
[29] Shogren (1998).
[30] "Japan Apologizes to Koreans for Occupation" (1998).
[31] "Menem's Visit to Britain; Views from Argentina and the Falkland Islands about ..." (1998).

January 7, 1999: A U.S. federal judge approves a June 1998 settlement between the U.S. government and Latin American Japanese World War II internees. The settlement includes an official apology from President Clinton and reparations of $5,000 each.[32]

March 10, 1999: President Clinton expresses remorse for U.S. support of right-wing governments in Guatemala that killed at least tens of thousands of rebels and Mayans.[33]

September 8, 2000: The head of the U.S. Federal Bureau of Indian Affairs, Kevin Gover, apologizes for the bureau's "legacy of racism and inhumanity."[34]

April 2001: President George W. Bush states that the United States is "very sorry for the loss of a Chinese pilot and for an American spy plane's emergency landing on Chinese soil." However, the United States did not accept responsibility for the April 1 midair collision.[35]

May 24, 2001: Prime Minister Junichiro Koizumi apologizes, on behalf of the government, to lepers "for the pain and suffering that patients were forced to endure" as a result of the government's policy of isolation. The government also "said that it would not contest a May 11 district court ruling that ordered the authorities to pay $15 million to 127 plaintiffs who challenged the repressive law that kept them isolated for decades."[36]

July 10, 2001: Polish President Aleksander Kwasniewski apologizes, on behalf of himself and the Polish people, for the participation of Polish citizens in the massacre of fellow Jewish citizens during World War II. The apology affirmed that Poles, and not Nazi soldiers, committed the crime.[37]

May 2002: Governor Mark Warner of Virginia describes that state's sterilization program "a shameful effort in which state government should have not been involved."[38]

---

[32] Zeuthen (1999).
[33] Broder (1999).
[34] Kelley (2000).
[35] Sanger and Meyers (2001).
[36] Sims (2001).
[37] Fisher (2001).
[38] Stern (2005).

December 2002: Oregon Governor John Kitzhaber apologizes for more than 2,600 sterilizations "performed under the authority of state law between 1917 and 1983."[39]

January 8, 2003: South Carolina Governor Jim Hodges apologizes for the state's forced sterilization program of women and blacks, dating from the 1930s through the 1960s. Over 250 people are estimated to have been sterilized.[40]

February 11, 2003: Premier Gordon Campbell of the provincial government of British Columbia apologizes to Aboriginal peoples, stating that provincial institutions have "failed aboriginal peoples across our province."[41]

March 11, 2003: California Governor Gray Davis apologizes for the state's forced sterilization program, dating from 1909 to the late 1940s. Approximately twenty thousand people are estimated to have been sterilized.[42]

June 4, 2003: Treaty Negotiations Minister Margaret Wilson offers "a formal Crown apology to the Ngati Ruanui of South Taranaki for acknowledged Treaty breaches."[43]

January 2004: At a ceremony marking the 1904–6 massacres of the Herero people during the colonial war, Wolfgang Massing, Germany's ambassador to Namibia, tells those Herero gathered that "he wished to 'express how deeply we regret this unfortunate past. 'He called the massacres the 'darkest chapter in our colonial history.' The statement was Germany's strongest ever expression of contrition for the killings." The German government refuses to pay reparations. In 2000, "Hereros in New York City filed a lawsuit in the United States on the behalf of the tribe, demanding $4 billion in reparations from the German government and German companies."[44]

February 24, 2007: The Virginia General Assembly expresses, through a roll-call vote, "profound regret" for slavery and for the treatment of Native Americans. This apology resolution for

---

[39] Ibid.
[40] Freiden (2003).
[41] Reuters (2003).
[42] Feist (2003).
[43] Wilson (n.d.)
[44] Donnelly (2004).

slavery is the first passed by a U.S. state legislature. Specifically, the resolution read, in part, "Resolved by the House of Delegates, the Senate concurring, that the General Assembly hereby acknowledge with profound regret the involuntary servitude of Africans and the exploitation of Native Americans and call for reconciliation among all Virginians."[45]

Governments

1945 and subsequently: Postwar Germany offers "moral and material reparations" to surviving Jews and the state of Israel.[46]

June 1983: The Commission on Wartime Relocation and Internment of Civilians recommends that Congress pass legislation providing an official apology and compensation to interned Japanese Americans.[47]

August 10, 1988: The Civil Liberties Act apologizes on behalf of the people of the United States for the internment of Japanese Americans during World War II. The Act also authorizes $1.25 billion for payments of $20,000 to each of the roughly sixty thousand internees still alive and for the establishment of a $50 million foundation to promote the cultural and historical concerns of Japanese Americans.[48]

September 22, 1988: The Canadian prime minister apologizes in the House of Commons to Japanese Canadians for their internment during World War II and announces that individual survivors will be eligible for $21,000 in compensation.[49]

November 15, 1993: The U.S. House passes U.S. Public Law 103–150: "To acknowledge the 100th anniversary of the January 17, 1893 overthrow of the Kingdom of Hawaii, and to offer an apology to native Hawaiians on behalf of the United States for the overthrow of the Kingdom of Hawaii."[50]

November 1995: Queen Elizabeth II approves legislation that "apologizes unreservedly" to the Maori of New Zealand for taking their

---

[45] Deans (2007).
[46] Pross (1998).
[47] Hatamiya (1993: 1).
[48] Ibid. (181–90).
[49] Torpey (2006: 81).
[50] U.S. Congress, Senate (1993).

land in 1863. The legislation included a payment of $112 million and the return of 39,000 acres to the Tainui people.[51]

May 26, 1997: Australian Federal Parliament "tables" report on the forced removal of Aboriginal children. The Report recommends apology. Nearly all state parliaments offer one; the prime minister and the Northern Territory Parliament refuse.[52]

January 7, 1998: The Canadian government formally apologizes for its historic treatment of indigenous persons and establishes a "healing fund."[53]

August 27, 1999: Australian Prime Minister John Howard and the Federal Parliament express regret for past mistreatment of Aborigines.[54]

February 5, 2002: The Belgium government expressed "its profound and sincere regrets and its apologies" for its "role in the assassination of Patrice Lumumba, the first prime minister of its former colony Congo in 1961." Foreign Minister Louis Michel also "announced the creation of a $3.5 million fund in Mr. Lumumba's name to promote democracy in Congo...."[55] (In November 2001, a parliamentary commission to inquiry about Belgium involvement concluded that Belgium bore a "moral responsibility" in the assassination, but did not recommend an apology.[56] It left the decision to apologize to Parliament and the government.)

Religious Institutions

1965: In a declaration entitled "Nostra Aetate," the Second Vatican Council reverses the traditional condemnation of Jews as the murderers of Jesus.[57]

August 17, 1986: The United Church of Canada officially apologizes to Canada's native peoples for past wrongs inflicted by the church.[58]

---

[51] "Elizabeth II to Approve Maori Land Settlement" (1995).
[52] "PM's Apology Draws Protest" (1997).
[53] DePalma (1998).
[54] "Australia Apologizes for Treatment of Aborigines." NY Times, August 27, 1999.
[55] Agence France-Presse (2002).
[56] Agence France-Presse (2001).
[57] Metzger (2005).
[58] Tavuchis (1991: 109–10).

October 31, 1992: The Catholic Church begs pardon for placing
Galileo Galilei under lifelong house arrest in 1633.[59]

November 1994: The Catholic Church announces a commitment
"to repent of past ecclesiastical sins as prelude to the celebration of Christianity's third millennium." "It is time," John
Paul said, "to examine the past with courage, to assign responsibility where it is due in a review of the long history of
humanity."[60]

1995: Pope John Paul asks forgiveness for Counter-Reformation
stake burnings.[61]

March 1995: The Jesuits' general congregation apologizes for abet-
ting "male domination" and pledged "solidarity with women."[62]

May 1995: Pope John Paul II begs forgiveness in the Czech Republic for the Church's role in the religious wars that followed the
Protestant Reformation.[63]

June 1995: The Southern Baptist Convention apologizes to African
Americans "for defending slavery in the antebellum South and for
condoning 'racism in our lifetime.'"[64]

July 10, 1995: In an open letter to "every woman," Pope John Paul
II apologizes for the Church's stance against women's rights and
for the historical denigration of women.[65]

September 30, 1997: The French Roman Catholic Church apologizes for its role during the Holocaust and its silence during the
Vichy Regime.[66]

March 16, 1998: The Vatican apologizes for its silence and inaction
during the Holocaust.[67]

September 2, 1999: Pope John Paul II asks forgiveness for the
past errors of the Catholic Church but did not specify any such
errors.[68]

---

[59] "Um, Sorry about That" (1997).
[60] Woodward (1995).
[61] "Um, Sorry about That" (1997).
[62] Woodward (1995).
[63] Ibid.
[64] Ibid.
[65] "Um, Sorry about That" (1997).
[66] Ibid.
[67] Bohlen (1998); Elie (1998).
[68] "Pope Repeats an Apology" (1999).

Organized Groups and Individual Citizens

April 1994: German Christians apologize to the Dutch for the Nazi invasion of the Netherlands in World War II.[69]

March 1995: On the thirtieth anniversary of the Selma–Montgomery march for voting rights, former Alabama governor George Wallace apologizes to civil rights advocates for resisting desegregation.[70]

May 1998: In Australia, individual citizens sign "sorry books" as a way of expressing regret and sorrow for government policies toward Aboriginal Australians.

July 1999: After a "Reconciliation Walk" across Europe, several hundred members of a Christian group apologize to religious leaders in Jerusalem for the mass killings of Muslims, Jews, and Byzantine Christians nine hundred years ago during the Crusades.[71]

December 16, 2000: White South Africans present a "Declaration of Commitment by White South Africans" on the occasion of the annual Reconciliation Day. The declaration seeks to encourage all white South Africans to acknowledge that they were beneficiaries under apartheid.[72]

Nongovernmental Organizations and Institutions

1995: The International Red Cross apologizes for its "moral failure" in not denouncing Nazi atrocities in World War II.[73]

Private Institutions

January 2005: Bank JP Morgan Chase apologizes "for its subsidiaries' involvement in the slave trade 200 years ago, admitting that it accepted slaves as loan collateral and ended up owning several hundred."[74] The bank's letter, signed by the chief executive

---

[69] Woodward (1995).
[70] Bragg (1995).
[71] Sharrock (1999).
[72] Cauvin (2000)
[73] Mitchell (1998: 46).
[74] Teather (2005).

officer William Harrison, read in part: "We apologise to the African-American community, particularly those who are the descendants of slaves, and to the rest of the American public for the role that Citizens' Bank and Canal Bank played. The slavery era was a tragic time in US history and in our company's history."[75]

June 1, 2005: Wachovia Corporation Bank issues an apology for the bank's ties to slavery. An internal investigation of the bank's history found that two of its predecessor banks either owned slaves or used slaves as collateral.[76]

[75] Ibid.
[76] Fears (2005); Paul (2005).

Bibliography

"100th Anniversary of the Overthrow of the Hawaiian Kingdom." 1993. *Congressional Record*, October 27, p. S14479.

Advisory Board of the President's Initiative on Race. 1998. "One America in the 21st Century: Forging a New Future." Available online at http://www.ncjrs. gov/pdffiles/173431.pdf.

Agence France-Presse. 2001. "Report Reproves Belgium in Lumumba's Death," *New York Times*, November 17, p. A5.

Agence France-Presse. 2002. "Belgium: Apology for Lumumba Killing," *New York Times*, February 6, p. A6.

Aleinikoff, T. Alexander. 2002. *Semblances of Sovereignty: The Constitution, the State, and American Citizenship*. Cambridge: Harvard University Press.

Allen, James, et al. 2000. *Without Sanctuary: Lynching Photography in America*. Santa Fe: Twin Palms.

Altman, J. C., and B. H. Hunter. 2003. "Monitoring 'Practical' Reconciliation: Evidence from the Reconciliation Decade, 1991–2001," Discussion Paper No. 254, Centre for Aboriginal Economic Policy Research, Australian National University, November.

Altman, J. C., Biddle, N., and B. Hunter. 2004. "Indigenous Socioeconomic Change 1971–2001: A Historical Perspective," Discussion Paper No. 266, Centre for Aboriginal Economic Policy Research, Australian National University.

Alves, Dora. 1999. *The Maori and the Crown: An Indigenous People's Struggle for Self-Determination*. Westport: Greenwood Press.

Anderssen, Erin, and Edward Greenspon. 1998. "Federal Apology Fails to Mollify Native Leaders," *Globe and Mail*, January 8, p. A4.

"Apology to Natives Gets Wide Support in Poll." 1998. *Vancouver Sun*, January 9, p. A2.

Armitage, Andrew. 1995. *Comparing the Policy of Aboriginal Assimilation: Australia, Canada, and New Zealand.* Vancouver: University of British Columbia Press.

Asada, Sadao. 1997. "The Mushroom Cloud and National Psyches," in *Living with the Bomb: American and Japanese Cultural Conflict in the Nuclear Age,* eds. Laura Hein and Mark Selden. Armonk: M. E. Sharpe.

Assembly of First Nations. 2006. "Royal Commission on Aboriginal People at 10 Years: A Report Card." Available online at http://www.afn.ca/cmslib/general/afn_rcap.pdf.

Attwood, Bain, ed. 1996. *In the Age of Mabo: History, Aborigines and Australia.* St. Leonards: Allen & Unwin.

_____. 2003. *Rights for Aborigines.* St. Leonards: Allen & Unwin.

Attwood, Bain, and S. G. Foster, eds. 2003. *Frontier Conflict: The Australian Experience.* Canberra: National Museum of Australia.

Attwood, Bain, and Andrew Markus. 1997. *The 1967 Referendum, or When Aborigines Didn't Get the Vote.* Canberra: Aboriginal Studies Press.

_____. 1999. *The Struggle for Aboriginal Rights: A Documentary History.* St. Leonards: Allen & Unwin.

Aubry, Jack. 1998a. "Peace Offering Gets Mixed Reaction," *Gazette* (Montreal), January 8, p. B5.

_____. 1998b. "Public Backs Apology to Aboriginals," *Gazette* (Montreal), January 9, p. A10.

_____. 2006. "Tories Replace Aboriginal Accord: Two-Year Plan, One-Fourth the Cost," *Gazette* (Montreal), May 3, p. A6.

"Australia Apologizes for Treatment of Aborigines." 1999. *New York Times,* August 27.

Australian Commonwealth Government. 2002. "Commonwealth Government Response to the Council for Aboriginal Reconciliation Final Report." Canberra.

Australian Electoral Commission (AEC) Info Centre. 2006. "Electoral Milestones/Timeline for Indigenous Australians." Available online at http://www.aec.gov.au/_content/When/history/ab_time.htm, accessed July 10.

Bailey, Sue. 2004. "Martin Outlines New Deal for Canada's Aboriginals; Goal Is Native Self-Government," *Windsor Star* (Ontario), April 20, p. A6.

Bakewell, Peter. 1997. *A History of Latin America.* Oxford: Blackwell.

Barkan, Elazar. 2000. *The Guilt of Nations: Restitution and Negotiating Historical Injustices.* New York: W. W. Norton.

Barkan, Elazar, and Alexander Karn, eds. 2006. *Taking Wrongs Seriously: Apologies and Reconciliation.* Stanford: Stanford University Press.

Bartlett, Richard H. 1988. *The Indian Act of Canada,* 2nd ed. Saskatchewan: University of Saskatchewan Native Law Centre.

Bass, Gary Jonathan. 2000. *Stay the Hand of Vengeance: The Politics of War Crimes Tribunals.* Princeton: Princeton University Press.

Bassett, C. Jeanne. 1994. "Comments: House Bill 591: Florida Compensates Rosewood Victims and Their Families for a Seventy-One-Year-Old Injury," *Florida State University Law Review* 22: 503–23.

Bazyler, Michael J. 2002. "The Holocaust Restitution Movement in Comparative Perspective," *Berkeley Journal of International Law* 20: 11–44.

———. 2003. *Holocaust Justice: The Battle for Restitution in America's Courts.* New York: New York University Press.

Beale, Sara Sun. 2000. "Federalizing Hate Crimes: Symbolic Politics, Expressive Law, or Tool for Criminal Enforcement?" *Boston University Law Review* 80: 1227–81.

Bean, Clive, et al. 1997. *The Politics of Retribution: The 1996 Federal Election.* St. Leonard's: Allen & Unwin.

Behrendt, Larissa. 2000."The Protection of Indigenous Rights: Contemporary Canadian Comparisons," Research Paper 27, Parliament of Australia, Parliamentary Library.

———. 2003. *Achieving Social Justice: Indigenous Rights and Australia's Future.* Sydney: Federation Press.

Bennett, Scott. 1996. *Winning and Losing: Australian National Elections.* Carlton South: Melbourne University Press.

———. 1999. *White Politics and Black Australians.* St. Leonards: Allen & Unwin.

Berger, Michael. 1993. "The Hidden Japanese," *New Leader*, September 6, p. 13.

Berlin, Ira. 2001."Overcome by Slavery," *New York Times*, July 13, p. A21.

Bieder, Robert E. 1986. *Science Encounters the Indian, 1820–1880: The Early Years of American Ethnology.* Norman: University of Oklahoma Press.

"Black Power on the March." 1988. *Sun* (Melbourne), January 27.

Blight, David. 2001. *Race and Reunion: The Civil War in American Memory.* Cambridge: Harvard University Press.

Bobo, Lawrence D., Michael C. Dawson, and Devon Johnson. 2001. "Enduring Two-Ness," *Public Perspective*, May/June: 12–16.

Bohlen, Celestine. 1992. "Russian Files Show Stalin Ordered Massacre of 20,000 Poles in 1940," *New York Times*, October 15, p. A1.

———. 1998. "Vatican Repents Failure to Save Jews from Nazis," *New York Times*, March 17, p. A1.

Bonnell, Andrew G., and Martin Crotty. 2004. "An Australian 'Historikerstreit?'" Review Article, *Australian Journal of Politics and History* 50: 425–33.

Boven, Theo van. 1996. "Revised Set of Basic Principles and Guidelines on the Right to Reparation for Victims of Gross Violations of Human Rights and Humanitarian Law." UN Doc:E/CN4/Sub 2/1996/17, May 24.

Bradford, William. 2005. "Beyond Reparations: Justice as Indigenism," *Human Rights Review*, April–June: 5–79.

Bragg, Rick. 1995. "Wallace Offers Apology at March Re-enactment," *Houston Chronicle*, March 11, p. A14.

Branscombe, Nyla R., and Bertjan Dooseje, eds. 2004. *Collective Guilt: International Perspectives.* New York: Cambridge University Press.

Brantlinger, Patrick. 2003. *Dark Vanishings: Discourse on the Extinction of Primitive Races, 1800–1930.* Cambridge: Cambridge University Press.

Brash, Don. 2004. "Nationhood." *New Zealand Herald*, January 1.

"Brash's Race Card Trumps Labour Treaty of Waitangi: Policy," 2005. *Press* (Christchurch), September 13, p. 4.

Brennan, Frank. 1998. *The Wik Debate: Its Impact on Aborigines, Pastoralists and Miners.* Sydney: University of New South Wales.

Broder, John M. 1999. "Clinton Offers His Apologies to Guatemala," *New York Times*, March 11, p. A1.

Brooks, Roy L., ed. 1999. *When Sorry Isn't Enough: The Controversy over Apologies and Reparations for Human Injustice.* New York: New York University Press.

———. 2004. *Atonement and Forgiveness: A New Model for Black Reparations.* Berkeley: University of California Press.

Brophy, Alfred L. 2002. *Reconstructing the Dreamland: The Tulsa Riot of 1921.* New York: Oxford University Press.

Brown, Michael E., and Sumit Ganguly, eds. 1997. *Government Policies and Ethnic Relations in Asia and the Pacific.* Cambridge: MIT Press.

Brysk, Allison. 2000. *From Tribal Village to Global Village.* Stanford: Stanford University Press.

Buck, Christopher. 2006. "'Never Again': Kevin Gover's Apology for the Bureau of Indian Affairs," *Wicazo SA Review*, Spring: 97–126.

Burgmann, Verity. 1993. *Power and Protest: Movements for Change in Australian Society.* St. Leonards: Allen & Unwin.

Burns, John F. 1997. "Queen Bows Head over Massacre in India," *New York Times*, October 15, p. A6.

Buruma, Ian. 2005. "A Sorry State: A New Breed of Rightwing Patriots Say That Japan Has Apologized Enough for War Crimes." *Financial Times Weekend Magazine*, May 28, p. 18.

Bushinsky, Jay. 1995. "Asking Forgiveness Is Just First Step." *Chicago Sun-Times*, March 6, p. 25.

Byrnes, Giselle. 2004. *The Waitangi Tribunal and New Zealand History.* Oxford: Oxford University Press.

Cairns, Alan C. 2000. *Citizens Plus: Aboriginal Peoples and the Canadian State.* Vancouver: University of British Columbia Press.

———. 2003. "Coming to Terms with the Past," in *Politics and the Past: On Repairing Historical Injustices*, ed. John Torpey. Lanham: Rowman & Littlefield, pp. 63–90.

California Department of Insurance, Slavery Era Insurance Registry. 2002. "Report to the California Legislature." Available online at http://www.insurance.ca.gov.

Canada Indian and Northern Affairs. n.d. Available online at http:www.ainc-inac.gc.ca/gs/schl_e.html.

Cardinal, Harold. 1969. *The Unjust Society.* Vancouver: Douglas & McIntyre.

Carens, Joseph H. 2000. *Culture, Citizenship, and Community: A Contextual Exploration of Justice as Evenhandedness.* New York: Oxford University Press.

Carty, R. Kenneth, William Cross, and Lisa Young. 2000. *Rebuilding Canadian Party Politics.* Vancouver: University of British Columbia Press.

Castellano, Marlene Brant. 1999. "Renewing the Relationship: A Perspective on the Impact of the Royal Commission on Aboriginal Peoples," in *Aboriginal Self-Government in Canada*, 2nd ed., ed. John H. Hylton. Saskatoon: Purich, pp. 92–111.

Cauvin, Henri E. 2000. "In Africa, a Mea Culpa for Apartheid Tests Whites," *New York Times*, December 17, p. A23.

Chesterman, John, and Brian Galligan. 1997. *Citizens without Rights: Aborigines and Australian Citizenship*. Melbourne, Victoria: Cambridge University Press.

"Chiefs Asked to Accept Apology, Money." 1998. *Globe and Mail*, March 10, p. A6.

Chrétien, Honourable Jean, Minister of Indian Affairs and Northern Development. 1969. *Statement of the Government of Canada on Indian Policy*. Ottawa.

Christian, William, and Colin Campbell. 1990. *Political Parties and Ideologies in Canada*, 3rd ed. Toronto: McGraw-Hill Ryerson.

Clarke, Jennifer. 2001. "Case Note: *Cubillo v. Commonwealth*," *Melbourne University Law Review* 25: 218–94.

Clarkson, Stephen. 2005. *The Big Red Machine: How the Liberal Party Dominates Canadian Politics*. Vancouver: University of British Columbia Press.

Coates, Ken S. 1998. "International Perspectives on Relations with Indigenous Peoples," in *Living Relationships: Kokiri Ngatahi: The Treaty of Waitangi in the New Millennium*, eds. Ken Coates and P. G. McHugh. Wellington: Victoria University Press, pp. 19–103.

Coates, Ken S., and P. G. McHugh, eds. 1998. *Living Relationships: Kokiri Ngatahi: The Treaty of Waitangi in the New Millennium*. Wellington: Victoria University Press.

Cohen, Felix S. [1941] 1988. *Handbook of Federal Indian Law*. Buffalo: William S. Hein.

Cohen, Richard. 1998. "A Fitting Apology," Op-Ed, *Washington Post*, March 31, p. A17.

"Cold Comfort: Japan." 1996. *Economist*, May 18, p. 36.

Cook, Curtis, and Juan D. Lindau, eds. 2000. *Aboriginal Rights and Self-Government*. Montreal: McGill-Queen's University Press.

Cornell, Stephen. 1988. *The Return of the Native: American Indian Political Resurgence*. New York: Oxford University Press.

Cott, Donna Lee Van. 2000. *The Friendly Liquidation of the Past: The Politics of Diversity in Latin America*. Pittsburgh: University of Pittsburgh Press.

———. 2005. *From Movements to Parties in Latin America: The Evolution of Ethnic Parties*. New York: Cambridge University Press.

Council for Aboriginal Reconciliation. 2000. "Reconciliation" (final report of the Council of Aboriginal Reconciliation to the prime minister and the Commonwealth Parliament). December.

Coyne, Andrew. 1998. "Two, Three, Many Nations: Behind the Apology to Aborigines, Is Ottawa Preparing a Negotiations Binge?" *Time*, January 19, pp. 43–4.

Cunningham, Michael. 1999. "Saying Sorry: The Politics of Apology," *Political Quarterly* 70: 285–93.

Dahl, Robert. 1989. *Democracy and Its Critics*. New Haven: Yale University Press.

Dalrymple, William. 2005. "India: The War over History," *New York Review of Books*, April 7, pp. 62–5.

Davidson, Alastair.1997. *From Subject to Citizen: Australian Citizenship in the Twentieth Century*. Melbourne: Cambridge University Press.

Davis, David Brion. 2001. "The Enduring Legacy of the South's Civil War Victory," *New York Times*, August 26, section 4, p. 1.

Dawson, Michael C., and Rovana Popoff. 2004. "Reparations: Justice and Greed in Black and White," *DuBois Review* 1: 47–91.

Deans, Bob. 2007. "Virginia Regrets Role in Slavery, Abuse of Native Americans," *Atlanta Journal-Constitution*, February 25, p. 3A.

Dew, Charles B. 2001. *Apostles of Disunion: Southern Secession Commissioners and the Causes of the Civil War*. Charlottesville: University Press of Virginia.

DePalma, Anthony. 1998. "Indigenous Tribes in Canada Receive a Formal Apology," *New York Times*, January 8, p. A1.

DiAlto, Stephanie. 2002. "Frame Wars: The Case of "Reconciliation" with Native Hawaiians and Native Americans." Presented at the annual meeting of the American Political Science Association, Boston, August 29–September 1.

Dickason, Olive Patricia. 1997. *Canada's First Nations: A History of Founding Peoples from Earliest Times*, 2nd ed. Oxford: Oxford University Press.

Dippie, Brian. 1982. *The Vanishing American: White Attitudes and U.S. Indian Policy*. Middletown: Wesleyan University Press.

Dodds, Graham G. 1999 "Political Apologies and Public Discourse." University of Pennsylvania. Unpublished paper.

————. 2003. "Political Apologies and Public Discourse," in *Public Discourse in America: Conversation and Community in the Twenty-First Century*, eds. Judith Rodin and Stephen P. Steinberg. Philadelphia: University of Pennsylvania Press, pp. 135–60.

Dodson, Mick. 1999. "The Human Rights Situation of Indigenous Peoples in Australia," *Indigenous Affairs* 1.

Dodson, Patrick. 2004. "Why I've Changed My Mind," *Australian*, December 7.

Donnelly, John. 2004. "Wounds of Colonialism Reopen in Namibia, German Apology for Massacres Poses Questions," *Boston Globe*, February 8, p. A10.

Dow, Coral, and Dr. John Gardiner-Garden. 1998. "Indigenous Affairs in Australia, New Zealand, Canada, United States of America, Norway and Sweden," Background Paper No. 15 1997–98, Department of the Parliamentary Library, Canberra.

Dudden, Alexis. 2005. "Apologizing for the Past between Japan and Korea," in *Partisan Histories*, eds. Max Paul Friedman and Padraic Kenny. New York: Palgrave Macmillan, pp. 39–54.

Durie, Mason. 1998. *Te Mana, Te Kawanatanga: The Politics of Maori Self-Determination*. Auckland: Oxford University Press.

Editorial. 1998. "A Path from Shame and Dependence," *Vancouver Sun*, January 8, p. A18.

Editorial. 2004. "The Long Trail to Apology," *New York Times*, June 28, p. A18.

Editorial. 2006. "Closure, at Least, on Residential Schools," *Gazette* (Montreal), May 1, p. A16.

Elie, Paul. 1998. "John Paul's Jewish Dilemma," *New York Times Sunday Magazine*, April 26, pp. 34–9.

"Elizabeth II to Approve Maori Land Settlement." 1995. *New York Times*, November 2, p. A11.

Elster, Jon. 2004. *Closing the Books: Transitional Justice in Historical Perspective*. New York: Cambridge University Press.

Environics Research Group. 1998. *First Nations Issues Study Preliminary Report*. December 10.

"Ex-Students Want Apology for Residential School Abuse." 2006. *Gazette* (Montreal), July, 26, p. A13.

Fallow, Michael. 2005. "A Sorry State of Affairs," *Southland Times* (New Zealand), February 26, p. 3.

Fears, Darryl. 2002. "Slaves' Descendants Sue Firms," *Washington Post*, September 4, p. A22.

———. 2005. "Seeking More Than Apologies for Slavery: Activists Hope Firms' Disclosure of Ties Will Lead to Reparations," *Washington Post*, June 20, p. A01.

Feist, Paul. 2003. "Davis Apologizes for State's Sterilization Program; Those with Hereditary Flaws Were Victims," *San Francisco Chronicle*, March 12, p. A20.

Fickling, David. 2003. "One Country, Two Histories: Conservative Australian Historians Rewrite Accepted View That Colonists Massacred Aborigines," *Guardian* (London), January 27, p. 19.

Field, Norma. 1995. "The Stakes of Apology," *Japan Quarterly* 42: 405–18.

Fisher, Ian. 2001. "At Site of Massacre, Polish Leader Asks Jews for Forgiveness," *New York Times*, July 11, p. A1.

Flanagan, Tom. 2000. *First Nations? Second Thoughts*. Montreal: McGill-Queen's University Press.

Fleras, Augie, and Jean Leonard Elliott. 1992. *The Nations Within: Aboriginal-State Relations in Canada, the United States, and New Zealand*. Toronto: Oxford University Press.

Fleras, Augie, and P. Spoonley. 1999. *Recalling Aotearoa: Indigenous Politics and Ethnic Relations in New Zealand*. Auckland: Oxford University Press.

Fletcher, Christine. 1997. "Federalism and Indigenous Peoples in Australia," in *Government Policies and Ethnic Relations in Asia and the Pacific*, eds. Michael E. Brown and Sumit Ganguly. Cambridge: MIT Press, pp. 395–420.

Forum. 2000. "Making the Case for Racial Reparations," *Harper's Magazine*, November, pp. 37–51.

Foss, Clive. 1992. "The Turkish View of Armenian History: A Vanishing Nation," in *The Armenian Genocide: History, Politics, Ethics*, ed. Richard G. Hovannisian. New York: St. Martin's Press, pp. 250–79.

"France Admits Role in Deporting Jews, Country Shares Responsibility for 'Criminal Folly'." 1995. *Toronto Star*, July 17, p. A2.

Fredrickson, George M. 2004."America's Original Sin," *New York Review of Books*, March 25: 34–6.

Freiden, Jaymi. 2003. "S. Carolina Issues Apology for Years of Sterilizations; Forced Procedure Used into the 1960s," *San Diego Union-Tribune*, January 9, p. A8.

Frideres, James S. 1998. Aboriginal Peoples in Canada: Contemporary Conflicts. Scarborough: Prentice Hall.

Furi, Megan, and Jill Wherrett. [1996] 2003. *Indian Status and Band Membership Issues*. Ottawa: Library of Parliament, Parliamentary Research Branch.

Gallagher, Gary W., and Alan T. Nolan. 2000. *The Myth of the Lost Cause and Civil War History*. Bloomington: Indiana University Press.

Gardiner-Garden, John. 1999. "From Dispossession to Reconciliation." Research Paper 27, Parliament of Australia Parliamentary Library, Canberra.

George, Alexander L., and Andrew Bennett. 2005. *Case Studies and Theory Development in the Social Sciences*. Cambridge: MIT Press.

"Germany Urges Herero to Drop Lawsuit." 2004. *Deutsche Welle*, May 8. Available online at http://www.dw-world.de/.

Ghannam, Jeffrey. 2000. "Repairing the Past," *ABA Journal*, November, pp. 39–70.

Gibney, Mark, and Erik Roxstrom. 2001."The Status of State Apologies," *Human Rights Quarterly* 23: 911–39.

Gibson, James L. 2004. *Overcoming Apartheid: Can Truth Reconcile a Divided Nation?* New York: Russell Sage Foundation.

_____. 2005. "The Truth about Truth and Reconciliation in South Africa," *International Political Science Review* 26: 341–61.

_____. 2006."The Contributions of Truth to Reconciliation: Lessons from South Africa," *Journal of Conflict Resolution* 50: 409–32.

Glaberson, William. 2004. "Putting a Price on Holocaust Survivors' Hopes." *New York Times*, March 13, p. B15.

Glynn, Carroll J., et al. 2004. *Public Opinion*, 2nd ed. Boulder: Westview Press.

Gordon, Michael, and Claire Harvey. 1997. "PM's Advice on Payouts in Question." *Weekend Australian*, May 31–June 1, p. 2.

Gordon-Reed, Annette. 1997. *Thomas Jefferson and Sally Hemmings: An American Controversy*. Charlottesville: University Press of Virginia.

Gover, Kevin. 2000. "Remarks of Kevin Gover, Assistant Secretary for Indian Affairs, Department of the Interior, at the Ceremony Acknowledging the 175th Anniversary of the Establishment of the Bureau of Indian Affairs." Available online at http://www.doi.gov/bia/as-ia/175gover.htm.

Grattan, Michelle, ed. 2000. *Reconciliation: Essays on Australian Reconciliation*. Melbourne: Black Inc.

Green, Shane. 2003. "Sex Slaves Fail in Compensation Bid," *The Age*, March 27, p. 15.

Greiff, Pablo de, ed. 2006. *The Handbook of Reparations*. New York: Oxford University Press.

Gross, Emma R. 1989.*Contemporary Federal Policy toward American Indians*. New York: Greenwood Press.

Guembe, María José. 2006. "Economic Reparations for Grave Human Rights Violations: The Argentinean Experience," in *The Handbook of Reparations*, ed. Pablo de Greiff. New York: Oxford University Press, pp. 21–54.

Hall, Tony. 1997. H. Con. Res. 96, June 12, 1997, 105th Congress.

Hatamiya, Leslie T. 1993. *Righting a Wrong: Japanese Americans and the Passage of the Civil Liberties Act of 1988*. Stanford: Stanford University Press.

Havemann, Paul. 1995. "'What's in the Treaty?' Constitutionalizing Maori Rights in Aotearoa/New Zealand 1975–1993," in *Legal Pluralism and the Colonial Legacy*, ed. Kayleen Hazlehurst. Aldershot: Avebury, pp. 73–101.

————, ed. 1999. Indigenous Peoples' Rights in Australia, Canada, and New Zealand. Auckland: Oxford University Press.

Hawaii Advisory Committee to the U.S. Commission on Civil Rights. 2001. *Reconciliation at the Crossroads: The Implications of the Apology Resolution and Rice v. Cayetano for Federal and State Programs Benefiting Native Hawaiians*. Summary report.

Hazlehurst, Kayleen M., ed. 1995. *Legal Pluralism and the Colonial Legacy*. Aldershot: Avebury.

Hein, Laura Elizabeth, and Mark Seldon, eds. 1997. *Living with the Bomb: American and Japanese Cultural Conflicts in the Nuclear Age*. Armonk: M. E. Sharpe.

Herf, Jeffrey. 1997. *Divided Memory: The Nazi Past in the Two Germanys*. Cambridge: Harvard University Press.

Herron, Senator the Hon. John, Minister for Aboriginal and Torres Strait Islander Affairs. 2000. "Inquiry into the Stolen Generation." Federal Government Submission to the Senate Legal and Constitutional References Committee, Canberra.

Hijino, Ken. 2002. "Japan's Cabinet Give to Fund for Comfort Women," *Financial Times* (London), July 3, p. 12.

Hirsch, James S. 2002. *Riot and Remembrance: The Tulsa Race War and Its Legacy*. Boston: Houghton Mifflin.

————. 2003. "Can Justice Be Done in Tulsa?" *Washington Post*, March 16, p. B02.

Hodgson, Dorothy L. 2002. "Introduction: Comparative Perspectives on the Indigenous Rights Movement in Africa and the Americas," *American Anthropologist* 104: 1037–49.

Holmes, Steven A. 1997. "Idea of Apologizing for Slavery Loses Steam, at Least for Now," *New York Times*, August 6, p. A15.

Hooker, Juliet. 2005. "Indigenous Inclusion/Black Exclusion: Race, Ethnicity and Multicultural Citizenship in Latin America," *Journal of Latin American Studies* 37: 285–310.

Howard, Hon. John. 1997. "Opening Ceremony Speech: The Prime Minister," Council for Aboriginal Reconciliation Convention, Melbourne, May 26–8. Available online at http://www.austlii.edu.au/au/other/IndigLRes/car/1997/4/pmspoken.html.

———. 2000. "Practical Reconciliation," in *Reconciliation: Essays on Australian Reconciliation*, ed. Michelle Gratton. Melbourne: Black Inc., pp. 88–96.

———. 2004. *Transcript of the Prime Minister, Joint Press Conference with Senator Amanda Vanstone*. Canberra: Parliament House. Available online at http://www.pm.gov.au/news/interviews/Interview795.html.

Hugo, Graeme. 2002. "Australian Immigration Policy: The Significance of the Events of September 11," *International Immigration Review* 26: 37–40.

Human Rights and Equal Opportunity Commission. 1997. *Bringing Them Home: National Inquiry into the Separation of Aboriginal and Torres Strait Islander Children from their Families*. Canberra: Commonwealth of Australia.

Hunter, B. H., and R. G. Schwab. 2003. "Practical Reconciliation and Continuing Disadvantage in Indigenous Education," *Drawing Board: An Australian Review of Public Affairs* 4: 83–98.

Hurley, Mary C., and Jill Wherrett. [1999] 2000a. "Aboriginal Self-Government." PRB 99–19E. Library of Parliament, Parliamentary Research Branch, Ottawa. Available online at http://www.parl.gc.ca/information/library/PRBpubs/962-e.htm.

———. [1999] 2000b. "The Report of the Royal Commission on Aboriginal Peoples." PRB 99–24–3. Library of Parliament, Parliamentary Research Branch, Ottawa. Available online at http://www.parl.gc.ca/information/library/PRBpubs/prb9924-e.htm.

Hylton, John H., ed. 1999. *Aboriginal Self-Government in Canada*, 2nd ed. Saskatoon: Purich.

Iggers, George G. 1997. Historiography in the Twentieth Century. Hanover: Wesleyan University Press.

Indian Residential Schools Resolution Canada. n.d. Statistics page. Available online at http://www.irsr-rqpi.gc.ca/english/statistics.html, accessed October 1, 2005.

Irving Saulwick & Associates. 2000. "Research into Issues Related to a Document of Reconciliation." Council for Aboriginal Reconciliation. Report No. 2, Indigenous Qualitative Research. Available online at http://www.austlii.edu.au/au/other/IndigLRes/car/.

Ivison, Duncan. 2000. "Political Community and Historical Injustice," *Australasian Journal of Philosophy* 78: 360–73.

Ivison, Duncan. 2002. *Postcolonial Liberalism*. Cambridge: Cambridge University Press.

Ivison, Duncan, Paul Patton, and Will Sanders. 2000. "Introduction," in *Political Theory and the Rights of Indigenous Peoples*, eds. Duncan Ivison, Paul Patton, and Will Sanders. New York: Cambridge University Press, pp. 1–21.

"Japan Apologizes to Koreans for Occupation." 1998. *Washington Post*, October 8, p. A28.

"Japan: Koreans' Plea Rejected." 1999. *New York Times*, August 31, p. A10.

Jenson, Jane, and Martin Papillon. 2000. "Challenging the Citizenship Regime: The James Cree and Transnational Action," *Politics and Society* 28: 245–64.

Jhappan, C. Radha. 1990. "Indian Symbolic Politics: The Double-Edged Sword of Publicity," *Canadian Ethnic Studies* 22:19–39.

Jonas, Dr. William. 2000. "Reconciliation and Human Rights," Australian Human Rights and Equal Opportunity Commission: Aboriginal & Torres Strait Islander Social Justice Report. Available online at http://www.hreoc.gov.au/social_justice/index.html.

Jupp, James. 1995. "From 'White Australia' to 'Part of Asia': Recent Shifts in Australian Immigration Policy towards the Region," *International Migration Review* 29: 207–29.

———. 1997. "The Ethnic Dimension," in *The Politics of Retribution: The 1996 Australian Federal Election*, eds. Clive Bean et al. St. Leonards: Allen & Unwin, pp. 80–7.

Kalt, Joseph P., and Joseph William Singer. 2004. "Myths and Realities of Tribal Sovereignty: The Law and Economics of Indian Self-Rule." Research Working Paper Series RWP04–016. Harvard University John F. Kennedy School of Government Faculty, Cambridge.

Kelley, Matt. 2000. "Indian Affairs Head Makes Apology," *Excite.News*, September 8.

Kettner, James H. 1978. *The Development of American Citizenship, 1608–1870*. Chapel Hill: University of North Carolina Press.

Kidd, Rosalind. 2000. *Black Lives, Government Lies*. Sydney: University of New South Wales Press.

Klinkner, Philip A., and Rogers M. Smith. 1999. *The Unsteady March*. Chicago: University of Chicago Press.

Kolbert, Elizabeth. 2006. "Dead Reckoning: The Armenian Genocide and the Politics of Silence," *New Yorker*, November 6, pp. 120–4.

Kymlicka, Will. 2001. *Politics in the Vernacular: Nationalism, Multiculturalism, and Citizenship*. New York: Oxford University Press.

Legg, Michael. 2002. "Indigenous Australians and International Law: Racial Discrimination, Genocide and Reparations," *Berkeley Journal of International Law* 20: 387–436.

Lehman, Russ, and Alyssa Macy. "Native Vote 2004: A National Survey and Analysis to Increase the Native Vote in 2004 and the Results Achieved," First American Education Project, National Congress of American Indians. Available online at http://www.ncai.org.

Lemont, Eric. N/A. "Developing Effective Processes of American Indian Constitutional and Governmental Reform: Lessons from the Cherokee Nation of Oklahoma, Hualapai Nation, Navajo Nation and Northern Cheyenne Tribe." Harvard Project on American Indian Economic Development. Available online at http://www.ksg.harvard.edu/hunap.

Lewin, Tamar. 2001. "Calls for Slavery Restitution Getting Louder," *New York Times*, June 4, p. A15.

Libesman, Heidi. 2005. "In Search of a Postcolonial Theory of Normative Integration: Reflections on A. C. Cairns' Theory of *Citizens Plus*," *Canadian Journal of Political Science* 38: 955–76.

Lind, Jennifer M. 2004. "Apologies in International Politics," Dartmouth College. Unpublished paper.

Lyall, Sarah. 1997. "The Irish Famine and the English." *New York Times*, June 8, section 4, p. 2.

Macintyre, Stuart, and Anna Clark. 2003. *The History Wars*. Carlton, Victoria: Melbourne University Press.

Magin, Janis L. 2006. "Hawaiians Weigh Options as Native-Status Bill Stalls." *New York Times*, June 11, p. 37.

Maier, Charles S. 1988. *The Unmasterable Past: History, Holocaust, and German National Identity*. Cambridge: Harvard University Press.

Mallet, Robyn K., and Janet K. Swim. 2004. "Collective Guilt in the United States: Predicting Support for Social Policies That Alleviate Social Injustice," in *Collective Guilt: International Perspectives*, eds. Nyla R. Branscombe and Bertjan Dooseje. New York: Cambridge University Press, pp. 56–74.

Manne, Robert. 2001. "In Denial: The Stolen Generations and the Right," *Australian Quarterly Essay* 1, pp. 1–113

Manne, Robert, ed. 2003. *Whitewash: On Keith Windschuttle's Fabrication of Aboriginal History*. Melbourne: Black Inc. Agenda.

Manuel, George, and Michael Poslums. 1974. *The Fourth World: An Indian Reality*. New York: Free Press.

"Maori Warn of Battle over Water." 2006. *Press* (Christchurch), August 2, p. 1.

Markus, Andrew. 1994. *Australian Race Relations*. St. Leonards: Allen & Unwin.

Martin, D. F. 2001. "Is Welfare Dependency 'Welfare Poison'? An Assessment of Noel Pearson's Proposals for Aboriginal Welfare Reform," Discussion Paper No. 213, Centre for Aboriginal Economic Policy Research, Australian National University.

Mason, W. Dale. 2000. *Indian Gaming: Tribal Sovereignty and American Politics*. Norman: University of Oklahoma Press.

Masumi, Fukatsu. 1995. "The Eclipse of Showa Taboos and the Apology Resolution," *Japanese Quarterly* 42: 419–25.

Matthews, Gregory H. 2005. "Apologies Can Make All the Difference in Dispute Resolution," *Legal Intelligencer*, June 1, p. 5.

McAdam, Doug. 1999. *Political Process and the Development of Black Insurgency 1930 –1970*, 2nd ed. Chicago: University of Chicago Press.

McAllister, Ian. 1992. *Political Behaviour: Citizens, Parties and Elites in Australia*. Melbourne: Longman Cheshire.

McBeath, Gerald. 1992. "Political Structure and Native Self-Government in the United States, Canada, and Australia," in *Indigenous Rights in the Pacific and North America: Race and Nation in the Late Twentieth Century*, eds. Henry Reynolds and Richard Nile. London: University of London, Sir Robert Menzies Centre for Australian Studies.

McCool, Daniel, Susan M. Olson, and Jennifer L. Robinson. 2007. *Native Vote: American Indians, the Voting Rights Act, and the Right to Vote*. New York: Cambridge University Press.

McDonald, Michael. 1976. "Aboriginal Rights," in *Contemporary Issues in Political Philosophy*, eds. William R. Shea and John King-Farlow. New York: Science History, pp. 27–48.

McGarty, Craig, et al. 2005. "Group-Based Guilt as a Predictor of Commitment to Apology," *British Journal of Social Psychology* 44: 659–80.

McGraw, Kathleen M. 1998. "Manipulating Public Opinion with Moral Justification," *Annals, American Association for Political and Social Science* 560: 129–42.

McGregor, Russell. 1996. "An Aboriginal Caucasian: Some Uses for Racial Kinship in Early Twentieth Century Australia," *Australian Aboriginal Studies* 1: 11–20.

———. 1997. *Imagined Destinies: Aboriginal Australians and the Doomed Race Theory, 1880–1939*. Carlton South: Melbourne University Press.

———. 2004. "Governance, Not Genocide: Aboriginal Assimilation in the Postwar Era," in *Genocide and Settler Society: Frontier Violence and Stolen Indigenous Children in Australian History*, ed. A. Dirk Moses. New York: Berghahn, pp. 290–307.

McKenna, Mark. 1997–8. "Different Perspectives on Black Armband History." Research Paper 5, Parliament of Australia, Parliamentary Library, Canberra.

McNeil, Kent. 2001. *Emerging Justice? Essays on Indigenous Rights in Canada and Australia*. Saskatoon: University of Saskatchewan Native Law Centre.

"Menem's Visit to Britain: Views from Argentina and the Falkland Islands about . . ." 1998. *Guardian* (London), October 31, p. 6.

Metzger, Yona. 2005. "Yesterday, Today and Tomorrow: Catholic-Jewish Relations 40 Years after Nostra Aetate," *America*, October 24, p. 12.

Milloy, Courtland. 1994. "Triumph of Justice in Florida," *Washington Post*, April 17, p. B1.

Milloy, James S. 1999. *A National Crime: The Canadian Government and the Residential School System, 1879–1986*. Winnipeg: University of Manitoba Press.

Mitchell, Emily. 1998. "Apologies: Who's Sorry Now?" *Index on Censorship* 3: 46–7.

Mofina, Rick. 2002. "Anglican Church to Pay up to $25M for Native Abuse: Church to Pay 30%, Government 70%, of Residential School Abuse Claims," *Ottawa Citizen*, November 21, p. A6.

Mollison, Andrew. 2004a. "U.S. Apology to Indians Considers Bill, 'Acknowledges Years of Official Depredations,'" *Seattle Post-Intelligencer*,

May 25. Available online at http://seattlepi.nwsource.com/national/174821_indian25.html.

———. 2004b. "Congress Considers Apology to Indians," *Atlanta Journal-Constitution*, May 25, p. 10A.

Morley, James W. 1965. *Japan and Korea: America's Allies in the Pacific*. New York: Walker.

Morse, Bradford W. 1999. "The Inherent Right of Aboriginal Governance," in *Aboriginal Self-Government in Canada*, 2nd ed., ed. John H. Hylton. Saskatoon: Purich, p. 16–44.

Moses, A. Dirk. 2001."Coming to Terms with Genocidal Pasts in Comparative Perspective: Germany and Australia," *Aboriginal History* 25: 91–115.

———, ed. 2004. *Genocide and Settler Society: Frontier Violence and Stolen Indigenous Children in Australian History*. New York: Berghahn.

Mowbray, Rebecca. 2005. "Bank Reveals Slavery Link; 2 La. Firms Named," *Times-Picayune*, January 21, p. 1.

Mukae, Ryuji. 1996. "Japan's Diet Resolution on World War II: Keeping History at Bay," *Asian Survey* 36: 1011–30.

Mulgan, Richard. 2005. *Politics in New Zealand*, 3rd ed. Auckland: Auckland University Press.

Murphy, Dean E. 1994. "German President Apologizes; Leader Asks Forgiveness for W.W. II Acts against Poland," *Houston Chronicle*, August 2, p. A13.

———. 2005. "Bill Giving Native Hawaiians Sovereignty Is Too Much for Some, Too Little for Others," *New York Times*, July 17, p. 14.

Murray, Maureen. 2003. "Native Protest Slams New Legislation," *Toronto Star*, March 21, p. B4.

NAACP Washington Bureau. 2004. "How Congress Voted: NAACP Civil Rights, Federal Legislative Record Card, 108th Congress 2003–2004."

Neal, Terry M. 2005. "Symbolic Lynching Resolution Forced Concrete Political Choice," *Washington Post*, June 2. Available online at http://www.washingtonpost.com.

Neill, Rosemary. 2002. *White Out: How Politics Is Killing Black Australia*. Crows Nest: Allen & Unwin.

Newspoll Market Research. 2000. "Summary of Findings: Quantitative Research into Issues Relating to the Document of Reconciliation." Council for Aboriginal Reconciliation. Available online at http://www.austlii.edu.au/au/other/IndigLRes/car/.

Newspoll, Saulwick & Muller, and Hugh Mackay. 2000. "Public Opinion on Reconciliation: Snap Shot, Close Focus, Long Lens," in *Reconciliation: Essays on Australian Reconciliation*, ed. Michelle Grattan. Melbourne: Black Inc., pp. 33–52.

New Zealand Electoral Commission. 2005. "Maori and the Vote." Available online at http://www.elections.org.nz/study/history/maori-vote.html.

New Zealand Electoral Commission and the Ministry of Maori Development. n.d. "Maori Roll or General Roll? It's Your Choice." Available online at http://www.elections.org.nz/elections/esyst/mroll.html.

Nichols, Roger L. 1998. *Indians in the United States and Canada: A Comparative History*. Lincoln: University of Nebraska Press.

Nobles, Melissa. 2005. "The Myth of Latin American Multiracialism." *Daedalus*, Winter: 82–7.

Norberry, Jennifer. 2001–2. "Voters and the Franchise: the Federal Story." Research Paper No.17, Parliament of Australia, Parliamentary Library, Canberra.

O'Connor, Colleen. 2004. "Who's Sorry Now? An Orgy of Apologies Spreading across the World," *Denver Post*, April 15, p. L-01.

O'Neill, Barry. 1999. *Honor, Symbols, and War*. Ann Arbor: University of Michigan Press.

Ogletree, Charles J., Jr. 2002. "Litigating the Legacy of Slavery," *New York Times*, Op-Ed, March 31, section 4, p. 9.

Oliver, W. H. 2001."The Future behind Us," in *Histories, Power and Loss: Uses of the Past – A New Zealand Commentary*, eds. Andrew Sharp and Paul McHugh. Wellington: Bridget Williams, pp. 9–29.

Onishi, Norimitsu. 2005a. "In Japan's New Texts, Lessons in Rising Nationalism," *New York Times*, April 17, p. 4.

_____. 2005b. "A War Shrine, for a Japan Seeking a Not Guilty Verdict," *New York Times*, June 22. Available online at http://www.nytimes.com/2005/06/22/international/asia/22letter.html?.

Parliament of New South Wales Legislative Council, Standing Committee on Social Issues. 1997. "Aboriginal Representation in Parliament Issues Paper."

Patton, Paul. 2005."Historic Injustice and the Possibility of Supersession," *Journal of Intercultural Studies* 26: 255–66.

Paul, Peralte C. 2005. "Wachovia Apologizes for Its Ties to Slavery," *Atlanta Journal-Constitution*, June 2, p. 3E.

Pells, Eddie. 1997. "Ala. Syphilis Victims Meet Clinton Today," *Boston Globe*, May 16, p. A3.

Peterson, Nicholas, and Will Sanders, eds. 1998. *Citizenship and Indigenous Australians: Changing Conceptions and Possibilities*. Melbourne: Cambridge University Press.

Pevar, Stephen L. 1992. *The Rights of Indians and Tribes*. Carbondale: Southern Illinois University Press.

"PM's Apology Draws Protest." 1997. *Sydney Morning Herald*, May 27, p. A1.

Pocock, J. P. A. 2001. "The Treaty between Histories," in *Histories, Power and Loss: Uses of the Past – A New Zealand Commentary*, eds. Andrew Sharp and Paul McHugh. Wellington: Bridget Williams, pp. 75–95.

Pollara Research and Earnscliffe Research and Communications. 2001. "Summary of Key Findings." Indian Residential Schools Resolution Canada. Available online at http://www.irsr.gc.ca/english/polling_10_02.html.

"Pope Repeats an Apology." 1999. *New York Times*, September 2, p. A8.

Pratt, Angela. 2003. "Make or Break? A Background to the ATSIC Changes and the ATSIC Review," Current Issues Brief No. 29, Parliament of Australia, Parliamentary Library, Canberra.

Pritchard, Sarah.1998. "The International Covenant on Civil and Political Rights and Indigenous Peoples," in *Indigenous Peoples, the United Nations and Human Rights*, ed. Sarah Pritchard. Leichhardt: Federation Press, pp. 184–202.

———, ed. 1998. *Indigenous Peoples, the United Nations and Human Rights.* Leichhardt: Federation Press.

Pross, Christian. 1998. *Paying for the Past: The Struggle over Reparations for Surviving Victims of the Nazi Terror.* Baltimore: Johns Hopkins University Press.

Radio Free Europe/ Radio Liberty. 2005. "Erdogan Urges France to Drop Armenian Genocide Recognition." 2005. February 4. Available online at http://www.rferl.org.

Ray, Arthur J. 2003. "Aboriginal Title and Treaty Rights Research: A Comparative Look at Australia, Canada, New Zealand and the United States," *New Zealand Journal of History* 37: 5–21.

Reed, Terrell. 2002. "Sins of the Past," *Black Enterprise*, June.

"Resident Schools, National Scandal." 1998. *Globe and Mail*, January 8, p. A16.

Reuters. 2003. "British Columbia Apologizes to Its Indians," *New York Times*, February 12, p. A7.

Reynolds, Henry. 1996. *Aboriginal Sovereignty: Three Nations, One Australia?* St. Leonards: Allen & Unwin.

———. 1999. *Why Weren't We Told? A Personal Search for the Truth about Our History.* Ringwood: Viking.

———. 2001. *An Indelible Stain? The Question of Genocide in Australia's History.* Ringwood: Viking.

Riley, Mark. 2003a. "Sorry, But the PM Says the Culture Wars Are Over," *Sydney Morning Herald*, September 10, p. 1.

———. 2003b. "Sorry Issue Is Unreconciled," *Sydney Morning Herald*, September 12, p. 4.

Robinson, Randall. 2000. *The Debt: What America Owes to Blacks.* New York: Dutton.

Roorda, Eric Paul. 1998. *The Dictator Next Door: The Good Neighbor Policy and the Trujillo Regime in the Dominican Republic, 1930–1945.* Durham: Duke University Press.

Rose, Deborah Bird. 2003. "Oral Histories and Knowledge," in *Frontier Conflict: The Australian Experience*, eds. Bain Attwood and S. G. Foster. Canberra: National Museum of Australia.

Rose, Michael, ed. 1996. *For the Record: 160 Years of Aboriginal Print Journalism.* St. Leonards: Allen & Unwin.

Royal Commission on Aboriginal Peoples. 1993. *Partners in Confederation: Aboriginal Peoples, Self-Government, and the Constitution.* Ottawa: Canadian Government Publishing.

———. 1997. *For Seven Generations: An Information Legacy of the Royal Commission on Aboriginal Peoples.* 5 vol. CD-ROM. Ottawa: Libraxus.

Russell, Dan. 2000. *A People's Dream: Aboriginal Self-Government in Canada*. Vancouver: University of British Columbia Press.

Russell, Peter, and Roger Jones. 1997. "Aboriginal Peoples and Constitutional Reform," in *For Seven Generations: An Information Legacy of the Royal Commission on Aboriginal Peoples* CD-ROM, ed. Royal Commission on Aboriginal Peoples. Ottawa: Libraxus.

Salzberger, Ronald P., and Mary C. Turck, eds. 2004. *Reparations for Slavery: A Reader*. Lanham: Rowman & Littlefield.

Sanger, David E., and Steven Lee Meyers. 2001. "Collision with China: Washington; Delicate Diplomatic Dance Ends Bush's First Crisis," *New York Times*, April 12, p. A1.

Schouls, Tim. 2003. *Shifting Boundaries: Aboriginal Identity, Pluralist Theory, and the Politics of Self-Government*. Vancouver: University of British Columbia Press.

Senate Legal and Constitutional References Committee. 2000. *Healing: A Legacy of Generations*. Canberra: Senate of Australia.

———. 2003. *Reconciliation: Off Track*. Canberra: Senate of Australia.

Sharp, Andrew. 1997a. "Civil Rights, Amelioration, and Reparation in New Zealand," in *Government Policies and Ethnic Relations in Asia and the Pacific*, eds. Michael Brown and Sumit Ganguly. Cambridge: MIT Press, pp. 421–56.

———. 1997b. *Justice and the Maori: The Philosophy and Practice of Maori Claims in New Zealand since the 1970s*. Auckland: Oxford University Press.

———. 2001. "Recent Juridical and Constitutional Histories of Maori," in *Histories, Power and Loss: Uses of the Past- A New Zealand Commentary*, eds. Andrew Sharp and Paul McHugh. Wellington: Bridget Williams, pp. 31–60.

Sharp, Andrew, and Paul McHugh, eds. 2001. *Histories, Power and Loss: Uses of the Past – A New Zealand Commentary*. Wellington: Bridget Williams.

Sharrock, David. 1999. "Nine Hundred Years Later, a Christian Apology for Crusades; Thousands Expected in Israel to Seek Forgiveness from Jews, Muslims," *Globe and Mail*, July 3, p. A18.

Shelby, Tommie. 2005. *We Who Are Dark: The Philosophical Foundations of Black Solidarity*. Cambridge: Harvard University Press.

Shepard, Scott. 2005. "Critics: Frist Vetoed Roll Call on Anti-Lynching Vote," *Palm Beach Post*, June 15.

Shogren, Elizabeth. 1998. "Clinton Condemns Silence on Rwanda," *Chicago Sun-Times*, March 26, p. 24.

Shriver, Donald. 1995. *An Ethic for Enemies: Forgiveness in Politics*. New York: Oxford University Press.

Silva, Alexandre da. 2005. "Hawaiians Unite against Ruling, But Also against Themselves," *Associated Press State & Local Wire*, August 3.

Sims, Calvin. 2001. "Japan Apologizes to Lepers and Declines to Fight Isolation Ruling," *New York Times*, May 24, p. A3.

Singleton, Gwynneth. 2000. *The Howard Government: Australian Commonwealth Administration 1996–1998*. Sydney: University of New South Wales Press.

Smith, Roger W. 1992. "The Armenian Genocide: Memory, Politics, and the Future," in *The Armenian Genocide: History, Politics, Ethics*, ed. Richard G. Hovannisian. New York: St. Martin's Press, pp. 1–20.

Smith, Rogers M. 2003. *Stories of Peoplehood: The Politics and Morals of Political Membership*. New York: Cambridge University Press.

Sorrenson, Keith. 1993. "The Position of Indigenous People in National Constitutions," in *Speeches from the Conference, Council for Aboriginal Reconciliation, Canberra, June 4–5*, pp. 28–37.

Sorrenson, M. P. K. 1989. "Towards a Radical Reinterpretation of New Zealand History: The Role of the Waitangi Tribunal," in *Maori and Pakeha Perspectives of the Treaty of Waitangi*, ed. I. H. Kawharu. Auckland: Oxford University Press, pp. 158–78.

Speirs, Rosemary. 1998. "PM Must Take the Lead: Government's Apology to Indians Should Have Come from Chrétien," *Gazette* (Montreal), January 9, p. B3.

Steffenhagen, Janet. 1998. "Apology to Abused Natives Elicits Powerful Emotions," *Vancouver Sun*, January 8, p. A3.

Stephenson, M. A., ed. 1995. *Mabo: The Native Title Legislation: A Legislative Response to the High Court's Decision*. Queensland: University of Queensland Press.

Stern, Alexandra Minna. 2005. "Eugenics and Historical Memory in America," *History Compass* 3: 1–11.

Stolberg, Sheryl Gay. 2005a. "Senate Issues Apology over Failure on Lynching Law," *New York Times*, June 1, p. 15.

————. 2005b. "The Senate Apologizes, Mostly," *New York Times*, June 19, section 4, p. 3.

Stout, David. 2000. "Indian Office No Place for John Wayne," *New York Times*, September 22, p. A14.

Struck, Doug. 2002a. "Increasingly, Japanese Look Back in Anger: On Anniversary of Defeat in WWII, an Unrepentant View Is Gaining Favor," *Washington Post*, August 16, p. A15.

————. 2002b. "Japan Expected to Aid N. Korea; Communists Seek $10 Billion in World War II Reparations," *Washington Post*, September 14, p. A12.

Summers, John. 2000–1. "The Parliament of the Commonwealth of Australia and Indigenous Peoples, 1901–1967." Research Paper No. 10. Parliament of Australia, Parliamentary Library, Canberra.

Swardson, Anne. 1997. "Swiss Regrets Remarks on Jewish Demands," *Washington Post*, January 16, p. A28.

Tarrow, Sidney. 1994. *Power in Movement: Social Movements, Collective Action and Politics*. Cambridge: Cambridge University Press.

Tate, Katherine. 2003. *Black Faces in the Mirror: African Americans and Their Representatives in the U.S. Congress*. Princeton: Princeton University Press.

Tavuchis, Nicholas. 1991. *Mea Culpa: A Sociology of Apology and Reconciliation*. Stanford: Stanford University Press.

Taylor, Kevin. 2004. "Poll: Maori Equal, Special," *New Zealand Herald*, February 28.

Teather, David. 2005. "Bank Admits It Owned Slaves," *Guardian* (London), January 22, p. 17.

Teitel, Ruti. 1997. "Transitional Jurisprudence: The Role of Law in Political Transformation," *Yale Law Journal* 106: 2009–80.

———. 2000. *Transitional Justice*. New York: Oxford University Press.

Temple, Philip. 2004. "New Book on Treaty Takes Political Line," *New Zealand Herald*, July 15.

"The Leaders' Apologies." 1993. *Guardian* (London), October 13, p. 25.

"The Long Trail to Apology." 2004. *New York Times*, June 28, p. A18.

"The Race Debate: Maori Say Paychecks Are Part of Treaty." 2004. *New Zealand Herald*, February 28.

Thomas, Edward K. 2005. "Testimony on an Apology to Native Americans." Submitted to U.S. Senate Committee on Indian Affairs, May 25.

Thomas-Lester, Avis. 2005. "Repairing Senate's Record on Lynching," *Washington Post*, June 11, p. A1.

Thompson, Elizabeth. 2006. "'Let the Government Hear from Canadians': Former PM Defends Bill to Close the Gap between Aboriginals, other Canadians," *Gazette* (Montreal), June 2, p. A10.

Thornton, Emily. 1995. "Final Mea Culpa?" *Far Eastern Economic Review*, August 24, p. 18.

Tobias, John L. 1983. "Protection, Civilization, Assimilation: An Outline History of Canada's Indian Policy," in *As Long as the Sun Shines and Water Flows: A Reader in Canadian Native Studies*, eds. Ian A. L. Getty and Antoine S. Lussier. Vancouver: University of British Columbia Press, pp. 39–64.

Torpey, John, ed. 2003. *Politics and the Past: On Repairing Historical Injustices*. Lanham: Rowman & Littlefield.

———. 2006. *Making Whole What Has Been Smashed: On Reparations Politics*. Cambridge: Harvard University Press.

Totsuka, Etsuro. 1999. "Translations: Commentary on a Victory for 'Comfort Women,'" *Pacific Rim Law and Policy* 8: 47–6.

Trigger, Bruce G. 1985. *Natives and Newcomers: Canada's "Heroic Age" Reconsidered*. Kingston: McGill-Queen's University Press.

Tsosie, Rebecca. 2006. "The BIA's Apology to Native Americans: An Essay on Collective Memory and Collective Conscience," in *Taking Wrongs Seriously*, eds. Elazar Barkan and Alexander Karn. Stanford: Stanford University Press, pp. 185–212.

Turner, Charles C. 2005. *The Politics of Minor Concerns: American Indian Policy and Congressional Dynamics*. Lanham: University Press of America.

"Um, Sorry about That." 1997. *Time*. October 13. Available online at http://www.time.com/time/magazine/article/0.9171.987181.00.html.

U.S. House of Representatives. 1997. "Resolution Apologizing for Slavery." June 1. Available online at http://thomas.loc.gov/, accessed July 23, 2004.

U.S. House of Representatives, Senate. 1993. "To Acknowledge the 100th Anniversary of the January 17, 1893 Overthrow of the Kingdom of Hawaii, and to Offer an Apology to Native Hawaiians on Behalf of the United States for the Overthrow. . . ." 103rd Congress, S. J. Res.19. Available online at http://www.thomas.gov.

U.S. Congress. 2000. H. Con. Res. 356, June 19, 106th Congress, 2nd session.

Utley, Robert M. 1984. *The Indian Frontier of the American West, 1865–1890.* Albuquerque: University of New Mexico Press.

Waitangi Tribunal. n.d. "Frequently Asked Questions." Available online at http://www.waitangi-tribunal.govt.nz/about/frequentlyaskedquestions. asp#3, accessed August 7, 2006.

Waldmeir, Patti. 2001. "Slavery Reparations Case Heads to Court," *Financial Times*, September 2, p. 3.

Waldrep, Christopher. 2000. "War of Words: The Controversy over the Definition of Lynching, 1899–1940," *Journal of Southern History* 1: 75–100.

Waldron, Jeremy. 1992. "Superseding Historic Injustice," *Ethics* 103: 4–28.

———. 2002. "Redressing Historical Injustice," *University of Toronto Law Journal* 52: 135–60.

———. 2004. "The Palestinian Refugees and the Right of Return: Theoretical Perspectives: Settlement, Return, and the Supersession Thesis," *Theoretical Inquiries in Law* 5: 237–68.

Wallace, Anthony F. C. 1999. *Jefferson and the Indians: The Tragic Fate of the First Americans.* Cambridge: Harvard University Press.

Ward, Alan. 1999. *An Unsettled History: Treaty Claims in New Zealand Today.* Wellington: Bridget Williams.

Watson, Jamal. 2001. "Blacks, Jews Found Still to Have Rifts," *Boston Globe*, August 16, p. A3.

Watts, Jonathan. 1998. "'Comfort Women' Win Damages in Landmark Ruling; Breakthrough for Japan's Sex Slaves," *Guardian* (London), April 28, p. 15.

Weaver, Sally M. 1981. *Making Canadian Indian Policy: The Hidden Agenda 1968–1970.* Toronto: University of Toronto Press.

———. 1990. "A New Paradigm in Canadian Indian Policy for the 1990s," *Canadian Ethnic Studies* 22: 12–18.

Weisman, Steven R. 1997. "India Wrestles with the Raj: A Queen's Gesture of Penitence Reignites a 50-Year-Old Debate," *New York Times*, October 26, section 4, p. 14.

"What's Eating Pakeha." 2004. *New Zealand Herald*, February 21.

"Who's Sorry Now?" 1993. *Time*, September 13. Available online at http://www.time.com.

Wiencek, Henry. 2003. *An Imperfect God: George Washington, His Slaves, and the Creation of America.* New York: Farrar, Straus & Giroux.

Wilkie, Curtis. 1997. "Divisions Arise on Slavery Apology," *Boston Globe*, June 29, p. A13.

Wilkins, David E. 1997. *American Indian Sovereignty and the U.S. Supreme Court: The Masking of Justice*. Austin: University of Texas Press.

———. 2002. *American Indian Politics and the American Political System*. Lanham: Rowman & Littlefield.

Williams, John A. 1969. *Politics of the New Zealand Maori: Protest and Cooperation, 1891–1909*. Seattle: University of Washington Press.

Williams, Linda Faye. 2003. *The Constraint of Race: Legacies of White Skin Privilege in America*. University Park: Pennsylvania State University Press.

Williamson, Edwin. 1992. *The Penguin History of Latin America*. Allen Lane: Penguin Press.

Wilson, Honorable Margaret. n.d. Available online at http://www.Beehive. govt.nz.

Windschuttle, Keith. 2002. *The Fabrication of Aboriginal History*. Sydney: Macleay Press.

Winsor, Hugh. 1998. "Chrétien Skipped His Share of Moment," *Globe and Mail*, January 9, p. A4.

Wolfe, Patrick. 2001. "Land, Labor, and Difference: Elementary Structures of Race," *American Historical Review*, June. Available online at http://www. historycooperative.org/journals/ahr/106.3/aho00866.html, accessed January 12, 2006.

Wood, Gordon S. 2003. "Slaves in the Family," *New York Times Book Review*, December 14, p. 10.

Woodward, Kenneth L., 1995. "Who's Sorry Now?" *Newsweek*, July 17, p. 65.

Yamamoto, Eric K. 1999. *Interracial Justice: Conflict and Reconciliation in Post-Civil Rights America*. New York: New York University Press.

Yashar, Deborah J. 1999. "Democracy, Indigenous Movements, and the Postliberal Challenge in Latin America," *World Politics* 52: 76–104.

———. 2005. *Contesting Citizenship in Latin America: The Rise of Indigenous Movements and the Postliberal Challenge*. New York: Cambridge University Press.

Yoshibumi, Wakamiya. 1999. *The Postwar Conservative View of Asia*. Tokyo: LTCB International Library Foundation.

Young, Audrey. 2004. "Clark Set to Go on Inquiry into Place of Treaty," *New Zealand Herald*, March 11.

Young, Iris Marion. 1995. "Polity and Group Difference: A Critique of the Ideal of Universal Citizenship," in *Theorizing Citizenship*, ed. Ronald Beiner. Albany: State University of New York Press, pp. 175–207.

Zeuthen, Kasper. 1999. "WWII Internees get 5,000 Dollars, Official Apology," *Daily Yomiuri* (Tokyo), January 9, p. 3.

Zweig, Ronald W. 2001. *German Reparations and the Jewish World*, 2nd ed. London: Frank Cass.

Index